THE GREATEST MILITARY GAMBLE
OF WORLD WAR II, AND ALMOST
THE GREATEST DISASTER.

ARNHEM

where the most prestigious Allied generals
gambled with their reputations and the lives
of their finest troops.

ARNHEM

where Germany's most brilliant military
commander was called back into service by
Hitler to achieve a miracle—and came close
to succeeding.

ARNHEM

where over twice as many Allied soldiers fell
than at Normandy, and where feats of near-
incredible heroism were commonplace.

ARNHEM

where a war that was almost won was almost
lost.

A BRIDGE TOO FAR

CORNELIUS RYAN

POPULAR LIBRARY • NEW YORK

POPULAR LIBRARY EDITION

FOR THEM ALL

MAPS BY RAFAEL PALACIOS

The photographs in this book are from the collection of the author, who gratefully acknowledges the assistance of the Imperial War Museum in London, the U.S. Department of Defense, the Dutch Historical Military Archives, the Dutch Municipal Archives, and the many individuals who provided photographs of events and themselves.

CONTENTS

CONTENTS

8

On the narrow corridor that would carry the armored drive, there were five major bridges to take. They had to be seized intact by airborne assault. It was the fifth, the crucial bridge over the Lower Rhine at a place called Arnhem, sixty-four miles behind the German lines, that worried Lieutenant General Frederick Browning, Deputy Commander, First Allied Airborne Army. Pointing to the Arnhem bridge on the map he asked, "How long will it take the armor to reach us?" Field Marshal Montgomery replied briskly, "Two days." Still looking at the map, Browning said, "We can hold it for four." Then he added, "But, sir, I think we might be going a bridge too far."

> The final conference at Montgomery's Headquarters on Operation Market-Garden, September 10, 1944, as recalled by participants. The quotes come from Major General Roy E. Urquhart's memoirs, *Arnhem*.

FOREWORD

OPERATION MARKET-GARDEN

September 17–24, 1944

Shortly after 10 A.M. on Sunday, September 17, 1944, from airfields all over southern England the greatest armada of troop-carrying aircraft ever assembled for a single operation took to the air. In this, the 263rd week of World War II, the Supreme Allied Commander, General Dwight David Eisenhower, unleashed Market-Garden, one of the most daring and imaginative operations of the war. Surprisingly, Market-Garden, a combined airborne and ground offensive, was authored by one of the most cautious of all the Allied commanders, Field Marshal Bernard Law Montgomery.

Market, the airborne phase of the operation, was monumental: it involved almost five thousand fighters, bombers, transports and more than 2500 gliders. That Sunday afternoon, at exactly 1:30 P.M., in an unprecedented daylight assault, an entire Allied airborne army, complete with vehicles and equipment, began dropping behind the German lines. The target for this bold and historic invasion from the sky: Nazi-occupied Holland.

On the ground, poised along the Dutch-Belgian border, were the Garden forces, massed tank columns of the British Second Army. At 2:35 P.M., preceded by artillery and led by swarms of rocket-firing fighters, the tanks began a dash up the backbone of Holland along a strategic route the paratroopers were already fighting to capture and hold open.

Montgomery's ambitious plan was designed to sprint the troops and tanks through Holland, springboard across the Rhine and into Germany itself. Operation Market-Garden, Montgomery reasoned, was the lightning stroke needed to topple the Third Reich and effect the end of the war in 1944.

Part One

THE RETREAT

☼ 1 ☼

IN THE THOUSAND-YEAR-OLD Dutch village of Driel, people listened intently. Even before dawn, restless sleepers woke and lights came on behind shuttered windows. Initially there was only a sense of something unaccountable taking place somewhere beyond the immediate, physical surroundings. Gradually vague impressions took form. In the far distance came a muted, continuous mutter.

Barely audible, but persistent, the sound reached the village in waves. Unable to identify the subtle noise, many listened instinctively for some change in the flow of the nearby Lower Rhine. In Holland, half of which lies below sea level, water is the constant enemy, dikes the major weapon in a never-ending battle that has gone on since before the eleventh century. Driel, sitting in a great bend of the Lower Rhine, southwest of Arnhem, capital of Gelderland, has an ever-present reminder of the struggle. A few hundred yards to the north, protecting the village and the region from the restless 400-yard-wide river, a massive dike, topped by a road, rises at places more than twenty feet high. But this morning the river gave no cause for alarm. The Neder Rijn swept peacefully toward the North Sea at its customary speed of two miles per hour. The sounds reverberating off the stone face of the protective dike came from another, far more ruthless, enemy.

As the sky lightened and the sun began to burn off the mist, the commotion grew louder. From roads due east of Driel the villagers could clearly hear the sound of traffic—traffic that seemed to grow heavier by the minute. Now their uneasiness turned to alarm, for there was no doubt about the identity of the movement: in this fifth year of World War II and after fifty-one months of Nazi occupation, everyone recognized the rumble of German convoys.

Even more alarming was the size of the procession. Some people later recalled that only once before had they heard such a flow of traffic—in May, 1940, when the Germans had invaded the Netherlands. At that time, swarming across the Reich frontier ten to fifteen miles from Driel, Hitler's mechanized armies had reached the main highways and spread swiftly throughout the country. Now, over those same roads convoys seemed once more to be moving endlessly.

Strange sounds came from the nearest main road—a two-lane highway connecting Arnhem, on the northern bank of the Lower Rhine, with the eighth-century city of Nijmegen, on the broad river Waal, eleven miles to the south. Against the low background throb of engines, people could plainly identify individual noises which seemed curiously out of place in a military convoy—the scrape of wagon wheels, the whir of countless bicycles and the slow, unpaced shuffling of feet.

What kind of convoy could this be? And, more important, where was it heading? At this moment in the war Holland's future could well depend on the answer to that question. Most people believed the convoys carried heavy reinforcements—either pouring into the country to bolster the German garrison or rushing south to halt the Allied advance. Allied troops had liberated northern France with spectacular speed. Now they were fighting in Belgium and were said to be close to the capital, Brussels, less than one hundred miles away. Rumors persisted that powerful Allied armored units were driving for the Dutch border. But no one in Driel could tell for sure exactly the direction the convoys were taking. Distance and the diffusion of sound made that impossible. And because of the nightly curfew the villagers were unable to leave their houses to investigate.

Plagued by uncertainty, they could only wait. They could not know that shortly before dawn the three young soldiers who constituted little Driel's entire German garrison had left the village on stolen bicycles and pedaled off into the mist. There was no longer any military authority in the village to enforce the curfew regulations.

Unaware, people kept to their homes. But the more curious among them were too impatient to wait and decided to risk using the telephone. In her home at 12 Honingveldsestraat, next to her family's jam-and-preserves factory, young Cora Baltussen called friends in Arnhem. She could scarcely believe their eyewitness report. The convoys were *not* heading south to the western front. On this misty morning, September 4, 1944, the Germans and their supporters appeared to be fleeing from Holland, traveling in anything that would move.

The fighting that everyone had expected, Cora thought, would now pass them by. She was wrong. For the insignificant village of Driel, untouched until now, the war had only begun.

�֎ 2 ✲

FIFTY MILES SOUTH, in towns and villages close to the Belgian border, the Dutch were jubilant. They watched incredulously as the shattered remnants of Hitler's armies in northern France and Belgium streamed past their windows. The collapse seemed infectious; besides military units, thousands of German civilians and Dutch Nazis were pulling out. And for these fleeing forces all roads seemed to lead to the German border.

Because the withdrawal began so slowly—a trickle of staff cars and vehicles crossing the Belgian frontier—few Dutch could tell exactly when it had started. Some believed the retreat began on September 2; others, the third. But by the fourth, the movement of the Germans and their followers had assumed the characteristics of a rout, a frenzied exodus that reached its peak on September 5, a day later to be known in Dutch history as *Dolle Dinsdag*, "Mad Tuesday."

Panic and disorganization seemed to characterize the German flight. Every kind of conveyance was in use. Thronging the roads from the Belgian border north to Arnhem and beyond were trucks, buses, staff cars, half-track vehicles, armored cars, horse-drawn farm carts and civilian automobiles running on charcoal or wood. Everywhere throughout the disorderly convoys were swarms of tired, dusty soldiers on hastily commandeered bicycles.

There were even more bizarre forms of transportation. In the town of Valkenswaard, a few miles north of the Belgian frontier, people saw heavily laden German troopers laboriously pushing along on children's scooters. Sixty miles away, in Arnhem, crowds standing on the Amsterdamseweg watched as a massive black-and-silver hearse pulled by two plodding farm horses passed slowly by. Crowded in the casket space in back were a score of disheveled, exhausted Germans.

Trudging in these wretched convoys were German soldiers from many units. There were Panzer troops, minus tanks, in their black battle suits; Luftwaffe men, presumably all that remained of German air force units that had been shattered in either France or Belgium; Wehrmacht soldiers from a score of divisions; and Waffen SS troops, their skull-and-crossbones insignia a macabre identification. Looking at these apparently leaderless, dazed troops moving aimlessly along, young Wilhelmina Coppens in St. Oedenrode thought that "most of them had no idea where they were or even where they were going." Some soldiers, to the bitter amusement of Dutch bystanders, were so disoriented that they asked for directions to the German frontier.

In the industrial town of Eindhoven, home of the giant Philips electrical works, the population had heard the low sound of

18

artillery fire from Belgium for days. Now, watching the dregs of the beaten German army thronging the roads, people expected Allied troops to arrive within hours. So did the Germans. It appeared to Frans Kortie, twenty-four-year-old employee in the town's finance department, that these troops had no intention of making a stand. From the nearby airfield came the roar of explosions as engineers blew up runways, ammunition dumps, gasoline storage tanks and hangars; and through a pall of smoke drifting across the town, Kortie saw squads of troops rapidly working to dismantle heavy antiaircraft guns on the roofs of the Philips buildings.

All through the area, from Eindhoven north to the city of Nijmegen, German engineers were hard at work. In the Zuid Willemsvaart Canal running below the town of Veghel, Cornelis de Visser, an elementary-school teacher, saw a heavily loaded barge blown skyward, shooting out airplane engine parts like a deadly rain of shrapnel. Not far away, in the village of Uden, Johannes de Groot, forty-five-year-old car-body builder, was watching the retreat with his family when Germans set fire to a former Dutch barracks barely 300 yards from his home. Minutes later heavy bombs stored in the building exploded, killing four of de Groot's children, aged five to eighteen.

In places such as Eindhoven, where school buildings were set ablaze, fire brigades were prevented from operating and whole blocks were burned down. Still, the sappers, in contrast to the fleeing columns on the roads, gave evidence of following some definite plan.

The most frantic and confused among the escapees were the civilians, German, Dutch, Belgian and French Nazis. They got no sympathy from the Dutch. To farmer Johannes Hulsen at St. Oedenrode, they looked "scared stiff"; and they had reason to be, he thought with satisfaction, for with the Allies "snapping at their heels these traitors knew it was *Bijltjesdag* ['Hatchet Day']."

The frantic flight of Dutch Nazis and German civilians had been triggered by the *Reichskommissar* in Holland, the notorious fifty-two-year-old Dr. Arthur Seyss-Inquart, and by the ambitious and brutal Dutch Nazi Party leader, Anton Mussert. Nervously watching the fate of the Germans in France and Belgium, Seyss-Inquart on September 1 ordered the evacuation of German civilians to the east of Holland, closer to the Reich border. The fifty-year-old Mussert followed suit, alerting members of his Dutch Nazi Party. Seyss-Inquart and Mussert were themselves among the first to leave: they moved from The Hague east to Apeldoorn, fifteen miles north of Arnhem.° Mussert rushed his family even closer to the Reich, moving them into the frontier region at Twente, in the province of Overijssel. At first most of the German and Dutch civilians moved at a leisurely pace. Then a sequence of events produced bedlam. On September 3 the British captured Brussels. The next day Antwerp fell. Now, British tanks and troops were only miles from the Dutch border.

On the heels of these stunning victories, the aged Queen of the Netherlands, Wilhelmina, told her people in a radio broadcast from London that liberation was at hand. She announced that her son-in-law, His Royal Highness Prince Bernhard, had been named Commander in Chief of the Netherlands Forces and would also assume leadership of all underground resistance groups. These factions, comprising three distinct organizations ranging politically from the left to the extreme right, would now be grouped together and officially known as *Binnenlandse Strijdkrachten* (Forces of the Interior). The thirty-three-year-old Prince Bernhard, husband of Princess Juliana, heir to the throne, followed the Queen's announcement with one of his own. He asked the underground to have armlets ready "displaying in distinct letters the word 'Orange,'" but not to use them "without my order." He warned them to "refrain in the enthusiasm of the moment from premature and independent actions, for these would compromise yourselves and the military operations underway."

° Seyss-Inquart was terrified. At Apeldoorn, he took to his underground headquarters—a massive concrete and brick bunker constructed at a cost of more than $250,000—complete with conference rooms, communications and personal suites. It still exists. Scratched on the concrete exterior near the entrance are the figures "6 1/4," the nickname for the hated commissioner. The Netherlanders couldn't resist it; in Dutch, Seyss-Inquart and "6 1/4" sound almost the same—*zes en een kwart.*

Next, a special message was broadcast from General Dwight D. Eisenhower, Supreme Commander of the Allied Forces, confirming that freedom was imminent. "The hour of liberation the Netherlands have awaited so long is now very near," he promised. And within a few hours these broadcasts were followed by the most optimistic statement of all, from the prime minister of the Dutch government in exile, Pieter S. Gerbrandy. He told his listeners, "Now that the Allied armies, in their irresistible advance, have crossed the Netherlands frontier . . . I want all of you to bid our Allies a hearty welcome to our native soil. . . ."

The Dutch were hysterical with joy, and the Dutch Nazis fled for their lives. Anton Mussert had long boasted that his party had more than 50,000 Nazis. If so, it seemed to the Dutch that they all took to the roads at the same time. In scores of towns and villages all over Holland, Nazi-appointed mayors and officials suddenly bolted—but often not before demanding back pay. The mayor of Eindhoven and some of his officials insisted on their salaries. The town clerk, Gerardus Legius, thought their posture ridiculous, but he didn't even feel badly about paying them off. Watching them scurry out of town "on everything with wheels" he wondered: "How far can they get? Where can they go?" There was also a run on the banks. When Nicolaas van de Weerd, twenty-four-year-old bank clerk, got to work in the town of Wageningen on Monday, September 4, he saw a queue of Dutch Nazis waiting outside the bank. Once the doors were opened they hurriedly closed accounts and emptied safety deposit boxes.

Railway stations were overrun by terrified civilians. Trains leaving for Germany were crammed to capacity. Stepping off a train on its arrival in Arnhem, young Frans Wiessing was engulfed by a sea of people fighting to get aboard. So great was the rush that after the train left, Wiessing saw a mountain of luggage lying abandoned on the platform. In the village of Zetten, west of Nijmegen, student Paul van Wely watched as Dutch Nazis crowding the railroad station waited all day for a Germany-bound train, which never arrived. Women and children were crying and to Van Wely "the waiting room looked like a junk

21

store full of tramps." In every town there were similar incidents. Dutch collaborators fled on anything that would move. Municipal architect Willem Tiemans, from his office window near the great Arnhem bridge, watched as Dutch Nazis "scrambled like mad" to get onto a barge heading up the Rhine for the Reich.

Hour after hour the traffic mounted, and even during darkness it went on. So desperate were the Germans to reach safety that on the nights of September 3 and 4, in total disregard of Allied air attacks, soldiers set up searchlights at some crossroads and many overloaded vehicles crawled by, headlights blazing. German officers seemed to have lost control. Dr. Anton Laterveer, a general practitioner in Arnhem, saw soldiers throwing away rifles —some even tried to sell their weapons to the Dutch. Joop Muselaars, a teen-ager, watched a lieutenant attempt to stop a virtually empty army vehicle, but the driver, ignoring the command, drove on through. Furious, the officer fired his pistol irrationally into the cobblestones.

Everywhere soldiers tried to desert. In the village of Eerde, Adrianus Marinus, an eighteen-year-old clerk, noticed a soldier jumping off a truck. He ran toward a farm and disappeared. Later Marinus learned that the soldier was a Russian prisoner of war who had been conscripted into the Wehrmacht. Two miles from Nijmegen, in the village of Lent on the northern bank of the Waal, Dr. Frans Huygen, while making his rounds, saw troops begging for civilian clothing, which the villagers refused. In Nijmegen deserters were not so abject. In many cases they demanded clothing at gunpoint. The Reverend Wilhelmus Peterse, forty-year-old Carmelite, saw soldiers hurriedly remove uniforms, change to suits and set off on foot for the German border. "The Germans were totally fed up with the war," recalls Garrit Memelink, Arnhem's Chief Forestry Inspector. "They were doing their damnedest to evade the military police."

With officers losing control, discipline broke down. Unruly gangs of soldiers stole horses, wagons, cars and bicycles. Some ordered farmers at gunpoint to haul them in their wagons toward Germany. All through the convoys the Dutch saw trucks, farm wagons, hand carts—even perambulators pushed by fleeing troops—piled high with loot filched from France, Belgium and Luxembourg. It ranged from statuary and furniture to lingerie. In Nijmegen soldiers tried to sell sewing machines, rolls of cloth, paintings, typewriters—and one soldier even offered a parrot in a large cage.

Among the retreating Germans there was no shortage of alcohol. Barely five miles from the German border in the town of Groesbeek, Father Herman Hoek watched horse-drawn carts loaded down with large quantities of wines and liquors. In Arnhem, the Reverend Reinhold Dijker spotted boisterous Wehrmacht troops on a truck drinking from a huge vat of wine which they had apparently brought all the way from France. Sixteen-year-old Agatha Schulte, daughter of the chief pharmacist of Arnhem's municipal hospital, was convinced that most of the soldiers she saw were drunk. They were throwing handfuls of French and Belgian coins to the youngsters and trying to sell bottles of wine, champagne and cognac to the adults. Her mother, Hendrina Schulte, vividly recalls seeing a German truck carrying another kind of booty. It was a large double bed—and in the bed was a woman.[*]

Besides the columns straggling up from the south, heavy German and civilian traffic was coming in from western Holland and the coast. It flooded through Arnhem and headed east for Germany. In the prosperous Arnhem suburb of Oosterbeek, Jan Voskuil, a thirty-eight-year-old chemical engineer, was hiding out at the home of his father-in-law. Learning that he was on a list of Dutch hostages to be arrested by the Germans, he had fled from his home in the town of Geldermalsen, twenty miles away, bringing his wife, Bertha, and their nine-year-old son. He had arrived in Oosterbeek just in time to see the evacuation. Jan's

[*] "Scenes were witnessed which nobody would ever have deemed possible in the German army," writes Walter Goerlitz, the German historian, in his *History of the German General Staff*. "Naval troops marched northward without weapons, selling their spare uniforms . . . They told people that the war was over and they were going home. Lorries loaded with officers, their mistresses and large quantities of champagne and brandy contrived to get get back as far as the Rhineland, and it was necessary to set up special courts-martial to deal with such cases."

father-in-law told him not to "worry anymore about the Germans; you won't have to 'dive' now." Looking down the main street of Oosterbeek, Voskuil saw "utter confusion." There were dozens of German-filled trucks, nose-to-tail, "all dangerously overloaded." He saw soldiers "on bicycles, pedaling furiously, with suitcases and grips looped over their handlebars." Voskuil was sure that the war would be over in a matter of days.

In Arnhem itself, Jan Mijnhart, sexton of the Grote Kerk—the massive fifteenth-century Church of St. Eusebius with a famed 305-foot-high tower—saw the *Moffen* (a Dutch nickname for the Germans, equivalent to the English "Jerry") filing through the town "four abreast in the direction of Germany." Some looked old and sick. In the nearby village of Ede an aged German begged young Rudolph van der Aa to notify his family in Germany that they had met. "I have a bad heart," he added, "and probably won't live much longer." Lucianus Vroemen, a teen-ager in Arnhem, noticed the Germans were exhausted and had "no fighting spirit or pride left." He saw officers trying, with little or no success, to restore order among the disorganized soldiers. They did not even react to the Dutch, who were yelling, "Go home! The British and Americans will be here in a few hours."

Watching the Germans moving east from Arnhem, Dr. Pieter de Graaff, forty-four-year-old surgeon, was sure he was seeing "the end, the apparent collapse of the German army." And Suze van Zweden, high-school mathematics teacher, had a special reason to remember this day. Her husband, Johan, a respected and well-known sculptor, had been in Dachau concentration camp since 1942 for hiding Dutch Jews. Now he might soon be freed, for obviously the war was nearly over. Suze was determined to witness this historic moment—the departure of the Germans and the arrival of the Allied liberators. Her son Robert was too young to realize what was happening but she decided to take her daughter Sonja, aged nine, into town. As she dressed Sonja, Suze said, "This is something you have to see. I want you to try and remember it all your life."

Everywhere the Dutch rejoiced. Dutch flags made their appearance. Enterprising merchants sold orange buttons and large stocks of ribbon to the eager crowds. In the village of Renkum there was a run on the local drapery shop, where manager Johannes Snoek sold orange ribbon as fast as he could cut it. To his amazement, villagers fashioned bows then and there and proudly pinned them on. Johannes, who was a member of the underground, thought "this was going a bit too far." To protect the villagers from their own excesses, he stopped selling the ribbon. His sister Maria, caught up in the excitement, noted happily in her diary that there was "a mood in the streets almost as though it was *Koninginnedag,* the Queen's birthday." Cheering crowds stood on sidewalks yelling, "Long live the Queen!" People sang the "Wilhelmus" (the Dutch national anthem) and "Oranje Boven!" ("Orange Above All!"). Cloaks flying, Sisters Antonia Stranzky and Christine van Dijk from St. Elisabeth's Hospital in Arnhem cycled down to the main square, the Velperplein, where they joined crowds on the terraces of cafés who were sipping coffee and eating potato pancakes as the Germans and Dutch Nazis streamed by.

At St. Canisius Hospital in Nijmegen, Sister M. Dosithèe Symons saw nurses dance with joy in the convent corridors. People brought out long-hidden radios and, while watching the retreat flood by their windows, listened openly for the first time in long months to the special Dutch service, Radio Orange, from London's BBC. So excited by the broadcasts was fruit grower Joannes Hurkx, in St. Oedenrode, that he failed to spot a group of Germans back of his house stealing the family bicycles.

In scores of places schools closed and work came to a halt. Employees at the cigar factories in Valkenswaard promptly left their machines and crowded into the streets. Streetcars stopped running in The Hague, the seat of government. In the capital, Amsterdam, the atmosphere was tense and unreal. Offices closed, and trading ceased on the stock exchange. Military units suddenly disappeared from the main thoroughfares, and the central station was mobbed by Germans and Dutch Nazis. On the outskirts of Amsterdam, Rotterdam and The Hague, crowds carrying

flags and flowers stood along main roads leading into the cities—
hoping to be the first to see British tanks coming from the south.

Rumors grew with every hour. Many in Amsterdam believed
that British troops had already freed The Hague, near the coast
about thirty miles to the southwest. In The Hague people
thought the great port of Rotterdam, fifteen miles away, had been
liberated. Rail travelers got a different story every time their
trains stopped. One of them, Henri Peijnenburg, a twenty-five-
year-old resistance leader traveling from The Hague to his home
in Nijmegen, a distance of less than eighty miles, heard at the
beginning of his journey that the British had entered the ancient
border city of Maastricht. In Utrecht he was told they had
reached Roermond. Then, in Arnhem he was assured that the
British had taken Venlo, a few miles from the German border.
"When I finally got home," he recalls, "I expected to see the Allies
in the streets, but all I saw were the retreating Germans." Peijnenburg felt confused and uneasy.

Others shared his concern—especially the underground high
command meeting secretly in The Hague. To them, tensely
watching the situation, Holland seemed on the threshold of
freedom. Allied tanks could easily slice through the country all
the way from the Belgian border to the Zuider Zee. The underground was certain that the "gateway"—through Holland, across
the Rhine and into Germany—was wide open.

The resistance leaders knew the Germans had virtually no
fighting forces capable of stopping a determined Allied drive.
They were almost scornful of the one weak and undermanned
division composed of old men guarding coastal defenses (they
had been sitting in concrete bunkers since 1940 without firing a
shot), and of a number of other low-grade troops, whose combat
capabilities were extremely doubtful, among them Dutch SS,
scratch garrison troops, convalescents and the medically unfit—
these last grouped into units aptly known as "stomach" and "ear"
battalions, because most of the men suffered from ulcers or were
hard of hearing.

To the Dutch the Allied move seemed obvious, invasion imminent. But its success depended on the speed of British forces driving from the south, and about this the underground high command was puzzled: they were unable to determine the precise extent of the Allied advance.

Checking on the validity of Prime Minister Gerbrandy's statement that Allied troops had already crossed the frontier was no simple matter. Holland was small—only about two thirds the size of Ireland—but it had a dense population of more than nine million, and as a result the Germans had difficulty controlling subversive activity. There were underground cells in every town and village. Still, transmitting information was hazardous. The principal, and most dangerous, method was the telephone. In an emergency, using complicated circuitry, secret lines and coded information, resistance leaders could call all over the country. Thus, on this occasion, underground officials knew within minutes that Gerbrandy's announcement was premature: British troops had not crossed the border.

Other Radio Orange broadcasts further compounded the confusion. Twice in a little more than twelve hours (at 11:45 P.M. on September 4 and again on the morning of September 5) the Dutch Service of the BBC announced that the fortress city of Breda, seven miles from the Dutch-Belgian border, had been liberated. The news spread rapidly. Illegal, secretly printed newspapers promptly prepared liberation editions featuring the "fall of Breda." But the Arnhem regional resistance chief, thirty-eight-year-old Pieter Kruyff, whose group was one of the nation's most highly skilled and disciplined, seriously doubted the Radio Orange bulletin. He had his communications expert Johannes Steinfort, a young telephone-company instrument maker, check the report. Quickly tying in to a secret circuit connecting him with the underground in Breda, Steinfort became one of the first to learn the bitter truth: the city was still in German hands. No one had seen Allied troops, either American or British.

Because of the spate of rumors, many resistance groups hurriedly met to discuss what should be done. Although Prince Bernhard and SHAEF (Supreme Headquarters Allied Expeditionary Forces) had cautioned against a general uprising, some underground members had run out of patience. The time had come, they believed, to directly confront the enemy and thus aid the advancing Allies. It was obvious that the Germans feared a general revolt. In the retreating columns, the underground noted, sentries were now sitting on the fenders of vehicles with rifles and submachine guns at the ready. Undeterred, many resistance men were eager to fight.

In the village of Ede, a few miles northwest of Oosterbeek, twenty-five-year-old Menno "Tony" de Nooy tried to persuade the leader of his group, Bill Wildeboer, to attack. It had long been planned, Tony argued, that the group should take over Ede in the event of an Allied invasion. The barracks at Ede, which had been used to train German marines, were now practically empty. De Nooy wanted to occupy the buildings. The older Wildeboer, a former sergeant major in the Dutch Army, disagreed. "I don't trust this situation," he told them. "The time is not yet ripe. We must wait."

Not all resistance movements were held in check. In Rotterdam, underground members occupied the offices of the water-supply company. Just over the Dutch-Belgian border in the village of Axel, the town hall with its ancient ramparts was seized and hundreds of German soldiers surrendered to the civilian fighters. In many towns Dutch Nazi officials were captured as they tried to bolt. West of Arnhem, in the village of Wolfheze, noted principally for its hospital for the mentally ill, the district police commissioner was seized in his car. He was locked up temporarily in the nearest available quarters, the asylum, for delivery to the British "when they arrived."

These were the exceptions. In general, underground units remained calm. Yet, everywhere they took advantage of the confusion to prepare for the arrival of Allied forces. In Arnhem, Charles Labouchère, forty-two, descendant of an old French family and active in an intelligence unit, was much too busy to bother about rumors. He sat, hour after hour, by the windows of an office in the neighborhood of the Arnhem bridge and, with a number of assistants, watched German units heading east and northeast along the Zevenaar and Zutphen roads toward Germany. It was Labouchère's job to estimate the number of troops and, where possible, to identify the units. The vital information he noted down was sent to Amsterdam by courier and from there via a secret network to London.

In suburban Oosterbeek, young Jan Eijkelhoff, threading his way unobtrusively through the crowds, cycled all over the area, delivering forged food ration cards to Dutchmen hiding out from the Germans. And the leader of one group in Arnhem, fifty-seven-year-old Johannus Penseel, called "the Old One," reacted in the kind of wily manner that had made him a legend among his men. He decided the moment had come to move his arsenal of weapons. Openly, with German troops all about, he and a few hand-picked assistants calmly drove up in a baker's van to the Municipal Hospital, where the weapons were hidden. Quickly wrapping the arms in brown paper they transported the entire cache to Penseel's home, whose basement windows conveniently overlooked the main square. Penseel and his coleader, Toon van Daalen, thought it was a perfect position from which to open fire on the Germans when the time came. They were determined to live up to the name of their militant subdivision—*Landelyke Knokploegen* ("Strong-arm Boys").

Everywhere men and women of the vast underground army poised for battle; and in southern towns and villages, people who believed that parts of Holland were already free ran out of their homes to welcome the liberators. There was a kind of madness in the air, thought Carmelite Father Tiburtius Noordermeer as he observed the joyful crowds in the village of Oss, southeast of Nijmegen. He saw people slapping one another on the back in a congratulatory mood. Comparing the demoralized Germans on the roads with the jubilant Dutch spectators, he noted "wild fear on the one hand and crazy, unlimited, joy on the other." "Nobody," the stolid Dutch priest recalled, "acted normally."

Many grew more anxious as time passed. In the drugstore on the main street in Oosterbeek, Karel de Wit was worried. He told his wife and chief pharmacist, Johanna, that he couldn't understand why Allied planes had not attacked the German traffic. Frans Schulte, a retired Dutch major, thought the general enthusiasm was premature. Although his brother and sister-in-law were overjoyed at what appeared to be a German debacle, Schulte was not convinced. "Things may get worse," he warned. "The Germans are far from beaten. If the Allies try to cross the Rhine, believe me, we may see a major battle."

✽ 3 ✽

Hitler's crucial measures were already underway. On September 4 at the Führer's headquarters deep in the forest of Görlitz, Rastenburg, East Prussia, sixty-nine-year-old Field Marshal Gerd von Rundstedt prepared to leave for the western front. He had not expected a new command.

Called abruptly out of enforced retirement, Von Rundstedt had been ordered to Rastenburg four days before. On July 2, two months earlier, Hitler had fired him as Commander in Chief West (or, as it was known in German military terms, OB West—*Oberbefehlshaber* West) while Von Rundstedt, who had never lost a battle, was trying to cope with the aftermath of Germany's greatest crisis of the war, the Allied invasion of Normandy.

The Führer and Germany's most distinguished soldier had never agreed on how best to meet that threat. Before the invasion, appealing for reinforcements, Von Rundstedt had bluntly informed Hitler's headquarters (OKW—Oberkommando der Wehrmacht)° that the Western Allies, superior in men, equipment and planes, could "land anywhere they want to." Not so, Hitler declared. The Atlantic Wall, the partly completed coastal

° Armed Forces High Command

fortifications which, Hitler boasted, ran almost three thousand miles from Kirkenes (on the Norwegian-Finnish frontier) to the Pyrenees (on the Franco-Spanish border) would make "this front impregnable against any enemy." Von Rundstedt knew only too well that the fortifications were more propaganda than fact. He summed up the Atlantic Wall in one word: "Humbug."

The legendary Field Marshal Erwin Rommel, renowned for his victories in the North African deserts in the first years of the war and sent by Hitler to command Army Group B under Von Rundstedt, was equally appalled by the Führer's confidence. To Rommel, the coastal defenses were a "figment of Hitler's *Wolkenkuckkucksheim* [cloud cuckoo land]." The aristocratic, tradition-bound Von Rundstedt and the younger, ambitious Rommel found themselves, probably for the first time, in agreement. On another point, however, they clashed. With the crushing defeat of his Afrika Korps by Britain's Montgomery at El Alamein in 1942 always in his mind, and well aware of what the Allied invasion would be like, Rommel believed that the invaders must be stopped on the beaches. Von Rundstedt icily disagreed with his junior—whom he sarcastically referred to as the "Marschall Bubi" ("Marshal Laddie"); Allied troops should be wiped out *after* they landed, he contended. Hitler backed Rommel. On D Day, despite Rommel's brilliant improvisations, Allied troops breached the "impregnable" wall within hours.

In the terrible days that followed, overwhelmed by the Allies, who enjoyed almost total air supremacy over the Normandy battlefield, and shackled by Hitler's "no withdrawal" orders ("Every man shall fight and fall where he stands"), Von Rundstedt's straining lines cracked everywhere. Desperately he plugged the gaps, but hard as his men fought and counterattacked, the outcome was never seriously in doubt. Von Rundstedt could neither "drive the invaders into the sea" nor "annihilate them" (the words were Hitler's).

On the night of July 1, at the height of the Normandy battle, Hitler's chief of staff, Field Marshal Wilhelm Keitel, called Von Rundstedt and plaintively asked, "What shall we do?" Characteristically blunt, Von Rundstedt snapped, "End the war, you fools. What else can you do?" Hitler's comment on hearing the remark was mild. "The old man has lost his nerve and can't master the situation any longer. He'll have to go." Twenty-four hours later, in a polite handwritten note, Hitler informed Von Rundstedt that, "in consideration of your health and of the increased exertions to be expected in the near future," he was relieved of command.

Von Rundstedt, the senior and most dependable field marshal in the Wehrmacht, was incredulous. For the five years of war his military genius had served the Third Reich well. In 1939, when Hitler cold-bloodedly attacked Poland, thereby igniting the conflict that eventually engulfed the world, Von Rundstedt had clearly demonstrated the German formula for conquest—*Blitzkrieg* ("lightning war")—when his Panzer spearheads reached the outskirts of Warsaw in less than a week. One year later, when Hitler turned west and with devastating speed overwhelmed most of western Europe, Von Rundstedt was in charge of an entire Panzer army. And in 1941 he was in the forefront again when Hitler attacked Russia. Now, outraged at the jeopardy to his career and reputation, Von Rundstedt told his chief of staff, Major General Gunther Blumentritt, that he had been "dismissed in disgrace by an amateur strategist." That "Bohemian corporal," he fumed, had used "my age and ill health as an excuse to relieve me in order to have a scapegoat." Given a free hand, Von Rundstedt had planned a slow withdrawal to the German frontier, during which, as he outlined his plans to Blumentritt, he would have "exacted a terrible price for every foot of ground given up." But, as he had said to his staff many times, because of the constant "tutelage from above," about the only authority he had as OB West was "to change the guard in front of the gate."°

From the moment of his recall and his arrival at the end of

° "Von Rundstedt was hurt by the implication in Hitler's letter that he had 'requested' relief," the late General Blumentritt told me in an interview. "Some of us at Headquarters actually thought he had, but this was not so. Von Rundstedt denied that he had ever asked to be relieved—or that he had ever thought of doing so. He was extremely angry—so angry in fact that he swore he would never again take a command under Hitler. I knew he did not mean it for, to Von Rundstedt, military obedience was unconditional and absolute."

August at the Rastenburg *Wolfsschanze* ("Wolf's Lair"), as it was named by Hitler, Von Rundstedt, at the Führer's invitation, attended the daily briefing conference. Hitler, according to the Deputy Chief of Operations General Walter Warlimont, greeted his senior field marshal warmly, treating him with "unwonted diffidence and respect." Warlimont also noted that throughout the long sessions Von Rundstedt simply sat "motionless and mono-syllabic."* The precise, practical field marshal had nothing to say. He was appalled by the situation.

The briefings clearly showed that in the east the Red Army now held a front more than 1,400 miles long, from Finland in the north to the Vistula in Poland, and from there to the Carpathian Mountains in Rumania and Yugoslavia. In fact, Russian armor had reached the borders of East Prussia, barely a hundred miles from the Führer's headquarters.

In the west Von Rundstedt saw that his worst fears had been realized. Division after division was now destroyed, the entire German line thrown helplessly back. Rear-guard units, although surrounded and cut off, still clung to vital ports such as Dunkirk, Calais, Boulogne, Le Havre, Brest, Lorient and St. Nazaire, forc-ing the Allies to continue bringing supplies in from the distant invasion beaches. But now, with the sudden, stunning capture of Antwerp, one of Europe's greatest deep seaports, the Allies might well have solved their supply problem. Von Rundstedt noted, too, that the tactic of *Blitzkrieg*, perfected by himself and others, was being borrowed with devastating effect by Eisenhower's armies. And Field Marshal Walter Model, the fifty-four-year-old new Commander in Chief, West (he took over on August 17), was clearly unable to bring order out of the chaos. His front had been ripped apart, slashed in the north by tanks of the British Second Army and the U.S. First Army driving through Belgium toward Holland; and, south of the Ardennes, armored columns of the U.S. Third Army under General George S. Patton were heading for Metz and the Saar. To Von Rundstedt the situation was no longer merely ominous. It was cataclysmic.

* Warlimont, *Inside Hitler's Headquarters*, 1939–45, p. 477.

NORTH SEA

ZUIDER ZEE

HOLLAND

GERMANY

RUHR
MONTGOMERY'S OBJECTIVE

Essen

Düsseldorf

Cologne

BELGIUM

Zwolle

IJSSEL R.

Apeldoorn

Ruurlo

HARMEL'S 10TH SS PANZER
(FRUNDSBERG) DIV.

BEGAN MOVING TO ARNHEM SEPT. 5–6

RHINE R.

Beekbergen

HARZER'S 9TH SS PANZER
(HOHENSTAUFEN) DIV.

ARNHEM

BITTRICH'S H.Q.

Oosterbeek
MODEL'S H.Q.
SEPT. 15

LOWER RHINE

NIJMEGEN

WAAL R.

Grave

MAAS R.

Vught
STUDENT'S H.Q.

WILHELMINA CANAL

WILLEMS CANAL

Son

EINDHOVEN

Neerpelt

Utrecht

Amsterdam

The Hague

Rotterdam

Tilburg

STUDENT'S FIRST
PARACHUTE ARMY

FRONT LINE
SEPT. 14/44

ESCAUT CANAL

MEUSE CANAL

DEMPSEY'S BR.
SECOND ARMY

ALBERT CANAL

Maastricht

MAAS R.

Bergen
op Zoom

Antwerp

Brussels

MONTGOMERY'S
BR. 21ST A.G.

Flushing

Breskens

VON ZANGEN'S
FIFTEENTH ARMY

Ghent

Bruges

Ostend

CRERAR'S CAN.
FIRST ARMY

THE FRONT, SEPT. 14, 1944

N

Reims

Miles
0   50
palacios

FRANCE

MEUSE R.

MEUSE R.

Verdun

PATTON'S U.S.
THIRD ARMY

Metz

MOSELLE R.

Luxembourg

Bastogne

BRADLEY'S
U.S. 12TH A.G

Malmedy

Liège

MEUSE R.

HODGES' U.S.
FIRST ARMY

OURTHE

GERMAN
SEVENTH ARMY

SIEGFRIED
LINE

BITTRICH'S
II SS PANZER CORPS

Trier

BLASCOWITZ'S
A.G G

SAAR

Saarbrücken

VON RUNDSTEDT'S
OB WEST

Arnberg

Koblenz

MOSEL R.

Bonn

RHINE R.

He had time to dwell on the inevitability of the end. Almost four days elapsed before Hitler allowed Von Rundstedt a private audience. During his wait the Field Marshal stayed in the former country inn reserved for senior officers in the center of the vast headquarters—a barbed-wire-enclosed enclave of wooden huts and concrete bunkers built over a catacomb of underground installations. Von Rundstedt vented his impatience at the delay on Keitel, the chief of staff. "Why have I been sent for?" he demanded. "What sort of game is going on?" Keitel was unable to tell him. Hitler had given Keitel no particular reason, short of an innocuous mention of the Field Marshal's health. Hitler seemed to have convinced himself of his own manufactured version for Von Rundstedt's dismissal on "health grounds" back in July. To Keitel, Hitler had merely said, "I want to see if the old man's health has improved."

Twice Keitel reminded the Führer that the Field Marshal was waiting. Finally, on the afternoon of September 4, Von Rundstedt was summoned to Hitler's presence, and, uncharacteristically, the Führer came to the point immediately. "I would like to entrust you once more with the western front."

Stiffly erect, both hands on his gold baton, Von Rundstedt merely nodded. Despite his knowledge and experience, his distaste for Hitler and the Nazis, Von Rundstedt, in whom the Prussian military tradition of devotion to service was ingrained, did not decline the appointment. As he was later to recall, "it would have been useless to protest anyway."*

Almost cursorily, Hitler outlined Von Rundstedt's task. Once more Hitler was improvising. Before D Day he had insisted that the Atlantic Wall was invulnerable. Now, to Von Rundstedt's dismay, the Führer stressed the impregnability of the Westwall—the long-neglected, unmanned but still formidable frontier fortifications better known to the Allies as the Siegfried Line.

* According to Walter Goerlitz, editor of *The Memoirs of Field Marshal Keitel* (Chapter 10, p. 347), Von Rundstedt said to Hitler, "My Führer, whatever you may command, I will do my duty to my last breath." My version of Von Rundstedt's reaction is based on the recollections of his former chief of staff, Major General Blumentritt. "I said nothing," Von Rundstedt told him. "If I'd opened my mouth, Hitler would have talked 'at me' for three hours."

Von Rundstedt, Hitler ordered, was not only to stop the Allies as far west as possible, but to counterattack for, as the Führer saw it, the most dangerous Allied threats were no more than "armored spearheads." Clearly, however, Hitler was shaken by the capture of Antwerp. Its vital port was to be denied the Allies at all costs. Thus, since the other ports were still in German hands, Hitler said, he fully expected the Allied drive to come to a halt because of overextended supply lines. He was confident that the western front could be stabilized and, with the coming of winter, the initiative regained. Hitler assured Von Rundstedt that he was "not unduly worried about the situation in the west."

It was a variation of a monologue Von Rundstedt had heard many times in the past. The Westwall, to Hitler, had now become an *idée fixe*, and Von Rundstedt once again was being ordered "not to give an inch," and "to hold under all conditions."

By ordering Von Rundstedt to replace Field Marshal Model, Hitler was making his third change of command of OB West within two months—from Von Rundstedt to Field Marshal Gunther von Kluge, to Model, and now once again to Von Rundstedt. Model, in the job just eighteen days, would now command only Army Group B under Von Rundstedt, Hitler said. Von Rundstedt had long regarded Model with less than enthusiasm. Model, he felt, had not earned his promotion the hard way; he had been elevated to the rank of field marshal too quickly by Hitler. Von Rundstedt thought him better suited to the job of a "good regimental sergeant major." Still, the Field Marshal felt that Model's position made little difference now. The situation was all but hopeless, defeat inevitable. On the afternoon of September 4, as he set out for his headquarters near Koblenz, Von Rundstedt saw nothing to stop the Allies from invading Germany, crossing the Rhine and ending the war in a matter of weeks.

On this same day in Wannsee, Berlin, Colonel General Kurt Student, fifty-four-year-old founder of Germany's airborne forces, emerged from the backwater to which he had been relegated for three long years. For him, the war had begun with great promise. His paratroops, Student felt, had been chiefly responsible for the capture of Holland in 1940, when some 4,000 of them dropped on the bridges of Rotterdam, Dordrecht and Moerdijk, holding the vital spans open for the main German invasion force. Student's losses had been incredibly low—only 180 men. But the situation was different in the 1941 airborne assault of Crete. There, losses were so high—more than a third of the 22,000-man force—that Hitler forbade all future airborne operations. "The day of parachute troops is over," the Führer said, and the future had dimmed for Student. Ever since, the ambitious officer had been tied to a desk job as commander of an airborne-training establishment, while his elite troopers were used strictly as infantry. With shattering abruptness, at precisely 3 P.M. on this critical September 4, Student emerged into the mainstream once again. In a brief telephone call, Colonel General Alfred Jodl, Hitler's operations chief, ordered him to immediately organize an army, which the Führer had designated as the "First Parachute Army." As the astounded Student listened, it occurred to him that "it was a rather high-sounding title for a force that didn't exist."

Student's troopers were scattered all over Germany, and apart from a few seasoned, fully equipped units, they were green recruits armed only with training weapons. His force of about ten thousand had almost no transportation, armor or artillery. Student didn't even have a chief of staff.

Nevertheless, Student's men, Jodl explained, were urgently needed in the west. They were to "close a gigantic hole" between Antwerp and the area of Liège-Maastricht by "holding a line along the Albert Canal." With all possible speed, Student was ordered to rush his forces to Holland and Belgium. Weapons and equipment would be issued at the "railheads of destination." Besides his paratroopers, two divisions had been earmarked for his new "army." One of them, the 719th, Student soon learned, was "made up of old men stationed along the Dutch coast who had not as yet fired a single shot." His second division, the 176th, was even worse. It consisted of "semi-invalids and convalescents who, for convenience, had been grouped together in separate battalions according to their various ailments." They even had special "diet" kitchens for those suffering from stomach trouble. Besides these units, he would get a grab bag of other forces scattered in Holland and Belgium—Luftwaffe troops, sailors and antiaircraft crews—and twenty-five tanks. To Student, the expert in paratroop warfare and supertrained airborne shock troops, his makeshift army was a "grotesque improvisation on a grand scale." Still, he was back in the war again.

All through the afternoon, by telephone and teletype, Student mustered and moved his men out. It would take at least four days for his entire force to reach the front, he estimated. But his toughest and best troops, rushed in special trains to Holland in what Student called a "blitz move," would be in position on the Albert Canal, as part of Model's Army Group B, within twenty-four hours.

Jodl's call and the information he himself had since gathered alarmed Student. It seemed apparent that his most seasoned group—the 6th Parachute Regiment plus one other battalion, together totaling about three thousand men—probably constituted the only combat-ready reserve in the whole of Germany. He found the situation ominous.

Frantically, Field Marshal Walter Model, Commander in Chief, West, tried to plug the yawning gap east of Antwerp and halt the disorderly retreat from Belgium into Holland. As yet no news of Von Rundstedt's appointment as his successor had reached him. His forces were so entangled, so disorganized that Model had all but lost control. He no longer had contact with the second half of his command, Army Group G in the south. Had General Johannes Blaskowitz, its commander, successfully withdrawn from France?

Model wasn't sure. To the harassed Field Marshal the predicament of Army Group G was secondary. The crisis was clearly in the north.

With dispatch and ferocity, Army Group B had been split in two by armored columns of the British and Americans. Of the two armies composing Army Group B, the Fifteenth was bottled up, its back to the North Sea, roughly between Calais and a point northwest of Antwerp. The Seventh Army had been almost destroyed, and thrown back toward Maastricht and Aachen. Between the two armies lay a 75-mile gap and the British had driven through it straight to Antwerp. Plunging along the same route were Model's own demoralized, retreating forces.

In a desperate effort to halt their flight, Model issued an emotional plea to his troops.

. . . With the enemy's advance and the withdrawal of our front, several hundred thousand soldiers are falling back—army, air force and armored units—troops which must re-form as planned and hold in new strong points or lines.

In this stream are the remnants of broken units which, for the moment, have no set objectives and are not even in a position to receive clear orders. Whenever orderly columns turn off the road to reorganize, streams of disorganized elements push on. With their wagons move whispers, rumors, haste, endless disorder and vicious self-interest. This atmosphere is being brought back to the rear areas, infecting units still intact and in this moment of extreme tension must be prevented by the strongest means.

I appeal to your honor as soldiers. We have lost a battle, but I assure you of this: We will win this war! I cannot tell you more at the present, although I know that questions are burning on your lips. Whatever has happened, never lose your faith in the future of Germany. At the same time you must be aware of the gravity of the situation. This moment will and should separate men from weaklings. Now every soldier has the same responsibility. When his commander falls, he must be ready to step into his shoes and carry on . . .

There followed a long series of instructions in which Model "categorically" demanded that retreating troops should immediately "report to the nearest command point," instill in others "confidence, self-reliance, self-control and optimism," and repudiate "stupid gossip, rumors and irresponsible reports." The enemy, he said, was "not everywhere at once" and, indeed, "if all the tanks reported by rumormongers were counted, there would have to be a hundred thousand of them." He begged his men not to give up important positions or demolish equipment, weapons or installations "before it is necessary." The astonishing document wound up by stressing that everything depended on "gaining time, which the Führer needs to put new weapons and new troops into operation."

Virtually without communications, depending for the most part on radio, Model could only hope that his Order of the Day reached all his troops. In the confusion he was not even sure of the latest position of his disorganized and shattered units; nor did he know precisely how far Allied tanks and troops had advanced. And where was the *Schwerpunkt* (main thrust) of the Allied drive—with the British and Americans in the north heading for the Siegfried Line and thence across the Rhine and into the Ruhr? Was it with Patton's massive U.S. Third Army driving for the Saar, the Siegfried Line and over the Rhine into Frankfurt?

Model's dilemma was the outgrowth of a situation that had occurred nearly two months earlier at the time of Von Rundstedt's dismissal and Hitler's swift appointment of Von Kluge as the old Field Marshal's successor. On sick leave for months from his command in Russia, Von Kluge happened to be making a courtesy call on the Führer at the precise moment when Hitler decided to dismiss Von Rundstedt. With no preamble, and possibly because Von Kluge happened to be the only senior officer in sight, Hitler had named the astonished Von Kluge Commander in Chief, West.

Von Kluge, a veteran front commander, took over on July 4. He was to last forty-four days. Exactly as predicted by Von Rundstedt, the Allied breakout occurred. "The whole western front has been ripped open," Von Kluge informed Hitler. Overwhelmed by the Allied tide pouring across France, Von Kluge, like Von

Rundstedt before him, found his hands tied by Hitler's insistent "no withdrawal" orders. The German armies in France were encircled and all but destroyed. It was during this period that another convulsion racked the Third Reich—an abortive assassination attempt on Hitler's life.

During one of the endless conferences at the Führer's headquarters, a time bomb in a briefcase, placed by Colonel Claus Graf von Stauffenberg beneath a table close to Hitler, exploded, killing and wounding many in the room. The Führer escaped with minor injuries. Although only a small elite group of officers were involved in the plot, Hitler's revenge was barbaric. Anyone connected with the plotters, or with their families, was arrested; and many individuals, innocent or not, were summarily executed.* Some five thousand people lost their lives. Von Kluge had been indirectly implicated, and Hitler also suspected him of trying to negotiate a surrender with the enemy. Von Kluge was replaced by Model and ordered to report immediately to the Führer. Before leaving his headquarters the despairing Von Kluge wrote a letter to Hitler. Then, en route to Germany, he took poison.

When you receive these lines I shall be no more [he wrote to the Führer]. . . . *I did everything within my power to be equal to the situation . . . Both Rommel and I, and probably all the other commanders here in the west with experience of battle against the Anglo-Americans, with their preponderance of material, foresaw the present developments. We were not listened to. Our appreciations were not dictated by pessimism, but from sober knowledge of the facts. I do not know whether Field Marshal Model, who has been proved in every sphere, will master the situation. From my heart I hope so. Should it not be so, however, and your new weapons . . . not succeed, then, my Führer, make up your mind to end the war. It is time to put an end to this frightfulness. . . . I have always admired your greatness . . . and*

---

* Hitler took advantage of his most senior officer, Von Rundstedt, once again by making him President of the Court of Honor that passed judgment on the officers suspected. Von Rundstedt quietly acceded to the Führer's request. "If I had not," he later explained, "I too might have been considered a traitor." Von Rundstedt's explanation has never satisfied many of his brother generals, who privately denounced him for bending to Hitler's request.

*your iron will . . . Show yourself now also great enough to put an
end to this hopeless struggle. . . .*

Hitler had no intention of conceding victory to the Allies, even
though the Third Reich that he had boasted would last a millen-
nium was undermined and tottering. On every front he was
attempting to stave off defeat. Yet each move the Führer made
seemed more desperate than the last.

Model's appointment as OB West had not helped. Unlike Von
Rundstedt or, briefly, Von Kluge, Model did not have the combat
genius of Rommel as support. After Rommel was badly wounded
by a strafing Allied plane on July 17, no one had been sent to
replace him.° Model did not at first appear to feel the need.
Confident that he could right the situation, he took on Rommel's
old command as well, becoming not only OB West but also Commander of Army Group B. Despite Model's expertise, the situation was too grave for any one commander.

At this time Army Group B was battling for survival along a
line roughly between the Belgian coast and the Franco-Luxem-
bourg border. From there, south to Switzerland, the remainder of
Model's command—Army Group G under General Blaskowitz—
had already been written off. Following the second Allied invasion on August 15, by French and American forces in the
Marseilles area, Blaskowitz' group had hurriedly departed southern France. Under continuous pressure they were now falling
back in disarray to the German border.

Along Model's disintegrating northern front, where Allied
armor had torn the 75-mile-wide gap in the line, the route from
Belgium into Holland and from there across Germany's vulnerable northwest frontier lay open and undefended. Allied forces
driving into Holland could outflank the Siegfried Line where the
massive belt of fortifications extending along Germany's frontiers
from Switzerland terminated at Kleve on the Dutch-German

° Rommel, who was also suspected by Hitler of being involved in the assassination
attempt, died three months later. While convalescing at his home, Hitler gave him
a choice: stand trial for treason or commit suicide. On October 14, Rommel swal-
lowed cyanide, and Hitler announced that the Reich's most popular field marshal
had "died of wounds sustained on the battlefield."

border. By turning this northern tip of Hitler's Westwall and crossing the Rhine, the Allies could swing into the Ruhr, the industrial heart of the Reich. That maneuver might well bring about the total collapse of Germany.

Twice in seventy-two hours Model appealed desperately to Hitler for reinforcements. The situation of his forces in the undefended gap was chaotic. Order had to be restored and the breach closed. Model's latest report, which he had sent to Hitler in the early hours of September 4, warned that the crisis was approaching and unless he received a minimum of "twenty-five fresh divisions and an armored reserve of five or six panzer divisions," the entire front might collapse, thereby opening the "gateway into northwest Germany."

Model's greatest concern was the British entry into Antwerp. He did not know whether the huge port, the second-largest in Europe, was captured intact or destroyed by the German garrison. The city of Antwerp itself, lying far inland, was not the crux. To use the port, the Allies needed to control its seaward approach, an inlet 54 miles long and 3 miles wide at its mouth, running into Holland from the North Sea past Walcheren Island and looping alongside the South Beveland peninsula. So long as German guns commanded the Schelde estuary, the port of Antwerp could be denied the Allies.

Unfortunately for Model, apart from antiaircraft batteries and heavy coastal guns on Walcheren Island, he had almost no forces along the northern bank. But on the other side of the Schelde and almost isolated in the Pas de Calais was General Gustav von Zangen's Fifteenth Army—a force of more than 80,000 men. Though pocketed—the sea lay behind them to the north and west, and Canadians and British were pressing in from the south and east—they nevertheless controlled most of the southern bank of the estuary.

By now, Model believed, British tanks, exploiting the situation, would surely be moving along the northern bank and sweeping it clear. Before long the entire South Beveland peninsula could be in their hands and sealed off from the Dutch mainland at its narrow base north of the Belgian border, barely 18 miles from Antwerp. Next, to open the port, the British would turn on the trapped Fifteenth Army and clear the southern bank. Von Zangen's forces had to be extricated.

Late in the afternoon of September 4 at Army Group B's headquarters southeast of Liège in the village of La Chaude Fontaine, Model issued a series of orders. By radio he commanded Von Zangen to hold the southern bank of the Schelde and reinforce the lesser ports of Dunkirk, Boulogne and Calais, which Hitler had earlier decreed were to be held with "fanatical determination as fortresses." With the remainder of his troops the hapless Von Zangen was to attack northeast into the avalanche of British armor. It was a desperate measure, yet Model saw no other course. If Von Zangen's attack was successful, it might isolate the British in Antwerp and cut off Montgomery's armored spearheads driving north. Even if the attack failed, Von Zangen's effort might buy time, slowing up the Allied drive long enough for reserves to arrive and hold a new front along the Albert Canal.

Exactly what reinforcements were on the way, Model did not know. As darkness fell he finally received Hitler's answer to his pleas for new divisions to stabilize the front. It was the terse news of his replacement as Commander in Chief, West, by Field Marshal von Rundstedt. Von Kluge had lasted forty-four days as OB West, Model barely eighteen. Normally temperamental and ambitious, Model reacted calmly on this occasion. He was more aware of his shortcomings as an administrator than his critics believed.° Now he could concentrate on the job he knew best:

° Twice Model informed Hitler of his inability to command both OB West and Army Group B. "We rarely saw him," OB West's Chief of Staff Blumentritt recalled. "Model hated paper work and spent most of his time in the field." Lieutenant General Bodo Zimmermann, OB West's operations chief, wrote after the war (OCMH MS 308, pp. 153–154) that though Model "was a thoroughly capable soldier," he often "demanded too much and that too quickly," hence "losing sight of what was practically possible." He had a tendency to "dissipate his forces," added Zimmermann, and "staff work suffered under his too-frequent absences and erratic, inconsistent demands."

being a front-line commander, solely in charge of Army Group B. But, among the flurry of frantic orders Model issued on this last day as OB West, one would prove momentous. It concerned the relocation of his II SS Panzer Corps.

The commander of the Corps, fifty-year-old Obergruppen-führer (Lieutenant General) Wilhelm Bittrich, had been out of touch with Model for more than seventy-two hours. His forces, fighting almost continuously since Normandy, had been badly mauled. Bittrich's tank losses were staggering, his men short on ammunition and fuel. In addition, because of the breakdown of communications, the few orders he had received by radio were already out of date when Bittrich got them. Uncertain of the enemy's movements and badly in need of direction, Bittrich set out on foot to find Model. He finally located the Field Marshal at Army Group B headquarters near Liège. "I had not seen him since the Russian front in 1941," Bittrich later recalled. "Monocle in his eye, wearing his usual short leather coat, Model was standing looking at a map and snapping out commands one after the other. There was little time for conversation. Pending official orders, which would follow, I was told to move my Corps head-quarters north into Holland." With all possible speed Bittrich was directed to "supervise the refitting and rehabilitation of the 9th and 10th SS Panzer divisions." The battered units, Model told him, were to "slowly disengage from the battle and immediately head north."[*]

The almost unknown Bittrich could hardly foresee the critical

---

[*] Understandably perhaps, German records of this period are vague and often inexplicable. Commands were issued, never received, re-sent, countermanded or changed. Considerable confusion exists about Model's order. According to Army Group B's war diary, movement orders for the 9th and 10th SS Panzer divisions were sent on the night of September 3. If so, they were never received. Also, it is recorded that Bittrich received his instructions forty-eight hours later to supervise the regrouping and rehabilitation of not only the 9th but the 2nd and 116th Panzer units. Curiously, the 10th is not mentioned. I can find no evidence that either the 2nd or 116th ever reached the Arnhem area. (It appears they continued fighting at the front.) According to Bittrich's own papers and logs, he received Model's orders orally on September 4 and duly directed only the 9th and 10th to proceed north. Both units, according to their commanders, began slowly withdrawing on September 5–6.

role his 9th and 10th SS Panzer divisions would play within the next two weeks. The site Model chose for Bittrich was in a quiet zone, at this point some seventy-five miles behind the front. By a historic fluke, the area included the city of Arnhem.

❊ 4 ❊

T HE HEADLONG RETREAT of the Germans out of Holland was slowing, although few of the jubilant Dutch realized it as yet. From the Belgian border north to Arnhem, roads were still choked, but there was a difference in the movement. From his post in the Provincial Building above the Arnhem bridge, Charles La-bouchère saw no letup in the flood of vehicles, troops and Nazi sympathizers streaming across the bridge. But a few blocks north of Labouchère's location, Gerhardus Gysbers, a seller of antique books, saw a change take place. German troops entering Arnhem from the west were not moving on. The compound of the Willems Barracks next to Gysbers' home and the streets in the immediate vicinity were filling with horse-drawn vehicles and disheveled soldiers. Gysbers noted Luftwaffe battalions, antiaircraft personnel, Dutch SS and elderly men of the 719th Coastal Division. It was clear to Arnhem's resistance chief, Pieter Kruyff, that this was no temporary halt. These troops were not heading back into Germany. They were slowly regrouping; some horse-drawn units of the 719th were starting to move south. Kruyff's chief of intelligence for the Arnhem region, thirty-three-year-old Henri Knap, unobtrusively cycling through the area, spotted the subtle change, too. He was puzzled. He wondered if the optimistic broadcasts from London were false. If so, they were cruel deceptions. Everywhere he saw the Dutch rejoicing. Everyone knew that Montgomery's troops had taken Antwerp. Surely Holland would be liberated within hours. Knap could see the Germans were re-organizing. While they still had little strength, he knew that if the British did not come soon that strength would grow.

In Nijmegen, eleven miles to the south, German military police were closing off roads leading to the German frontier. Elias Broekkamp, a wine importer, saw some troops moving north toward Arnhem, but the majority were being funneled back and traffic was being broken up, processed and fanned out. As in Arnhem, the casual spectator seemed unaware of the difference. Broekkamp observed Dutch civilians laughing and jeering at what they believed to be the Germans' bewildering predicament.

In fact the predicament was growing much less. Nijmegen was turning into a troop staging area, once more in the firm control of German military.

Farther south, in Eindhoven, barely ten miles from the Belgian border, the retreat had all but stopped. In the straggling convoys moving north there were now more Nazi civilians than troops. Frans Kortie, who had seen the Germans dismantling antiaircraft guns on the roofs of the Philips factories, noted a new develop-ment. In a railway siding near the station he watched a train pulling flatcars into position. On the cars were heavy antiaircraft guns. Kortie experienced a feeling of dread.

Far more disheartening for observant Dutch was the discovery that reinforcements were coming in from Germany. In Tilburg, Eindhoven, Helmond and Weert, people saw contingents of fresh troops arrive by train. Unloaded quickly and formed up, they set out for the Dutch-Belgian border. They were not regular Wehr-macht soldiers. They were seasoned, well-equipped and disci-plined, and their distinctive helmets and camouflaged smocks instantly identified them as veteran German paratroopers.

❊ 5 ❊

B<small>Y LATE AFTERNOON</small> of September 5 Colonel General Kurt Student's first paratroop formations were digging in at points along the north side of Belgium's Albert Canal. Their haste was almost frantic. Student, on his arrival at noon, had discovered that Model's "new German line" was strictly the 80-foot-wide water barrier itself. Defense positions had not been prepared. There were no strong points, trenches or fortifications. And, to make matters worse for the defenders, Student noted, "almost everywhere the southern bank dominated the northern side." Even the bridges over the canal were still standing. Only now were engineers placing demolition charges. In all the confusion no one apparently had ordered the crossings destroyed.

Nevertheless, Student's timetable was well planned. The "blitz move" of his airborne forces was a spectacular success. "Considering that these paratroopers were rushed in from all over Germany, from Güstrow in Mecklenburg to Bitsch in Lothringen," he later recalled, "and arms and equipment, brought in from still other parts of Germany, were waiting for them at the railheads, the speed of the move was remarkable." Student could only admire "the astonishing precision of the general staff and the entire German organization." Lieutenant General Karl Sievers' 719th Coastal Division had made good time, too. Student was heartened to see their columns heading for positions north of Antwerp "clattering down the roads to the front, their transports and artillery pulled by heavy draft horses."* Hour by hour, his

---

* Despite the confusion, horse-lover Student took the time to note in his diary that "these huge animals were Clydesdale, Percheron, Danish and Frisian types."

hastily formed First Parachute Army was arriving. Also, by extraordinary good fortune, help had come from a most unexpected source.

The headlong retreat from Belgium into Holland had been slowed and then virtually stopped by the doggedness and ingenuity of one man: Lieutenant General Kurt Chill. Because his 85th Infantry Division was almost totally destroyed, Chill had been ordered to save whatever remained and move back into Germany. But the strong-willed general, watching the near-panic on the roads and prompted by Model's Order of the Day, decided to disregard orders. Chill concluded that the only way to avert catastrophe was to organize a line along the Albert Canal. He welded what remained of his 85th Division with the remnants of two others and quickly dispersed these men to strategic points on the northern bank of the canal. Next, he turned his attention to the bridges and set up "reception centers" at their northern exits. In twenty-four hours Chill succeeded in netting thousands of servicemen from nearly every branch of the German armed forces. It was a "crazy-quilt mob,"* including Luftwaffe mechanics, military-government personnel, naval coastal units and soldiers from a dozen different divisions, but these stragglers, armed at best with rifles, were already on the canal when Student arrived.

Student called Chill's virtuoso performance in halting the near-rout "miraculous." With remarkable speed he had established a defense line of sorts, helping to buy a little time for all of Student's forces to arrive. This would still take several days. Even with the boost from Chill, Student's patchwork First Parachute Army might total at best 18,000–20,000 men, plus some artillery,

---

Contrary to general belief, Hitler's armies, unlike the Allies', were never totally motorized. Even at the pinnacle of German strength more than 50 percent of their transport was horse-drawn.

* Charles B. MacDonald, *The Siegfried Line Campaign*, p. 124. Published in the official U.S. Army History series, MacDonald's volume and Martin Blumenson's *Breakout and Pursuit* together give the most accurate military picture of the German debacle in the west and the events that followed. Another valuable work on the period, more vivid perhaps because it was written shortly after the war, is Milton Shulman's *Defeat in the West*.

antiaircraft guns and twenty-five tanks—hardly the equivalent of an American division. And racing toward this scanty force—so thin that Student could not even man the 75-mile Antwerp-Maastricht gap, let alone close it—were the awesome armored forces of the British Second Army and part of the U.S. First Army. Student was outgunned and outnumbered; about all that stood between him and disaster was the Albert Canal itself.

At what point along it would the enemy attack? Student's line was vulnerable everywhere, but some areas were more critical than others. He was particularly concerned about the sector north of Antwerp, where the weak 719th Coastal Division was only now taking up position. Was there still time to take advantage of the 80-foot-wide water barrier and turn it into a major defense line that would delay the Allies long enough for additional reinforcements to reach the canal? This was Student's greatest hope.

He expected to be attacked at any moment, yet there were still no reports of Allied armor. Student was particularly surprised that there was almost no enemy contact north of Antwerp. He had by now expected that British tanks, after capturing the city, would strike north, cut off the Beveland peninsula, and smash into Holland. It seemed to Student that the British had slowed down. But why?

Four times in eighteen days the vast complex of the German Supreme Headquarters in the West had been forced to move. Bombed, shelled, almost overrun by Allied tanks, OB West had finally come to a halt behind the borders of the Reich. And shortly after 2 P.M. on September 5 the new commander in chief found his headquarters in the little town of Aremberg near Koblenz.

Tired and irritable after his long journey, Field Marshal Gerd von Rundstedt dispensed with the usual military courtesies and fanfare that often accompanied a German change of command. Immediately he plunged into a series of staff conferences that were to last long into the evening. Officers not personally acquainted with the field marshal were startled by the speed of his takeover. To older hands, it was as though he had never been away. For everyone, the very presence of Von Rundstedt brought feelings of relief and renewed confidence.

Von Rundstedt's task was formidable, his problems were massive. He must produce, as quickly as possible, a strategic blueprint for the 400-mile western front running from the North Sea all the way to the Swiss border—a plan which Field Marshal Model had candidly found beyond his capability. With the battered forces at Von Rundstedt's disposal—Army Group B in the north and G in the south—he was expected to hold everywhere and even to counterattack, as Hitler had directed. Simultaneously, to stave off invasion of the Reich, he was to make a reality of Hitler's "impregnable" Siegfried Line—the long-obsolete, unfinished concrete fortifications which had lain neglected, unmanned, and stripped of guns since 1940. There was more, but on this afternoon Von Rundstedt gave first priority to the immediate problems. They were far worse than even he had anticipated.

The picture was bleak. Before his dismissal by Hitler in July, Von Rundstedt had command of sixty-two divisions. Now his operations chief, Lieutenant General Bodo Zimmermann, produced an ominous balance sheet. In the two army groups, he told the Field Marshal, there were "forty-eight 'paper' divisions, fifteen panzer divisions and four brigades with almost no tanks." So weak in men, equipment and artillery were these forty-eight divisions, Zimmermann said, that in his view they constituted "a combat power equivalent to only twenty-seven divisions." This force was less than "half the strength of the Allies." Von Rundstedt learned that his staff believed Eisenhower had at least sixty divisions, completely motorized and at full strength. (This estimate was wrong. Eisenhower had, at this moment, forty-nine divisions on the Continent.)

As for German panzer forces, they were virtually nonexistent. Along the entire front, against the Allies' estimated strength of more than two thousand tanks, there were only one hundred panzers left. The Luftwaffe had been virtually destroyed; above the battlefield, the Allies had complete aerial supremacy. Von Rundstedt's own grim summation was that in troops, most of whom were exhausted and demoralized, he was outnumbered more than 2 to 1; in artillery by 2½ guns to 1; in tanks, 20 to 1; and in planes, 25 to 1.° Besides there were grave shortages in gasoline, transportation and ammunition. Von Rundstedt's new chief of staff, General Siegfried Westphal, was later to recall, "The situation was desperate. A major defeat anywhere along the front—which was so full of gaps that it did not deserve the name—would lead to catastrophe if the enemy were to fully exploit the opportunities."

Lieutenant General Blumentritt, fully agreeing with Westphal's view, was even more specific.† In his opinion, if the Allies mounted "a major thrust resulting in a breakthrough anywhere," collapse would follow. The only capable troops Von Rundstedt had were those facing General George S. Patton's U.S. Third Army driving toward Metz and heading for the industrial region of the Saar. These forces might delay Patton, but they were not strong enough to stop him. Rather than waste precious time, it seemed to Blumentritt that the Allies would strike where the Germans were weakest—by attempting a powerful thrust in the north to cross the Rhine and move into the Ruhr. That drive, he believed, might be given priority by the Americans and the British, because, as he later put it, "He who holds northern Germany, holds Germany."

° German losses in men and matériel had been staggering. In the ninety-two days since the invasion of Normandy, 300,000 German troops had been killed or wounded or were missing; another 200,000 were surrounded, holding "last-ditch fortresses" such as ports or in the Channel Islands. Some 53 German divisions had been destroyed, and strewn across France and Belgium were vast quantities of matériel including at least 1,700 tanks, 3,500 guns, thousands of armored vehicles and horse-drawn or motorized transports and mountains of equipment and supplies ranging from small arms to vast ammunition dumps. The casualties included two field marshals and more than twenty generals.

† To Von Rundstedt's annoyance, General Blumentritt, who had long been his chief of staff and most trusted confidant, was replaced by General Westphal on September 5 and ordered back to Germany. Von Rundstedt protested the change, to no avail. Blumentritt did, however, attend the early conferences in Aremberg and did not leave the headquarters until September 8.

Von Rundstedt had already reached the same conclusion. Seizing the Ruhr was undoubtedly the major Allied objective. The British and Americans in the north were driving in that direction, toward the frontier at Aachen. There was little to stop them from penetrating the unmanned, outdated Siegfried Line, crossing Germany's last natural barrier, the vital Rhine, and striking into the Reich's industrial heart.

Von Rundstedt's analytical mind had seized on one more fact. Eisenhower's skilled and highly trained airborne forces, used so successfully in the Normandy invasion, had disappeared off German situation maps. They were not being used as infantry. Obviously these forces had been withdrawn, preparatory to another airborne operation. But where and when? It was logical that an airborne drop would coincide with a drive on the Ruhr. In Von Rundstedt's view such an attack might come at either of two key areas: behind the Westwall fortifications, or east of the Rhine to seize bridgeheads. In fact, Field Marshal Model, several days earlier, had expressed the same fear in a message to Hitler, stressing the possibility as an "acute threat." Equally, Von Rundstedt could not discount the possibility of the entire Allied front moving forward simultaneously toward the Ruhr *and* the Saar with airborne troops committed at the same time. The Field Marshal could see no solution to any of these impending threats. Allied opportunities were too many and too varied. His only option was to try to bring order out of chaos and to buy time by outguessing Allied intentions, if he could.

Von Rundstedt did not underestimate Eisenhower's intelligence of the German predicament. But, he pondered, was the Allied command really aware how desperate the situation was? The truth was that he was fighting, as he put it to Blumentritt, with "rundown old men" and the pillboxes of the Westwall would be "absolutely useless against an Allied onslaught." It was "madness," he said, "to defend these mouse holes for reasons of prestige." Nevertheless, the ghostly Siegfried Line must be given substance, its fortifications readied and manned. Tersely, Von

Rundstedt told his staff: "We must somehow hold for at least six weeks."

Studying each aspect of the situation confronting him, diagraming possible Allied moves and weighing each alternative, he noted that the most vigorous attacks were still being made by Patton, heading for the Saar. In the north British and American pressure was noticeably less. Von Rundstedt thought he detected an absence of movement, almost a pause, in that area. Turning his attention to Montgomery's front, as Blumentritt was later to remember, Von Rundstedt concentrated on the situation at Antwerp. He was intrigued by reports that, for more than thirty-six hours now, the British had mounted no drive north from the city, nor had they cut the South Beveland peninsula. Obviously, Antwerp's great harbor facilities would solve Allied supply problems. But they could not use the port if both sides of the 54-mile-long estuary leading to it remained in German hands. To the Field Marshal, it seemed clear that the letup he had noted was real; a definite Allied slowdown had occurred, particularly in Montgomery's area.

Throughout his career, Von Rundstedt had closely studied British military tactics; he had also, to his own misfortune, been able to observe American warfare at first hand. He had found the Americans more imaginative and daring in the use of armor, the British superb with infantry. In each case, however, commanders made the difference. Thus, Von Rundstedt considered Patton a far more dangerous opponent than Montgomery. According to Blumentritt, Von Rundstedt viewed Field Marshal Montgomery as "overly cautious, habit-ridden and systematic." Now the Field Marshal weighed the significance of Montgomery's tardiness. With the other Channel ports still in German hands, Von Rundstedt saw Antwerp as essential to Eisenhower's advance—so why had Montgomery not moved for thirty-six hours and apparently failed to secure the second-largest port in Europe? There could be only one reason: Montgomery was not ready to continue the attack. Von Rundstedt was certain that he would not depart from

VON RUNDSTEDT'S PLAN:
ESCAPE OF VON ZANGEN'S
FIFTEENTH ARMY BEGINS
SEPT. 6, 1944

0   Miles   15

SCHOUWEN

NORTH
SEA

N

NORTH
BEVELAND

WALCHEREN

SOUTH
BEVELAND

Flushing

Breskens

SCHELDE ESTUARY

VON ZANGEN'S HQ.

Axel

HOLLAND
BELGIUM

Bruges

FIFTEENTH ARMY POCKET, SEPT. 5, 1944

CANADIAN
FIRST ARMY

Ghent

Rotterdam

LOWER RHINE

WAAL R.

Dordrecht

MAAS R.

Vught

WILHELMINA CANAL

Breda

Tilburg

Bergen op Zoom

Woensdrecht

HOLLAND
BELGIUM

THE GREAT MISTAKE:
BRITISH FAIL TO CUT
ESCAPE ROUTE OF
VON ZANGEN'S
FIFTEENTH ARMY

FRONT LINE SEPT. 5, 1944

MEUSE - ESCAUT CANAL

Antwerp

ALBERT CANAL

SCHELDE R.

BRITISH
SECOND ARMY

palacios

habit. The British would never attack until the meticulous, detail-minded Montgomery was fully prepared and supplied. The answer therefore, Von Rundstedt reasoned, was that the British had overextended themselves. This was not a pause, Von Rundstedt told his staff. Montgomery's pursuit, he was convinced, had ground to a halt.

Quickly, Von Rundstedt turned his attention to Model's orders of the previous twenty-four hours. Because now, if his theory was right, Von Rundstedt saw a chance not only to deny the port of Antwerp to the Allies but, equally important, to save General Von Zangen's trapped Fifteenth Army, a force of more than 80,000 men—men that Von Rundstedt desperately needed.

From Model's orders he saw that, while Von Zangen had been told to hold the southern bank of the Schelde and reinforce the Channel ports, he had also been ordered to attack with the remainder of his troops northeast into the flank of the British drive—an attack scheduled to take place on the morning of the sixth. Without hesitation, Von Rundstedt canceled that attack. Under the circumstances, he saw no merit to it. Besides, he had a bolder, more imaginative plan. The first part of Model's orders could stand, because now holding the Channel ports was more important than ever. But instead of attacking northeast, Von Zangen was ordered to evacuate his remaining troops by sea, across the waters of the Schelde to the island of Walcheren. Once on the northern bank of the estuary, Von Zangen's troops could march eastward along the one road running from Walcheren Island, across the South Beveland peninsula until they reached the Dutch mainland north of Antwerp. Because of Allied air power, ferrying operations across the 3-mile mouth of the Schelde, between the ports of Breskens and Flushing, would have to take place at night. Nevertheless, with luck, a good portion of the Fifteenth Army might be safely withdrawn within two weeks. Von Rundstedt knew that the plan was hazardous, but he saw no other course, for, if successful, he would have almost an entire German army, battered though it might be, at his disposal. More than that he would still—unbelievably—control the vital port of

Antwerp. But the success of the operation would depend entirely on Von Rundstedt's hunch that Montgomery's drive had indeed come to a halt.

Von Rundstedt was sure of it. Further, he was banking on it that Montgomery's slowdown held a far deeper significance. Because of overextended communications and supply lines, he was convinced, the Allied breakneck pursuit had reached its limit. At the close of the conference, as Blumentritt was later to recall, "Von Rundstedt looked at us and suggested the incredible possibility that, for once, Hitler might be right."

Hitler's and Von Rundstedt's estimates of the situation, although only partly correct, were far more accurate than either realized. The precious time Von Rundstedt needed to stabilize his front was being provided by the Allies themselves. The truth was that the Germans were losing faster than the Allies could win.

✣6✣

EVEN AS VON RUNDSTEDT gambled desperately to save the trapped Fifteenth Army, Major General George Philip Roberts, commander of the British 11th Armored Division, 150 miles away in Antwerp, was jubilantly informing his superiors of a startling development. His men had captured not only the city but the huge port as well.

Together with the Guards Armored Division, Roberts' tanks had made an extraordinary dash of more than 250 miles in just five days. The spearhead of Lieutenant General Miles C. Dempsey's great British Second Army had been ordered by Lieutenant General Brian Horrocks, XXX Corps commander, to "keep going like mad." Leaving the Guards to capture Brussels, Roberts' division bypassed the city and in the early hours of September 4, with the courageous help of the Belgian underground, entered Antwerp. Now, some thirty-six hours later, after clearing the deep-sea complex of a stunned and panic-stricken enemy, Roberts reported that his men had captured Antwerp's huge 1,000-acre harbor area intact. Warehouses, cranes, bridges, 3½ miles of wharves, quays, locks, drydocks, rolling stock—and, unbelievably, even the all-important electrically controlled sluice gates, in full working order—had been seized.

German plans to demolish the port had failed. Explosives had been placed on major bridges and other key installations, but, overwhelmed by the spectacular speed of the British and resistance groups (among them Belgian engineers who knew exactly where the demolitions were planted), the disorganized German garrison never had a chance to destroy the vast harbor facilities.

The thirty-seven-year-old Roberts had brilliantly executed his orders. Unfortunately, in one of the greatest miscalculations of the European war, no one had directed him to take advantage of the situation—that is, strike north, grab bridgeheads over the Albert Canal in the northern suburbs, and then make a dash for the base of the South Beveland peninsula only eighteen miles away. By holding its 2-mile-wide neck, Roberts could have bottled up German forces on the isthmus, preparatory to clearing the vital northern bank. It was a momentous oversight.° The port of Antwerp, one of the war's major prizes, was secured; but its approaches, still held by the Germans, were not. This great facility, which could have shortened and fed Allied supply lines all

° The late B. H. Liddell Hart, the celebrated British historian, in his *History of the Second World War* wrote: "It was a multiple lapse—by four commanders from Montgomery downwards . . ." Charles B. MacDonald, the American historian in *The Mighty Endeavor*, agrees with Liddell Hart. He called the failure "one of the greatest tactical mistakes of the war." The best and most detailed account on the cost of Antwerp is undoubtedly R. W. Thompson, *The 85 Days*, and I agree with him that one of the main reasons for the missed opportunity was "weariness." Men of the 11th Armored, he wrote, "slept where they sat, stood or lay, drained of emotion, and in utter exhaustion." If we accept his theory it is doubtful that Roberts' 11th could have continued its drive with the same vigor. Nevertheless, Antwerp and its vital approaches, argues Thompson, might have been taken with ease "had there been a commander following the battle, hour by hour, day by day, and with the flexibility of command to see the prospect."

along the front, was useless. Yet nobody, in the heady atmosphere of the moment, saw this oversight as more than a temporary condition. Indeed, there seemed no need to hurry. With the Germans reeling, the mop-up could take place at any time. The 11th Armored, its assignment completed, held its positions awaiting new orders.

The magnificent drive of Dempsey's armored forces in the north, equaling that of Patton's south of the Ardennes, had run its course, though at this moment few realized it. Roberts' men were exhausted, short on gasoline and supplies. The same was true of the remainder of General Brian Horrocks' XXX Corps. Thus, on this same afternoon, the relentless pressure that had thrown the Germans back in the north, shattered and demoralized, suddenly relaxed. The blunder at Antwerp was compounded as the British came to a halt to "refit, refuel, and rest."

General Horrocks, the XXX Corps's capable and dynamic commander, was not even thinking about Antwerp.° Like Field Marshal Montgomery, commander of the British 21st Army Group, his attention was focused on another target: the crossing of the Rhine and a swift end to the war. Only a few hours earlier, elated at the verve and dash of his armies, Montgomery had cabled the Supreme Commander, General Dwight D. Eisenhower: "We have now reached a stage where a really powerful and full-blooded thrust towards Berlin is likely to get there and thus end the war."

In London, His Royal Highness, the Prince of the Netherlands conferred with Queen Wilhelmina and then telephoned his wife,

---

° Horrocks, in his memoirs, gives a very frank explanation. "My excuse is that my eyes were fixed entirely on the Rhine and everything else seemed of subsidiary importance. It never entered my head that the Schelde would be mined and that we would not be able to use Antwerp until the channel had been swept and the Germans cleared from the coastlines on either side. . . . Napoleon would, no doubt, have realized these things but Horrocks didn't." He also readily admits there was little opposition ahead of him and "we still had 100 miles of petrol per vehicle and one further day's supply within reach." There would have been "considerable risk" but "I believe that if we had taken the chance and carried straight on with our advance, instead of halting in Brussels, the whole course of the war in Europe might have been changed."

the Princess Juliana, in Canada. He urged her to fly immediately to England, ready to return to the Netherlands the moment the country was freed. Their long exile was about to end. The liberation, when it came, would be swift. They must be ready. Yet Bernhard was uneasy.

Over the past seventy-two hours messages reaching him from the resistance had again and again underscored the German panic in Holland and repeated the news that the retreat, begun on September 2, was still in progress. Now, on the fifth, underground leaders reported that although the Germans were still disorganized, the exodus appeared to be slowing down. Bernhard had also heard from the Dutch Prime Minister in exile. Prime Minister Gerbrandy was somewhat embarrassed. Obviously his September 3 broadcast was premature; Allied troops had most certainly not crossed the Dutch border as yet. The Prince and the Prime Minister pondered the reason. Why had the British not moved? Surely, from the underground messages they received, the situation in Holland was clear.

Bernhard had little military training and was dependent on his own advisers, yet he was puzzled.* If the Germans were still disorganized and, as his resistance leaders believed, a "thrust by a few tanks" could liberate the country "in a matter of hours"—why, then, didn't the British proceed? Perhaps Montgomery disbelieved the reports of the Dutch resistance because he considered them amateurish or unreliable. Bernhard could find no other explanation. Why else would the British hesitate, instead of instantly crossing the border? Although he was in constant touch

---

* The young Prince, although named Commander in Chief of the Netherlands Forces by the Queen, was quite frank in interviews with the author regarding his military background. "I had no tactical experience," he told me, "except for a course at the War College before the war. I followed this up with courses in England, but most of my military knowledge was learned in a practical way by reading and by discussions with my officers. However, I never considered myself experienced enough to make a tactical decision. I depended on my staff, who were very well qualified." Nevertheless Bernhard took his job very seriously. In his meticulously kept personal diary for 1944, which he kindly placed at my disposal, he recorded in minuscule handwriting each movement, almost minute by minute, from telephone calls and military conferences to official functions. During this period, based on his own notations, I would estimate that his average working day was about sixteen hours.

with his ministers, the United States ambassador at large, Anthony Biddle, and Eisenhower's chief of staff, Bedell Smith, and as a result was well aware that, at this moment, the advance was so fluid that the situation was changing almost hour by hour, nevertheless Bernhard thought he would like firsthand information. He made a decision: he would request permission of SHAEF to fly to Belgium and see Field Marshal Montgomery himself as soon as possible. He had every faith in the Allied high command and, in particular, Montgomery. Still, if something was wrong, Bernhard had to know.

At his spartan, tented headquarters in the Royal Palace Gardens at Laeken, a few miles from the center of Brussels, Field Marshal Bernard Law Montgomery impatiently waited for an answer to his coded "Personal for Eisenhower Eyes Only" message. Its urgent demand for a powerful and full-blooded thrust to Berlin was sent in the late hours of September 4. Now, by midday on September 5, the brusque, wiry fifty-eight-year-old hero of El Alamein waited for a reply and impatiently fretted about the future course of the war. Two months before the invasion of Normandy he had said, "If we do our stuff properly and no mistakes are made, then I believe that Germany will be out of the war this year." In Montgomery's unalterable opinion, a momentous strategic mistake had been made just before the Allies captured Paris and crossed the Seine. Eisenhower's "broad-front policy"—moving his armies steadily forward to the borders of the Reich, then up to the Rhine—may have been valid when planned before the invasion, but with the sudden disorderly collapse of the Germans, the Britisher believed, it was now obsolete. As Montgomery put it, that strategy had become "unstitched." And all his military training told him "we could not get away with it and . . . would be faced with a long winter campaign with all that that entailed for the British people."

On August 17 he had proposed to General Omar N. Bradley,

the U.S. 12th Army Group commander, a single-thrust plan. Both his own and Bradley's army group should stay "together as a solid mass of forty divisions, which would be so strong that it need fear nothing. This force should advance northeastward." Montgomery's 21st Army Group would clear the Channel coast, and secure Antwerp and southern Holland. Bradley's U.S. 12th Army Group, its right flank on the Ardennes, would head for Aachen and Cologne. The basic objective of Montgomery's proposed drive was to "secure bridgeheads over the Rhine before the winter began and to seize the Ruhr quickly." In all probability, he theorized, it would also end the war. Montgomery's plan called for three of Eisenhower's four armies—the British Second, the U.S. First and the Canadian First. The fourth, Patton's U.S. Third Army, at this moment making headlines around the world for its spectacular advances, Montgomery dismissed. He calmly suggested it should be brought to a halt.

Some forty-eight hours later Montgomery learned that Bradley, who he had believed was responsive to his own idea, actually favored an American thrust, a Patton drive toward the Rhine and Frankfurt. Eisenhower rejected both plans; he was not prepared to change his strategic concept. The Supreme Commander wanted to remain flexible enough to thrust both to the Ruhr and the Saar as the occasion permitted. To Montgomery, this was no longer the "broad-front policy" but a double-thrust plan. Everybody now, he felt, was "going his own way"—especially Patton, who seemed to be allowed enormous latitude. Eisenhower's determination to persist in his original concept revealed quite clearly, in Montgomery's opinion, that the Supreme Commander was "in fact, completely out of touch with the land battle."

Montgomery's view was based on a recent development which angered him and, he felt, demeaned his own role. He was no longer the over-all coordinator of the land battle. On September 1 Eisenhower had personally taken over command. Because the Supreme Commander believed Montgomery "a master of the set battle piece," he had given the British general operational control of the D-Day assault and the initial period of fighting thereafter.

Thus, General Omar N. Bradley's 12th Army Group was under Montgomery. Press stories appearing in the United States at the end of August revealing that Bradley's army group still operated under Montgomery created such a public furor that Eisenhower was promptly ordered by General George C. Marshall, U.S. Chief of Staff, to "immediately assume direct command" of all ground forces. American armies reverted back to their own command. The move caught Montgomery off base. As his chief of staff, General Francis de Guingand, later put it: "Montgomery . . . never, I believe, thought that the day would come so soon. Possibly he hoped that the initial command set up was there to stay for a long time. He was, I think, apt to give insufficient weight to the dictates of prestige and national feelings, or to the increasing contribution of America, in both men and arms . . . it was obvious, however, to most of us that it would have been an impossible situation for a British general and a British headquarters to retain command of these more numerous American formations indefinitely."[*] It may have been obvious to his staff but not to Montgomery. He felt publicly humiliated.[†]

It was hardly a secret that Monty and his superior, Sir Alan Brooke, Chief of the Imperial General Staff, were highly critical of Eisenhower. Both men considered him ambivalent and indecisive. In a letter to Montgomery on July 28, Brooke commented that Eisenhower had only "the very vaguest conception of war!" On another occasion he summarized the Supreme Commander as "a most attractive personality," but with "a very, very limited brain from a strategic point of view." Montgomery, never a man to mince words, saw "right from the beginning that Ike had simply no experience for the job," and while history, he felt, would record Eisenhower "as a very good Supreme Commander, as a field commander he was very bad, very bad."[‡] Angrily, Montgomery began promoting the idea of an over-all "Land

[*] Major General Francis de Guingand, *Generals at War*, pp. 100–101.
[†] Montgomery and the British public, as outraged as he, were somewhat mollified when George VI, at Churchill's strong urging, made Montgomery a field marshal on September 1.
[‡] Author's interview with Field Marshal Montgomery.

Forces Commander," a post sandwiched between the army groups and Eisenhower. He knew just the man for the job—himself. Eisenhower was well aware of the underground campaign. He remained calm. The Supreme Commander was, in his way, as obstinate as Montgomery. His orders from General Marshall were clear and he had no intention of entertaining the idea of any overall ground commander other than himself.

Montgomery had no opportunity to discuss his single-thrust plan or his thoughts about a land-forces commander directly with Eisenhower until August 23, when the Supreme Commander came to lunch at 21st Army Group headquarters. Then the fractious Montgomery, with extraordinary tactlessness, insisted on a private conversation with the Supreme Commander. He demanded that Eisenhower's chief of staff, General Bedell Smith, be excluded from the conference. Smith left the tent, and for an hour Eisenhower, grimly keeping his temper, was lectured by his subordinate on the need for "a firm and sound plan." Montgomery demanded that Eisenhower "decide where the main effort would be" so that "we could be certain of decisive results quickly." Again and again he pressed for the "single thrust," warning that if the Supreme Commander continued the "broad-front strategy with the whole line advancing and everyone fighting all the time, the advance would inevitably peter out." If that happened, Montgomery warned, "the Germans would gain time to recover, and the war would go on all through the winter and well into 1945. If we split the maintenance," Montgomery said, "and advance on a broad front we shall be so weak everywhere we'll have no chance of success." To his mind there was only one policy: "to halt the right and strike with the left, or halt the left and strike with the right." There could only be one thrust and everything should support it.

Eisenhower saw Montgomery's proposal as a gigantic gamble. It might produce speedy and decisive victory. It might instead result in disaster. He was not prepared to accept the risks involved. Nevertheless he found himself caught between Montgomery on one side and Bradley and Patton on the other—each advocating "the main thrust," each wanting to be entrusted with it.

Up to this point, Montgomery, notorious for his slow-moving, if successful, tactics, had yet to prove that he could exploit a situation with the speed of Patton; and at this moment Patton's army, far ahead of everyone else, had crossed the Seine and was racing toward Germany. Diplomatically, Eisenhower explained to Montgomery that, whatever the merits of a single thrust, he could hardly hold back Patton and stop the U.S. Third Army in its tracks. "The American people," said the Supreme Commander, "would never stand for it, and public opinion wins wars." Montgomery heatedly disagreed. "Victories win wars," he announced. "Give people victory and they won't care who won it."

Eisenhower was not impressed. Although he did not say so at the time, he thought Montgomery's view was "much too narrow," and that the Field Marshal did not "understand the over-all situation." Eisenhower explained to Montgomery that he wanted Patton to continue eastward so that a link-up might be effected with the American and French forces advancing from the south. In short, he made it quite clear that his "broad-front policy" would continue.

Montgomery turned for the moment to the subject of a land commander. "Someone must run the land battle for you." Eisenhower, Montgomery declared, should "sit on a very lofty perch in order to be able to take a detached view of the whole intricate problem, which involves land, sea, air, et cetera." He retreated from arrogance to humility. If the matter of "public opinion in America was involved," Montgomery declared, he would gladly "let Bradley control the battle and serve under him."

Eisenhower quickly dismissed the suggestion. Placing Bradley over Montgomery would be as unacceptable to the British people as the reverse would be to the Americans. As for his own role he could not, he explained, deviate from the plan to take personal control of the battle. But, in seeking a solution to some of the immediate problems, he was ready to make some concessions to Montgomery. He needed the Channel ports and Antwerp. They were vital to the entire Allied supply problem. Thus, for the moment, Eisenhower said, priority would be given to the 21st Army Group's northern thrust. Montgomery could use the Allied First Airborne Army in England—at the time SHAEF's only reserve. Additionally, he could have the support of the U.S. First Army moving on his right.

Montgomery had, in the words of General Bradley, "won the initial skirmish," but the Britisher was far from satisfied. It was his firm conviction that Eisenhower had missed the "great opportunity." Patton shared that view—for different reasons—when the news reached him. Not only had Eisenhower given supply priority to Montgomery at the expense of the U.S. Third Army, but he had also rejected Patton's proposed drive to the Saar. To Patton, it was "the most momentous error of the war."

In the two weeks since this clash of personalities and conflicting military philosophies had taken place, much had happened. Montgomery's 21st Army Group now rivaled Patton's in speed. By September 5, with his advance units already in Antwerp, Montgomery was more convinced than ever that his single-thrust concept was right. He was determined to reverse the Supreme Commander's decision. A crucial turning point in the conflict had been reached. The Germans, Montgomery was convinced, were teetering on the verge of collapse.

He was not alone in this view. On nearly every level of command, intelligence officers were forecasting the imminent end of the war. The most optimistic estimate came from the Combined Allied Intelligence Committee in London. The German situation had deteriorated to such an extent that the group believed the enemy incapable of recovery. There was every indication, their estimate said, that "organized resistance under the control of the German high command is unlikely to continue beyond December 1, 1944, and . . . may end even sooner." Supreme Headquarters shared this optimism. At the end of August, SHAEF's intelligence summary declared that "the August battles have done it and the enemy in the west has had it. Two and one half months of bitter fighting have brought the end of the war in Europe in sight, almost within reach." Now, one week later, they considered the

German army "no longer a cohesive force but a number of fugitive battle groups, disorganized and even demoralized, short of equipment and arms." Even the conservative director of military operations at the British War Office, Major General John Kennedy, noted on September 6 that "If we go at the same pace as of late, we should be in Berlin by the 28th. . . ."

In this chorus of optimistic predictions there seemed only one dissenting voice. The U.S. Third Army's intelligence chief, Colonel Oscar W. Koch, believed the enemy still capable of waging a last-ditch struggle and warned that "barring internal upheaval in the homeland and the remote possibility of insurrection within the Wehrmacht . . . the German armies will continue to fight until destroyed or captured."* But his own intelligence officer's cautious appraisal meant little to the Third Army's ebullient commander, Lieutenant General George S. Patton. Like Montgomery in the north, Patton in the south was now only one hundred miles from the Rhine. He too believed the time had come, as Montgomery had put it, "to stick our neck out in a single deep thrust into enemy territory," and finish off the war. The only difference lay in their views of who was to stick out his neck. Both commanders, flushed with victory and bidding for glory, now vied for that opportunity. In his zeal, Montgomery had narrowed his rivalry down to Patton alone: a British field marshal in charge of an entire army group was trying to outrace an American lieutenant general in charge of a single army.

But all along the front the fever of success gripped battle commanders. After the spectacular sweep across France and Belgium and with evidence of German defeat all around, men now confidently believed that nothing could stop the victorious surge from continuing through the Siegfried Line and beyond, into the heart of Germany. Yet, keeping the enemy off balance and disorganized demanded constant, unremitting Allied pressure. Supporting that pressure had now produced a crisis that few seemed aware of. The heady optimism bordered on self-deception

---

* For a more detailed version of Allied intelligence estimates see Dr. Forrest C. Pogue, *The Supreme Command*, pp. 244–45.

for, at this moment, Eisenhower's great armies, after a hectic dash of more than two hundred miles from the Seine, were caught up in a gigantic maintenance and supply problem. After six weeks of almost nonstop advance against little opposition, few noted the sudden loss of momentum. But as the first tanks approached Germany's threshold and at places began probing the Westwall itself, the advance began to slow. The Allied pursuit was over, strangled by its own success.

The chief problem crippling the advance was the lack of ports. There was no shortage of supplies, but these were stockpiled in Normandy, still being brought in across the beaches or through the only workable port, Cherbourg—some 450 miles behind the forward elements. Supplying four great armies in full pursuit from that far back was a nightmarish task. A lack of transportation added to the creeping paralysis. Rail networks, bombed in preinvasion days or destroyed by the French underground, could not be repaired fast enough. Gasoline pipelines were only now being laid and extended. As a result, everything from rations to gasoline was being hauled by road, and there was a frustrating shortage of trucks.

To keep abreast of the pursuit which, day by day, pushed farther east, every kind of vehicle was being pressed into service. Artillery, antiaircraft guns and spare tanks had been unloaded from their conveyors and left behind so that the conveyors could be used to carry supplies. Divisions had been stripped of their transport companies. The British had left one entire corps west of the Seine so that its transport could service the rest of the speeding army. Montgomery's difficulties mounted with the discovery that 1,400 British three-ton trucks were useless because of faulty pistons.

Now, in herculean efforts to keep the pursuit going without pause, a ceaseless belt of trucks—the "Red Ball Express"—hammered east, delivered their supplies and then swung back to the west for more, some convoys often making a grueling round trip of between six and eight hundred miles. Even with all available transport moving around the clock and with commanders in the field applying the most stringent economies, the supply demands of the armies could not be met. Taxed beyond its capabilities, the makeshift supply structure had almost reached the breaking point.

Besides the acute transportation problem, men were tired, equipment worn out after the catapultlike advance from Normandy. Tanks, half-tracks and vehicles of every description had been driven so long without proper maintenance that they were breaking down. Overshadowing everything was a critical shortage of gasoline. Eisenhower's armies, needing one million gallons per day, were receiving only a fraction of that amount.

The effect was critical. In Belgium, as the enemy fled before it, an entire corps of the U.S. First Army was halted for four days, its tanks dry. Patton's U.S. Third Army, more than a hundred miles ahead of everyone else, and meeting little opposition, was forced to halt for five days on the Meuse, because armored columns were out of gas. Patton was furious when he discovered that of the 400,000 gallons of gasoline ordered, he had received only 32,000 due to priority cutbacks. He promptly ordered his leading corps commander: "Get off your fanny as fast as you can and move on until your engines run dry, then get out and walk, goddammit!" To his headquarters staff, Patton raged that he was "up against two enemies—the Germans and our own high command. I can take care of the Germans, but I'm not sure I can win against Montgomery and Eisenhower." He tried. Convinced that he could bludgeon his way into Germany in a matter of days, Patton furiously appealed to Bradley and Eisenhower. "My men can eat their belts," he stormed, "but my tanks have gotta have gas."

The crushing defeat of the Germans in Normandy and the systematic and speedy annihilation of their forces following the breakout had caused the logistic crisis. On the assumption that the enemy would hold and fight on the various historic river lines, invasion planners had anticipated a more conservative advance. A pause for regrouping and massing of supplies, it was assumed, would take place after the Normandy beachhead had been secured and Channel ports captured. The lodgment area was expected to lie west of the river Seine which, according to the projected timetable, would not be reached until September 4 (D plus 90 days). The sudden disintegration of the enemy's forces and their headlong flight eastward had made the Allied timetable meaningless. Who could have foreseen that by September 4 Allied tanks would be two hundred miles east of the Seine and in Antwerp? Eisenhower's staff had estimated that it would take approximately eleven months to reach the German frontier at Aachen. Now, as tank columns approached the Reich, the Allies were almost seven months ahead of their advance schedule. That the supply and transportation system, designed for a much slower rate of progress, had stood up to the strain of the hectic pursuit at all was close to miraculous.

Yet, in spite of the critical logistic situation, no one was ready to admit that the armies must soon halt or that the pursuit was over. "Every commander from division upwards," Eisenhower later wrote, was "obsessed with the idea that with only a few more tons of supply, he could rush right on and win the war. . . . Each commander, therefore, begged and demanded priority over all others, and it was quite undeniable that in front of each were opportunities for quick exploitation that made the demands completely logical." Still, the optimism had infected even the Supreme Commander. It was obvious that he believed the impetus of the advance could be maintained long enough for the Allied armies to overrun the Siegfried Line before the Germans had a chance to defend it, for he saw signs of "collapse" on the "entire front." On September 4 he directed that Bradley's "12th Army Group will capture the Saar and the Frankfurt area." Montgomery's "21st Army Group will capture the Ruhr and Antwerp."

Even Patton seemed appeased by the announcement. Now he was sure that, given adequate supplies, his powerful U.S. Third Army could, by itself, reach the industrial Saar and then dash on all the way to the Rhine.° And in the unparalleled atmosphere of

---

° Patton's weekly press conferences were always newsworthy, but especially memorable for the General's off-the-record remarks, which, because of his colorful vocabulary, could never have been printed anyway. That first week of September, as a war correspondent for the London *Daily Telegraph,* I was present when, in victory that prevailed, Montgomery, with his coded message of September 4, once again doggedly pressed his case. This time he went far beyond his proposal of August 17 and his conversation with Eisenhower on August 23. Convinced that the Germans were broken, the commander of the British 21st Army Group believed that he could not only reach the Ruhr but race all the way to Berlin itself.

In his nine-paragraph message to Eisenhower, Montgomery spelled out again the reasons that convinced him that the moment had come for a "really powerful and full-blooded thrust." There were two strategic opportunities open to the Allies, "one via the Ruhr and the other via Metz and the Saar." But, he argued, because "we have not enough resources, two such drives could not be maintained." There was a chance for only one—his. That thrust, the northern one "via the Ruhr," was, in Montgomery's opinion, "likely to give the best and quickest results." To guarantee its success, Monty's single thrust would need "all the maintenance resources . . . without qualification." He was now clearly impatient of any other considerations. He was going on record both as to the worth of his own plan and his skill and belief in himself as the one man to carry it off. Other operations would have to get along with whatever logistic support remained. There could be no compromise, he warned the Supreme Commander. He dismissed the possibility of two drives, because "it would split our maintenance resources so that neither thrust is full-blooded" and as a result "prolong the war." As Montgomery saw the problem it was "very simple and clear-cut." But time was of "such vital importance . . . that a decision is required at once."

Acrid and autocratic, the most popular British commander since Wellington was obsessed by his own beliefs. Considering the acute logistic situation, he reasoned that his single-thrust theory was now more valid than it had been two weeks before. In

typical fashion, he expounded on his plans for the Germans. In his high-pitched voice and pounding the map, Patton declared that, "Maybe there are five thousand, maybe ten thousand, Nazi bastards in their concrete foxholes before the Third Army. Now, if Ike stops holding Monty's hand and gives me the supplies, I'll go through the Siegfried Line like shit through a goose."

his intractable way—and indifferent as to how the tone of his message might be received—Montgomery was not merely suggesting a course of action for the Supreme Commander; the Field Marshal was dictating one. Eisenhower must halt all other armies in their tracks—in particular Patton's—so that all resources could be put behind his single drive. And his Signal No. M-160 closed with a typical example of Montgomery's arrogance. "If you are coming this way perhaps you would look in and discuss it," he proposed. "If so, delighted to see you lunch tomorrow. Do not feel I can leave this battle just at present." That his closing words bordered on the insolent seemed not to occur to Montgomery in his anxiety that this last chance to finish off the Germans must not be lost. Limpetlike, he clung to his single-thrust plan. For now he was sure that even Eisenhower must realize that the time had come to strike the final blow.

In the bedroom of his villa at Granville on the western side of the Cherbourg peninsula, the Supreme Commander read Montgomery's Signal No. M-160 with angry disbelief. The fifty-five-year-old Eisenhower thought Montgomery's proposal "unrealistic" and "fantastic." Three times Montgomery had nagged him to exasperation about single-thrust schemes. Eisenhower thought he had settled the strategy conflict once and for all on August 23. Yet, now Montgomery was not only advocating his theory once again but was proposing to rush all the way to Berlin. Usually calm and congenial, Eisenhower now lost his temper. "There isn't a single soul who believes this can be done, except Montgomery," he exploded to members of his staff. At this moment, to Eisenhower's mind, the most urgent matter was the opening of the Channel ports, especially Antwerp. Why could Montgomery not understand that? The Supreme Commander was only too well aware of the glittering opportunities that existed. But, as he told the Deputy Supreme Commander, Marshal of the Royal Air Force Sir Arthur Tedder, and SHAEF's assistant chief of staff

Lieutenant General Frederick Morgan, for Montgomery "to talk of marching to Berlin with an army which is still drawing the great bulk of its supplies over the beaches is fantastic."

The Field Marshal's message could hardly have come at a worse time. The Supreme Commander was propped up in bed, his right knee in a cast, as a consequence of an injury of which Montgomery, at the moment, was unaware. Eisenhower had more cause than this, however, to be edgy. Leaving the main body of SHAEF in London, he had come to the Continent to take personal control on September 1, four days earlier. His small advance command headquarters at Jullouville near Granville was totally inadequate. Because of the phenomenal movement of his armies, Eisenhower was stranded more than four hundred miles from the front—and there were, as yet, no telephone or teletype facilities. Except for radio and a rudimentary courier system, he was unable to communicate immediately with his commanders in the field. The physical injury which added to these tactical discomforts had occurred after one of his routine flying visits to his principal commanders. On September 2, returning from a conference at Chartres with senior American generals, Eisenhower's plane, because of high winds and bad visibility, had been unable to land at the headquarters' airfield. Instead, it had put down—safely—on the beach near his villa. But then, trying to help the pilot pull the plane away from the water's edge, Eisenhower had badly wrenched his right knee. Thus, at this vital juncture in the war, as the Supreme Commander tried to take control of the land battle and with events happening so fast that immediate decisions were necessary, Eisenhower was physically immobilized.

Although Montgomery—or, for that matter, Bradley and Patton—might feel that Eisenhower "was out of touch with the land battle," only distance made that argument valid. His excellent, integrated Anglo-American staff was much more cognizant of the day-to-day situation in the field than his generals realized. And while he expected combat commanders to display initiative and boldness, only the Supreme Commander and his staff could view the over-all situation and make decisions accordingly. But it was true that, in this transitional period, while Eisenhower was assuming personal control, there appeared to be a lack of clear-cut direction, due in part to the complexity of the Supreme Commander's role. Coalition command was far from easy. Yet, Eisenhower, maintaining a delicate balance, and following to the letter the plans of the Combined Chiefs of Staff, made the system work. In the interest of Allied amity, he might modify strategy, but Eisenhower had no intention of throwing caution to the winds and allowing Montgomery, as the Supreme Commander later put it, to make a "single, knifelike drive toward Berlin."°

He had been more than tolerant with Montgomery, granting him concession after concession, often incurring the anger of his own American generals. Yet, it seemed that Monty "always wanted everything and he never did anything fast in his life."† Eisenhower said he understood Montgomery's peculiarities better than the Britisher realized. "Look, people have told me about his boyhood," Eisenhower recalled, "and when you have a contest between Eton and Harrow on one side and some of the lesser schools on the other, some of these juniors coming into the army

---

° In all fairness to Montgomery, it must be said that he, himself, never used this phrase. His idea was to throw forty divisions together and drive toward Berlin—certainly no knifelike thrust—but he has been credited with the remark and in my opinion it hurt his cause at SHAEF during the many strategic meetings that took place.

† To the author. In a taped interview, President Eisenhower almost relived for me his emotions at the time of this bitter argument with Montgomery. When I told him I had interviewed the Field Marshal, Eisenhower cut me short and said, "You don't have to tell me what he told you—he said I knew nothing about war—right? Look, I'm interested only in getting this thing down truthfully and logically, because any historian has to make deductions. . . . Personally, I don't believe I would put too much weight on what generals remember, including me. Because memory is a fallible thing . . . Goddammit, I don't know what you heard in Britain, but the British have never understood the American system of command. . . . When the whole damned thing [WW II] was done . . . I never heard from the British any goldarn paeans of praise. And you're not going to hear it now, particularly from people like Montgomery. . . . His associates—they've said things about him that I would never dream of repeating. . . . I don't care if he goes down as the greatest soldier in the world. He isn't, but if he goes down that way it's all right with me. . . . He got so damn personal to make sure that the Americans and me, in particular, had no credit, had nothing to do with the war, that I eventually just stopped communicating with him . . . I was just not interested in keeping up communications with a man that just can't tell the truth." The reader is urged to remember that never, during the war, did the Supreme Commander publicly discuss the Field Marshal, and his views expressed here are revealed for the first time.

felt sort of inferior. The man, all his life, has been trying to prove that he was somebody." Clearly, however, the Field Marshal's views reflected his British superiors' beliefs on how the Allies should proceed.

Understandable as this might be, Montgomery's arrogance in presenting such views invariably set American commanders' teeth on edge. As Supreme Commander, armed by the Combined Chiefs of Staff with sweeping powers, Eisenhower had one prime concern: to hold the Allies together and win the war swiftly. Although some of SHAEF's staff, including many Britishers, considered Montgomery insufferable and said so, Eisenhower never commented on him except in private to his chief of staff, Bedell Smith. But, in fact, the Supreme Commander's exasperation with Montgomery went far deeper than anyone knew. Eisenhower felt that the Field Marshal was "a psychopath . . . such an egocentric" that everything he had ever done "was perfect . . . he never made a mistake in his life." Eisenhower was not going to let him make one now. "Robbing the American Peter who is fed from Cherbourg," he told Tedder, "will certainly not get the British Paul to Berlin."

Nevertheless, Eisenhower was deeply disturbed at the widening rift between him and Britain's favorite general. Within the next few days, the Supreme Commander decided, he would meet with Montgomery in an effort to clarify what he considered to be a misunderstanding. Once more he would attempt to spell out his strategy and hope for agreement, however grudgingly it might come. In the interim before the meeting, he made one thing clear. He firmly rejected Montgomery's single-thrust plan and his bid for Berlin. On the evening of September 5, in a coded message to the Field Marshal, he said, "While agreeing with your conception of a powerful and full-blooded thrust toward Berlin, I do not agree that it should be initiated at this moment to the exclusion of all other maneuvers." As the Supreme Commander saw it, "the bulk of the German army in the west has now been destroyed," and that success should be exploited "by promptly breaching the Siegfried Line, crossing the Rhine on a wide front and seizing the

Saar and the Ruhr. This I intend to do with all possible speed."
These moves, Eisenhower believed, would place a "strangle hold
on Germany's main industrial areas and largely destroy her
capacity to wage war. . . ." Opening the ports of Le Havre and
Antwerp was essential, Eisenhower went on, before any "powerful thrust" into Germany could be launched. But, at the moment,
Eisenhower emphasized, "no relocation of our present resources
would be adequate to sustain a thrust to Berlin. . . ."

Eisenhower's decision took thirty-six hours to reach Montgomery, and then only the last half of the message arrived. The
concluding two paragraphs were received by Montgomery at 9
A.M. on the morning of September 7. The opening section did not
arrive until September 9, another forty-eight hours later. As
Montgomery saw it, Eisenhower's communication was one more
confirmation that the Supreme Commander was "too far removed
from the battle."

From the first fragment of the message that Montgomery received, it was abundantly clear that Eisenhower had rejected his
plan, for it contained the sentence, "No relocation of our present
resources would be adequate to sustain a thrust to Berlin." Montgomery immediately sent off a message disagreeing heatedly.

With the slackening of the pursuit, Montgomery's worst fears
were being realized. German opposition was stiffening. In his
message, focusing in particular on the shortage of supplies, Montgomery claimed that he was getting only half his requirements,
and "I cannot go on for long like this." He refused to be diverted
from his plan to drive to Berlin. The obvious necessity of immediately opening up the vital port of Antwerp was not even mentioned in his dispatch, yet he stressed that "as soon as I have a Pas
de Calais port working, I would then require about 2,500 additional three-ton lorries, plus an assured airlift averaging about
1,000 tons a day to enable me to get to the Ruhr and finally
Berlin." Because it was all "very difficult to explain," the Field

Marshal "wondered if it was possible" for Eisenhower to come and see him. Unshaken in his conviction that the Supreme Commander's decision was a grave error and confident that his own plan would work, Montgomery refused to accept Eisenhower's rejection as final. Yet he had no intention of flying to Jullouville in an attempt to change Eisenhower's mind. Such diplomacy was not part of his makeup, although he was fully aware that the only hope of selling his proposal was via a face-to-face meeting with the Supreme Commander. Outraged and seething, Montgomery awaited a reply from Eisenhower. The British Field Marshal was in near-seclusion, impatient and irritable, at the moment when Prince Bernhard arrived at the headquarters to pay his respects.

Bernhard had arrived in France on the evening of the sixth. With a small staff, three jeeps, his Sealyham terrier Martin and a bulging briefcase containing Dutch underground reports, he and his party flew to the Continent, guarded by two fighter planes, in three Dakotas with Bernhard at the controls of one. From the airfield at Amiens they drove to Douai, fifty miles north, and early on the seventh set out for Belgium and Brussels. At the Laeken headquarters the Prince was met by General Horrocks, introduced to Montgomery's staff and ushered into the presence of the Field Marshal. "He was in a bad humor and obviously not happy to see me," Bernhard recalled. "He had a lot on his mind, and the presence of royalty in his area was understandably a responsibility that he could easily do without."

The Field Marshal's renown as the greatest British soldier of the war had made him, in Bernhard's words, "the idol of millions of Britishers." And the thirty-three-year-old Prince was in awe of Montgomery. Unlike Eisenhower's relaxed, almost casual manner, Montgomery's demeanor made it difficult for Bernhard to converse easily with him. Sharp and blunt from the outset, Montgomery made it clear that Bernhard's presence in his area "worried" him. With justification untempered by tact or explanation, Montgomery told the Prince that it would be unwise for Bernhard to visit the headquarters of the Dutch unit—the Princess Irene Brigade—attached to the British Second Army, quartered in the area around Diest, barely ten miles from the front line. Bernhard, who, as Commander in Chief of the Netherlands Forces, had every intention of visiting Diest, for the moment did not respond. Instead, he began to discuss the Dutch resistance reports. Montgomery overrode him. Returning to the matter, he told the Prince, "You must not live in Diest. I cannot allow it." Irked, Bernhard felt compelled to point out that he was "serving directly under Eisenhower and did not come under the Field Marshal's command." Thus, from the start, as Bernhard remembers the meeting, "rightly or wrongly, we got off on the wrong foot." (Later, in fact, Eisenhower backed Montgomery regarding Diest, but he did say that Bernhard could stay in Brussels "close to 21st Army Group headquarters, where your presence may be needed.")

Bernhard went on to review the situation in Holland as reflected in the underground reports. Montgomery was told of the retreat and disorganization of the Germans, which had been going on since September 2, and of the makeup of the resistance groups. To the best of his knowledge, Bernhard said, the reports were accurate. Montgomery, according to the Prince, retorted, "I don't think your resistance people can be of much use to us. Therefore, I believe all this is quite unnecessary." Startled by the Field Marshal's bluntness, Bernhard "began to realize that Montgomery apparently did not believe *any* of the messages coming from my agents in Holland. In a way, I could hardly blame him. I gathered he was a bit fed up with misleading information that he had received from the French and Belgian resistance during his advance. But, in this instance, I knew the Dutch groups involved, the people who were running them and I knew the information was, indeed, correct." He persisted. Showing the Field Marshal the message file and quoting from report after report, Bernhard posed a question: "In view of this, why can't you attack right away?"

"We can't depend on these reports," Montgomery told him. "Just because the Dutch resistance claim the Germans have been retreating from September 2 doesn't necessarily mean they are still retreating." Bernhard had to admit the retreat "was slowing down," and there were "signs of reorganization." Still, in his opinion, there was valid reason for an immediate attack.

Montgomery remained adamant. "Anyway," he said, "much as I would like to attack and liberate Holland, I can't do it because of supplies. We are short of ammunition. We are short of petrol for the tanks and if we did attack, in all probability they would become stranded." Bernhard was astounded. The information he received in England from both SHAEF and his own advisers had convinced him that the liberation of Holland would be accomplished in a matter of days. "Naturally I automatically assumed that Montgomery, commander on the spot, knew the situation better than anyone else," Bernhard later said. "Yet we had absolutely every detail on the Germans—troop strength, the number of tanks and armored vehicles, the position of antiaircraft guns— and I knew, apart from immediate front-line opposition, that there was little strength behind it. I was sick at heart, because I knew that German strength would grow with each passing day. I was unable to persuade Montgomery. In fact, nothing I said seemed to matter."

Then Montgomery made an extraordinary disclosure. "I am just as eager to liberate the Netherlands as you are," he said, "but we intend to do it in another, even better way." He paused, thought a moment and then, almost reluctantly, said, "I am planning an airborne operation ahead of my troops." Bernhard was startled. Instantly a number of questions came to his mind. In what area were the drops planned? When would the operation take place? How was it being developed? Yet he refrained from asking. Montgomery's manner indicated he would say no more. The operation was obviously still in the planning stage and the Prince's impression was that only the Field Marshal and a few of his staff officers knew of the plan. Although he was given no more details, Bernhard was now hopeful that the liberation of Holland, despite Montgomery's earlier talk of lack of supplies, was imminent. He must be patient and wait. The Field Marshal's reputation was awesome. Bernhard believed in it and in the man himself. The Prince felt a renewal of hope, for "anything Montgomery did, he would do well."

Eisenhower, acceding to Montgomery's request, set Sunday, September 10, as the date for a meeting. He was not particularly looking forward to his meeting with Montgomery and the usual temperamental arguments he had come to expect from the Field Marshal. He was, however, interested in learning what progress had been made in one aspect of the Montgomery operation. Although the Supreme Commander must approve all airborne plans, he had given Montgomery tactical use of the First Allied Airborne Army and permission to work out a possible plan involving that force. He knew that Montgomery, at least since the fourth, had been quietly exploring the possibility of an airborne operation to seize a bridgehead across the Rhine.

Ever since the formation of the First Allied Airborne Army under its American commander, Lieutenant General Lewis Hyde Brereton, six weeks earlier, Eisenhower had been searching for both a target and a suitable opportunity to employ the force. To that end he had been pressing Brereton and the various army commanders to develop bold and imaginative airborne plans calling for large-scale mass attacks deep behind the enemy's lines. Various missions had been proposed and accepted, but all had been canceled. In nearly every case the speeding land armies had already arrived at the objectives planned for the paratroops.

Montgomery's original proposal had called for units of Brereton's airborne force to grab a crossing west of the town of Wesel, just over the Dutch-German border. However, heavy antiaircraft defenses in that area had forced the Field Marshal to make a change. The site he then chose was farther west in Holland: the Lower Rhine bridge at Arnhem—at this juncture more than seventy-five miles behind the German front lines.

By September 7, Operation Comet, as the plan was called, was in readiness; then bad weather, coupled with Montgomery's concern about the ever-increasing German opposition his troops were encountering, forced a postponement. What might have succeeded on the sixth or seventh seemed risky by the tenth. Eisenhower too was concerned; for one thing he felt that the launching of an airborne attack at this juncture would mean a delay in opening the port of Antwerp. Yet the Supreme Commander remained fascinated by the possibilities of an airborne attack.

The abortive operations, some of them canceled almost at the last minute, had created a major problem for Eisenhower. Each time a mission reached the jump-off stage, troop-carrier planes, hauling gasoline to the front, had to be grounded and made ready. This loss of precious air-supply tonnage brought cries of protest from Bradley and Patton. At this moment of relentless pursuit, the airlift of gasoline, they declared, was far more vital than airborne missions. Eisenhower, anxious to use the paratroopers and urged by Washington to do so—both General Marshall and General Henry H. Arnold, commander of the U.S. Army air forces, wanted to see what Brereton's new Allied Airborne Army could accomplish—was not prepared to ground his highly trained airborne divisions. On the contrary, he was insisting that they be used at the earliest opportunity.* In fact, it might be a way to catapult his troops across the Rhine at the very moment when the pursuit was slowing down. But on this morning of September 10, as he flew to Brussels, all other considerations were secondary in his mind to the opening of the vital port of Antwerp.

Not so Montgomery. Anxious and determined, he was waiting at Brussels airport as Eisenhower's plane touched down. With characteristic preciseness, he had honed and refined his arguments preparatory to the meeting. He had talked with General Miles C. Dempsey of the British Second Army, and Lieutenant General Frederick Browning, commander of the British I Airborne Corps, who was also deputy chief of the First Allied Airborne Army. Browning was waiting in the wings for the outcome of the conference. Dempsey, concerned at the ever-stiffening enemy resist-

* Pogue, *The Supreme Command*, p. 280.

ance before him and aware from the intelligence reports that new units were moving in, asked Montgomery to abandon the plan for an airborne attack on the bridge at Arnhem. Instead, he suggested concentrating on seizing the Rhine crossing at Wesel. Even in conjunction with an airborne mission, Dempsey contended, the British Second Army probably was not strong enough to drive due north to Arnhem by itself. It would be better, he believed, to advance in conjunction with the U.S. First Army northeast toward Wesel.

A drive into Holland was, in any case, now imperative. The British War Office had informed Montgomery that V-2's—the first German rockets—had landed in London on September 8. Their launch sites were believed to be somewhere in western Holland. Whether before or after receiving this information, Montgomery altered his plans. Operation Comet, as originally devised, called for only a division and a half—the British 1st Airborne and the Polish 1st Parachute Brigade; that force was too weak to be effective, he believed. As a result, he canceled Comet. In its place, Montgomery came up with an even more ambitious airborne proposal. As yet, only a few of the Field Marshal's upper-echelon officers knew about it and, apprehensive of General Bradley's influence with Eisenhower, they had taken great pains to see that no hint of the plan reached American liaison officers at the British headquarters. Like Eisenhower, Lieutenant General Browning and the headquarters of the First Allied Airborne Army in England were, at this moment, unaware of Montgomery's new airborne scheme.

Because of his injured knee, Eisenhower was unable to leave his plane, and the conference was held on board. Montgomery, as he had done on August 23, determined who should be present at the meeting. The Supreme Commander had brought his deputy, Air Chief Marshal Sir Arthur Tedder, and an assistant chief of staff, Lieutenant General Sir Humphrey Gale, in charge of administration. Curtly, Montgomery asked that Eisenhower exclude Gale from the conference while insisting that his own administrative and supply chief, Lieutenant General Miles Graham, remain. Another, less acquiescent superior might well have taken issue with Montgomery's attitude. Eisenhower patiently granted the Field Marshal's demand. General Gale left.

Almost immediately Montgomery denounced the Supreme Commander's broad-front policy. Constantly referring to a sheaf of Eisenhower's communications that had arrived during the previous week, he called attention to the Supreme Commander's inconsistencies in not clearly defining what was meant by "priority." He argued that his 21st Army Group was not getting the "priority" in supplies promised by Eisenhower; that Patton's drive to the Saar was being allowed to proceed at the expense of Montgomery's forces. Calmly Eisenhower answered that he had never meant to give Montgomery "absolute priority" to the exclusion of everyone else. Eisenhower's strategy, Montgomery reiterated, was wrong and would have "dire consequences." So long as these two "jerky and disjointed thrusts were continued," with supplies split between himself and Patton, "neither could succeed." It was essential, Montgomery said, that Eisenhower decide between him and Patton. So fierce and unrestrained was Montgomery's language that Eisenhower suddenly reached out, patted Montgomery's knee and told him, "Steady, Monty! You can't speak to me like that. I'm your boss." Montgomery's anger vanished. "I'm sorry, Ike," he said quietly.°

The uncharacteristic but seemingly genuine apology was not the end of the matter. Doggedly, though with less acrimony, Montgomery continued to argue for his "single thrust." Eisenhower listened intently and with sympathy to the arguments, but his own view remained unchanged. His broad-front advance would continue. He told Montgomery clearly why. As Eisenhower was later to recall,† he said, "What you're proposing is this—if I give you all of the supplies you want, you could go straight to Berlin—right straight to Berlin? Monty, you're nuts.

° In his memoirs, Montgomery, in discussing the meeting, says that "we had a good talk." But he does state that, during these days of strategy arguments, "Possibly I went a bit far in urging on him my own plan, and did not give sufficient weight to the heavy political burden he bore. . . . Looking back on it all I often wonder if I paid sufficient heed to Eisenhower's notions before refuting them. I think I did. Anyhow . . . I never cease to marvel at his patience and forbearance. . . ."

† To the author.

MARKET-GARDEN PLAN

○   Montgomery's Main Objective

●   Br. 1st Airborne Drop Zones

◉   U.S. 82nd Airborne Drop Zones

◑   U.S. 101st Airborne Drop Zones

⚌   Key Bridges

Amsterdam

NORTH SEA

N

The Hague

Rotterdam

Dordrecht

Moerdijk

SCHOUWEN

Breda

N. BEVELAND

Bergen op Zoom

WALCHEREN

Flushing

SOUTH BEVELAND

SCHELDE

ESTUARY

Breskens

FRONT LINE SEPT. 17/44

Antwerp

B   E   L   G

0   Miles   30

You can't do it. What the hell! If you try a long column like that in a single thrust you'd have to throw off division after division to protect your flanks from attack. Now suppose you did get a bridge across the Rhine. You couldn't depend for long on that one bridge to supply your drive. Monty, you can't do it."

Montgomery, according to Eisenhower, replied, "I'll supply them all right. Just give me what I need and I'll reach Berlin and end the war."

Eisenhower's rejection was firm. Antwerp, he stressed, must be opened before any major drive into Germany could even be contemplated. Montgomery then played his trump card. The most recent development—the rocket attack on London from sites in the Netherlands—necessitated an immediate advance into Holland. He knew exactly how such a drive should begin. To strike into Germany, Montgomery proposed to use almost the entire First Allied Airborne Army in a stunning mass attack.

His plan was an expanded, grandiose version of Operation Comet. Montgomery now wanted to use three and a half divisions—the U.S. 82nd and 101st, the British 1st Airborne and the Polish 1st Parachute Brigade. The airborne forces were to seize a succession of river crossings in Holland ahead of his troops, with the major objective being the Lower Rhine bridge at Arnhem. Anticipating that the Germans would expect him to take the shortest route and drive northeast for the Rhine and the Ruhr, Montgomery had deliberately chosen a northern "back door" route to the Reich. The surprise airborne attack would open a corridor for the tanks of his British Second Army, which would race across the captured bridges to Arnhem, over the Rhine and beyond. Once all this was accomplished, Montgomery could wheel east, outflank the Siegfried Line, and dash into the Ruhr.

Eisenhower was intrigued and impressed. It was a bold, brilliantly imaginative plan, exactly the kind of mass attack he had been seeking for his long-idle airborne divisions. But now the Supreme Commander was caught between the hammer and the anvil: if he agreed to the attack, the opening of Antwerp would temporarily have to be delayed and supplies diverted from Patton. Yet, Montgomery's proposal could revitalize the dying advance and perhaps propel the pursuit across the Rhine and into the Ruhr. Eisenhower, fascinated by the audaciousness of the plan, not only gave his approval,° but insisted that the operation take place at the earliest possible moment.

Yet the Supreme Commander stressed that the attack was a "limited one." And he emphasized to Montgomery that he considered the combined airborne-ground operation "merely an extension of the northern advance to the Rhine and the Ruhr." As Eisenhower remembered the conversation, he said to Montgomery, "I'll tell you what I'll do, Monty. I'll give you whatever you ask to get you over the Rhine because I want a bridgehead . . . but let's get over the Rhine first before we discuss anything else." Montgomery continued to argue, but Eisenhower would not budge. Frustrated, the Field Marshal had to accept what he called a "half measure," and on this note the conference ended.

After Eisenhower's departure, Montgomery outlined the proposed operation on a map for Lieutenant General Browning. The elegant Browning, one of Britain's pioneer airborne advocates, saw that the paratroopers and glider-borne forces were being called upon to secure a series of crossings—five of them major bridges including the wide rivers of the Maas, the Waal and the Lower Rhine—over a stretch approximately sixty-four miles long between the Dutch border and Arnhem. Additionally, they were charged with holding open the corridor—in most places a single highway running north—over which British armor would drive. All of the bridges had to be seized intact if the armored dash was to succeed. The dangers were obvious, but this was precisely the kind of surprise assault for which the airborne forces had been trained. Still, Browning was uneasy. Pointing to the most northern bridge over the Lower Rhine at Arnhem, he asked, "How long will it take the armor to reach us?" Montgomery replied briskly, "Two days." Still intent on the map, Browning said, "We can hold it for four." Then he added, "But sir, I think we might be going a bridge too far."

° Eisenhower told Stephen E. Ambrose, according to his book, *The Supreme Commander*, p. 518 fn.: "I not only approved . . . I insisted upon it. What we needed was a bridgehead over the Rhine. If that could be accomplished, I was quite willing to wait on all other operations. . . ."

THE PRIZE
*The most northern of all
crossings to be seized by
Anglo-American and Polish
airborne forces was the
Arnhem bridge over the
Lower Rhine. Assigned to
Major General Urquhart's
British 1st Airborne Division
and Major General
Sosabowski's Polish 1st
Parachute Brigade, it was the
key to Montgomery's plan
to end the war in 1944.
Photo shows bridge with long
boulevards stretching back to
the concert hall complex,
Musis Sacrum (left
foreground).*

The Bridges: Urquhart's men were also to capture the Arnhem railroad crossing and the pontoon bridge. The Germans blew up the former, and the middle section of the latter was found missing. Mystery surrounds RAF photo of pontoon bridge [LEFT] taken eleven days before attack: were Germans replacing or removing the center? No one could tell, but attack was ordered just the same.

Major General Gavin's 82nd Airborne swiftly captured the 1500-foot-long Grave bridge over the Maas River [OPPOSITE TOP] and, among others, the Heumen Canal bridge [OPPOSITE CENTER]. But due to confusion in orders and quick German reaction, they failed to capture on the first day Nijmegen bridge, over the Waal [BELOW], eleven miles from Arnhem. Crossing fell in combined Anglo-American attack on the 19th when the 82nd made a daring river assault which has been called a "second Omaha Beach landing."

South of 82nd's positions, Major General Taylor's 101st Airborne captured all bridges but one: the crossing at Son [BELOW] was blown up, throwing Market-Garden's schedule off by 36 hours.

Eisenhower and Montgomery were bitterly opposed on war strategy. Montgomery thought Supreme Commander indecisive with "no experience for the job"; Eisenhower considered Britain's popular Field Marshal "an egocentric who never made a mistake in his life."

New chief of First Allied Airborne Army, Lieutenant General Brereton, had never commanded paratroops before. He was in disagreement with British deputy, Lieutenant General Browning. Hours before attack planning began, Brereton received a letter of resignation from Browning.

Browning, Britain's foremost airborne authority, withdrew his resignation when named to command Market-Garden. He had never had operational control of an airborne corps before.

(*Left to right*) *Major General Adair, commander of Guards Armored Division; Field Marshal Montgomery; Lieutenant General Horrocks, whose XXX Corps tanks and infantry would make drive; and Major General Roberts, whose Eleventh Armored captured Antwerp but was halted to "refuel, refit and rest," thus allowing bulk of German Fifteenth Army to reach Holland and participate in Market-Garden offensive.*

*[*BELOW LEFT*] Major General Taylor, commander of the U.S. 101st Airborne, meets with Lieutenant General Ritchie, of 12th British Corps; and [*RIGHT*] General Dempsey, chief of Second British Army, confers with Major General Gavin, U.S. 82nd Airborne commander.*

Dutch intelligence man Henri Knap [TOP LEFT] with Arnhem underground chief Pieter Kruyff [RIGHT] warned London of Panzer divisions in Arnhem area on September 14th. · [CENTER] Major Brian Urquhart, Browning's intelligence chief, also spotted German tanks on RAF reconnaissance photos. Warnings went unheeded. · [LOWER LEFT] Major General "Roy" Urquhart, commander of British 1st Airborne, though veteran combat leader, was commanding paratroop division for first time. He was not only unaware of German armor but was forced to land his units from six to eight miles from crucial Arnhem bridge. Hardly had the attack begun than communications failed, and General Urquhart, cut off from headquarters behind German lines, was forced to hide out for 39 vital hours.

With Urquhart "missing," Brigadier Hicks [TOP LEFT] was forced to lead the division. · When 4th Parachute Brigade landed, September 18th, Brigadier Hackett [ABOVE RIGHT], because of seniority, challenged Hicks over division command. · Urquhart's Chief of Staff, Colonel Mackenzie [CENTER LEFT], calmed down arguing brigadiers · Meanwhile, unaware of true situation in Arnhem, General Sosabowski [CENTER RIGHT] and his Polish 1st Parachute Brigade were delayed more than two days because of bad weather. · Brigadier Lathbury [BELOW], commander of 1st Parachute Brigade, should have assumed division leadership, but was wounded and, like General Urquhart, considered "missing."

Holding northern approaches to Arnhem bridge and outnumbered by at least 10 to 1, Colonel John Frost [LEFT], with his men, in one of history's greatest feats of arms, held off elements of two German Panzer divisions. · Another bridge hero, Captain Eric Mackay [CENTER, AS HE IS TODAY], though almost out of ammunition, actually called on Germans to surrender. Wounded and captured, Mackay [BELOW, AT TILLER] refused to give up; he escaped and floated downstream to Nijmegen with companions.

Irish Guards tank group led the armored breakout from Dutch-Belgian border. Shown here are its commander, Colonel J. O. E. Vandeleur [ABOVE LEFT], and his cousin Giles, a battalion commander [ABOVE RIGHT]. [RIGHT] The two men as they appeared in 1944. The Germans succeeded in halting Vandeleur's tanks barely six miles short of Frost's men on Arnhem bridge.

RAF Flight Lieutenant Love [TOP], ground-to-air communications officer during tank drive, wondered why he had volunteered for job. · Lord Wrottesley [LEFT CENTER], who made first contact with Urquhart's isolated troops. · Lieutenant Hay [RIGHT CENTER], whose "Phantom" radio unit finally contacted ground forces for Urquhart. · Colonel Chatterton [RIGHT], Glider Pilot Regiment commander, who pressed for a daring glider coup-de-main on Arnhem bridge. Had his plan been adopted, the bridge might have been taken within hours. Instead, Chatterton was called "an assassin and a bloody murderer" for suggesting the idea.

In his division's last stand at Oosterbeek, Major Cain [ABOVE LEFT], though wounded again and again, continued to fight back against enemy tanks. · Miss Clair Miller [ABOVE RIGHT], of London's Hobson & Sons Ltd., made Browning's Pegasus flag, contrary to the Arnhem myth that it was the work of his wife, novelist Daphne du Maurier. Miss Miller also sewed 500 tiny compasses into troopers' uniforms, which later aided many in making an escape. · Major Lonsdale [BELOW LEFT], whose "Lonsdale Force" held out to the very end.

In the Anglo-American attack on Nijmegen bridge, 82nd Airborne's Major Cook [ABOVE RIGHT] led the unprecedented crossing of Waal River to seize bridge's northern end. · Simultaneously Lieutenant Colonel Vandervoort [ABOVE LEFT], together with British forces, attacked southern approaches.

Military Cross winner Lieutenant Gorman [ABOVE LEFT] had his "doubts" about the entire operation. He felt that no one was moving fast enough to rescue Frost's men on Arnhem bridge. · Lieutenant Wierzbowski [ABOVE RIGHT] was sent with a company to capture the bridge at Best, which was believed to be "lightly held." The area actually contained more than 1,000 German troops of the forgotten Fifteenth Army and in the end involved an entire regiment of the 101st Airborne.

Lieutenant Glover [ABOVE LEFT], who took his pet chicken, Myrtle, on the Arnhem jump. "Myrtle, the parachick" was killed and in the midst of the fighting was given a formal burial. · Major Deane-Drummond [ABOVE RIGHT], second in command, 1st Airborne Division Signals, had doubts that his communications would work, but like everyone else was "swept along with the prevailing attitude," which was "For God's sake, don't rock the boat." · Colonel Tucker [RIGHT], 504th regimental commander, whose units crossed Waal River, was appalled at slowness of British tanks. He had expected a special task force to make the eleven-mile dash to Arnhem and relieve bridge defenders. Instead, Tucker said, the British "stopped for tea."

Fired by Hitler after the Normandy débacle, Von Rundstedt [LEFT], the Reich's most competent Field Marshal, was recalled in September. The situation on the western front was so catastrophic that Von Rundstedt believed the Allies could invade the Reich and end the war within two weeks. His strategy in saving Fifteenth Army was major factor in defeating Montgomery's Market-Garden plan. Field Marshal Model [BELOW], whom Von Rundstedt called a "good regimental sergeant major," had been unable to halt Allied drive across western Europe, but by chance had moved the II SS Panzer Corps into the Arnhem area days before the airborne attack. Captured Market-Garden plans were in his hands within 48 hours, but, incredibly, Model refused to believe them.

II SS Panzer Corps commander, Lieutenant General Bittrich (shown above as he is today and in 1944), knew nothing of captured Market-Garden plans, but correctly deduced that main objective was Arnhem bridge.

The Reich's airborne expert, Colonel General Student (today and in 1944), was stunned by size of airborne drop and "only wished I had had such forces at my disposal."

The British landed virtually amidst two Panzer divisions in the Arnhem area, to the surprise of their commanders: Lieutenant Colonel Harzer (above as he is today and in 1944) of 9th SS "Hohenstaufen" Division; Major General Harmel (below) of 10th SS "Frundsberg" Division.

Double agent "King Kong" Lindemanns [RIGHT] crossed front lines to inform Germans of British ground attack on September 17th. Contrary to British newspaper reports after the war, Lindemanns knew nothing about scope of airborne attack.

Luftwaffe General Dessloch [ABOVE LEFT] was so worried about possibility of airborne attack that he refused to visit Model. The battalion of Major Krafft [ABOVE RIGHT] was by chance in position on the edge of British drop zones.

The first man at Model's headquarters in Tafelberg Hotel to learn of airborne drop barely two miles away was Lieutenant Sedelhauser [RIGHT]. "They are dropping in our laps," he was told.

Prince Bernhard [ABOVE] shown as he arrived in liberated Eindhoven and [OPPOSITE] as he is today. Neither Bernhard nor his general staff were consulted about terrain difficulty in the Market-Garden plan until it was too late, and detailed information which the Prince had from Dutch underground sources regarding German armor in Arnhem was discounted.

Expecting liberation, the Dutch in Oosterbeek found themselves caught up in brutal battle. "Montgomery will be here soon," optimistic Britishers told 17-year-old Anje van Maanen [LEFT]. · Jan Voskuil [ABOVE] could not rid himself of a "feeling of hopelessness." · Hendrika van der Vlist [BELOW] wrote in her diary that Oosterbeek had become "one of the bloodiest battlefields."

Kate ter Horst [ABOVE LEFT] *with son Michiel during war and* [RIGHT] *with husband, Jan, as they are today, courageously made her home available to British wounded. At one time during battle more than 300 casualties crowded the house. A former Dutch captain, Jan could not understand why the British failed to use Driel ferry* [BELOW] *to cross the Rhine. In Market-Garden planning the ferry was completely overlooked.*

The embryo concept (which thereafter would bear the code name "Operation Market-Garden"—"Market" covering the airborne drop and "Garden" for the armored drive) was to be developed with the utmost speed, Montgomery ordered. He insisted that the attack had to be launched in a few days. Otherwise, he told Browning, it would be too late. Montgomery asked: "How soon can you get ready?" Browning, at this moment, could only hazard a guess. "The earliest scheduling of the operation would be the fifteenth or sixteenth,"* he told the Field Marshal.

Carrying Montgomery's skeleton plan and weighed with the urgency of preparing for such a massive mission in only a few days, Browning flew back to England immediately. On landing at his Moor Park Golf Course base near Rickmansworth on the outskirts of London, he telephoned the First Allied Airborne headquarters, twenty miles away, and notified the commander, Lieutenant General Brereton, and his chief of staff, Brigadier General Floyd L. Parks. The time was 2:30 P.M., and Parks noted that Browning's message contained "the first mention of 'Market' at this headquarters."

The airborne commanders were not the only officers caught unaware. Montgomery's daring plan so impressed and surprised the Field Marshal's greatest critic, General Omar N. Bradley, that he later recalled, "Had the pious, teetotalling Montgomery wobbled into SHAEF with a hangover, I could not have been more astonished. . . . Although I never reconciled myself to the venture, I nevertheless freely concede that it was one of the most imaginative of the war."†

It was, but Montgomery remained unhappy. He now prodded

---

* Minutes of the first planning meeting, First Allied Airborne Army operational file 1014–1017.
† General Omar N. Bradley, *A Soldier's Story*, p. 416. Bradley also added, "I had not been brought into the plan. In fact, Montgomery devised and sold it to Ike several days before I even learned of it from our own liaison officer at 21st Army Group."

the Supreme Commander even further, reverting to the cautious, perfectionist thinking that was characteristic of his military career. Unless the 21st Army Group received additional supplies and transport for the "selected thrust," Montgomery warned Eisenhower, Market-Garden could not be launched before September 23 at the earliest, and might even be delayed until September 26. Browning had estimated that Market could be ready by the fifteenth or sixteenth, but Montgomery was concerned about Garden, the land operation. Once again he was demanding what he had always wanted: absolute priority, which to his mind would guarantee success. Eisenhower noted in his desk diary for September 12: "Monty's suggestion is simple—'give him everything.'" Fearing that any delay might jeopardize Market-Garden, Eisenhower complied. He promptly sent his chief of staff, General Bedell Smith, to see Montgomery; Smith assured the Field Marshal of a thousand tons of supplies per day plus transport. Additionally, Montgomery was promised that Patton's drive to the Saar would be checked. Elated at the "electric" response—as the Field Marshal called it—Montgomery believed he had finally won the Supreme Commander over to his point of view.

Although opposition before Montgomery's troops had stiffened, he believed that the Germans in Holland, behind the hard crust of their front lines, had little strength. Allied intelligence confirmed his estimate. Eisenhower's headquarters reported "few infantry reserves" in the Netherlands, and even these were considered to be "troops of low category." The enemy, it was thought, was still "disorganized after his long and hasty retreat . . . and though there might be numerous small bodies of Germans in the area," they were hardly capable of any great organized resistance. Montgomery now believed he could quickly crack the German defenses. Then, once he was over the Rhine and headed for the Ruhr, he did not see how Eisenhower could halt his drive. The Supreme Commander would have little choice, he reasoned, but to let him continue toward Berlin—thus ending the war, as Montgomery put it, "reasonably quickly." Confidently, Montgomery set Sunday, September 17, as D Day for

Operation Market-Garden. The brilliant scheme he had devised was to become the greatest airborne operation of the entire war.

Not everyone shared Montgomery's certainty about Market-Garden. At least one of his senior officers had reason to be worried. General Miles Dempsey, commander of the British Second Army, unlike the Field Marshal, did not dispute the authenticity of Dutch resistance reports. From these, Dempsey's intelligence staff had put together a picture indicating rapidly increasing German strength between Eindhoven and Arnhem, in the very area of the planned airborne drop. There was even a Dutch report that "battered panzer formations have been sent to Holland to refit," and these too were said to be in the Market-Garden area. Dempsey sent along this news to Browning's British I Airborne Corps, but the information lacked any back-up endorsement by Montgomery or his staff. The ominous note was not even included in intelligence summaries. In fact, in the mood of optimism prevailing at 21st Army Group headquarters, the report was completely discounted.

☆ 7 ☆

FIELD MARSHAL GERD VON RUNDSTEDT's high-risk gamble to rescue the remains of General Von Zangen's encircled Fifteenth Army in the Pas de Calais was paying off. Under cover of darkness, ever since September 6, a hastily assembled fleet consisting of two ancient Dutch freighters, several Rhine barges and some small boats and rafts had been plying back and forth across the three-mile mouth of the Schelde estuary ferrying men, artillery, vehicles and even horses.

Although powerful coastal guns on Walcheren Island protected against attack from the sea, the Germans were surprised that Allied naval forces made no effort to interfere. Major General Walter Poppe expected the convoy carrying his splintered 59th Infantry Division to be "blown out of the water." To him the one-hour trip between Breskens and Flushing "in completely darkened ships, exposed and defenseless, was a most unpleasant experience." The Allies, the Germans suspected, completely underestimated the size of the evacuation. Certainly they knew about it. Because both Von Rundstedt and Army Group B's commander, Field Marshal Walter Model, desperately in need of reinforcements, were demanding speed, some daylight trips had been made. Immediately, fighters pounced on the small convoys. Darkness, however unpleasant, was much safer.

The most hazardous part of the journey was on the Schelde's northern bank. There, under the constant threat of Allied air attack, Von Zangen's forces had to follow a single main road, running east from Walcheren Island, across the Beveland peninsula and into Holland. Part of the escape route, at the narrow neck joining the mainland, was only a few miles from Antwerp and British lines on the Albert Canal. Inexplicably the British even now made no serious effort to attack north, spring the trap, and cut the base of the isthmus. The escape route remained open. Although hammered by incessant Allied air attacks Von Zangen's Fifteenth Army would eventually reach Holland—at a most crucial moment for Montgomery's Market-Garden operation.

While the Fifteenth Army had been extricated more by calculated design than by luck, now the opposite occurred: fate, the unexpected and unpredictable, took a hand. Some eighty miles away the battered armored units of Lieutenant General Wilhelm Bittrich's elite, veteran II SS Panzer Corps reached bivouac areas in the vicinity of Arnhem. As directed by Field Marshal Model on September 4, Bittrich had slowly disengaged the 9th and 10th SS

Panzer divisions for "refitting and rehabilitation." Model had chosen the Arnhem area. The two reduced, but still tough, divisions were fanned out to the north, east and south of the town. Bittrich assigned the 9th SS to a huge rectangular sector north and northeast of Arnhem, where most of the division's men and vehicles were on high ground and conveniently hidden in a densely wooded national park. The 10th was encamped in a semicircle to the northeast, east and southeast. Thus, camouflaged and hidden in nearby woods, villages and towns—Beekbergen, Apeldoorn, Zutphen, Ruurlo and Doetinchem—both divisions were within striking distance of Arnhem; some units were within a mile or two of the suburbs. As Bittrich was later to recall, "there was no particular significance in Model choosing the Arnhem vicinity—except that it was a peaceful sector where nothing was happening."

The possibility that this remote backwater might have any strategic value to the Allies was obviously discounted. On the morning of September 11, a small group of Model's staff officers was dispatched in search of a new site for Army Group B's headquarters—in Arnhem.

One of Model's aides, his general headquarters administration and transportation officer, thirty-five-year-old Lieutenant Gustav Sedelhauser, later remembered that "we visited the 9th and 10th SS division headquarters at Beekbergen and Ruurlo and General Bittrich's command post at Doetinchem. Then we inspected Arnhem itself. It had everything we wanted: a fine road net and excellent accommodations. But it was not until we drove west to the outlying district of Oosterbeek that we found what we were looking for." In the wealthy, residential village just two and a half miles from the center of Arnhem was a group of hotels, among them the gracious, white Hartenstein, with its broad expanse of crescent-shaped lawn, stretching back into parklike surroundings where deer roamed undisturbed, and the smaller, two-story, tree-shaded Tafelberg with its glassed-in veranda and paneled rooms. Impressed by the facilities and, as Sedelhauser recalled, "especially the accommodations," the group promptly recommended

Oosterbeek to the chief of staff, Lieutenant General Hans Krebs, as "perfect for Army Group B's headquarters." Model approved the decision. Part of the staff, he decided, would live at the Hartenstein, while he would occupy the more secluded, less ostentatious Tafelberg. Lieutenant Sedelhauser was delighted. Since his tenure the headquarters had never remained anywhere for more than a few days, and now Sedelhauser "was looking forward to some peace and a chance to get my laundry done." By September 15, Model directed, Army Group B's headquarters was to be fully operational in Oosterbeek—approximately three miles from the broad expanse of heaths and pastureland where the British 1st Airborne Division was due to land on September 17.

Part Two

THE PLAN

❖ 1 ❖

IN THE EARLY EVENING of September 10, within hours of General Browning's meeting with Field Marshal Montgomery, Lieutenant General Lewis H. Brereton held the first basic planning conference on Operation Market. At his Sunninghill Park headquarters near the fashionable Ascot racecourse thirty-five miles from London, twenty-seven senior officers crowded into Brereton's large map-lined office. After General Browning briefed the group on Montgomery's plan, Brereton told them that, because there was so little time, "major decisions arrived at now must stand—and these have to be made immediately."

The task was monumental, and there were few guidelines. Never before had there been an attempt to send a mammoth airborne force, complete with vehicles, artillery and equipment, capable of fighting on its own, deep behind enemy front lines. In comparison with Market, previous airborne attacks had been small; yet months had gone into their planning. Now, to prepare for the greatest paratroop and glider-borne infantry operation ever conceived, Brereton and his planners had barely seven days.

Brereton's greatest concern was not the deadline, but the possibility that this operation, like its predecessors, might be canceled. His long-idle airborne troops were impatient for action, and a serious morale problem had developed as a consequence. For weeks his elite, highly trained divisions had stood down while ground forces on the Continent swept victoriously across France and Belgium. There was a widespread feeling that victory was so near that the war might end before the First Allied Airborne Army got into battle.

The General harbored no doubts about the ability of his staff to meet the tight, one-week Market schedule. There had been so many "dry runs" in developing previous airborne schemes that his headquarters and division staffs had reached a stage of high-speed efficiency. Additionally, much of the planning that had gone into Comet and other canceled operations could be readily adapted to Market. In preparing for the aborted Comet mission, for example, the British 1st Airborne Division and the Polish Brigade, charged with that operation, had made a thorough study of the Arnhem area. Still, most of the Market concept meant vastly expanded planning—and all of it was time-consuming.

General Brereton was outwardly confident and calm, but members of his staff noted that he smoked one cigarette after another. On his desk was a framed quotation which the General often pointed out to his staff. It read: "Where is the Prince who can afford so to cover his country with troops for its defense, as that 10,000 men descending from the clouds, might not, in many places, do an infinite deal of mischief before a force could be brought together to repel them?" It had been written in 1784 by Benjamin Franklin.

Brereton was fascinated by the vision of the eighteenth-century statesman and scientist. "Even after a hundred sixty years," he had told his staff, "the idea remains the same." But Franklin would have been bewildered by the complexities and size of Operation Market. To invade Holland from the sky, Brereton planned to land almost 35,000 men—nearly twice the number of paratroops and glider-borne infantry used in the invasion of Normandy.

To "grab the bridges with thunderclap surprise," as Brereton put it, and hold open the narrow, one-highway advance corridor for the British Garden ground forces—from their attack line near the Dutch-Belgian border to Arnhem sixty-four miles north—three and one half airborne divisions were to be used. Two would be American. Almost directly ahead of General Horrocks' XXX Corps tanks, Major General Maxwell D. Taylor's 101st Airborne Division was to capture canal and river crossings over a fifteen-mile stretch between Eindhoven and Veghel. North of them, Brigadier General James M. Gavin's veteran 82nd Division was charged with the area between Grave and the city of Nijmegen, approximately a ten-mile stretch. They were to seize crossings over the great Maas and Waal rivers, in particular the huge multispan bridge at Nijmegen, which, with its approaches, was almost a half-mile long. The single most important objective of Operation Market-Garden was Arnhem and its vital crossing over the 400-yard-wide Lower Rhine. The great concrete-and-steel, three-span highway bridge, together with its concrete ramps, was almost 2,000 feet long. Its capture was assigned to the British and Poles—Major General Robert "Roy" E. Urquhart's 1st Airborne Division and, under his command, Major General Stanislaw Sosabowski's Polish 1st Parachute Brigade. Arnhem, lying farthest away from the Garden forces, was the prize. Without the Rhine crossing, Montgomery's bold stroke to liberate Holland, outflank the Siegfried Line and springboard into Germany's industrial Ruhr would fail.

To carry the huge force to targets three hundred miles away, an intricate air plan had to be designed. Three distinct operations were required: transportation, protection and resupply. No fewer than twenty-four different airfields would be needed for takeoff. Brereton planned to use every operable glider in his command—an immense fleet of more than 2,500. Besides hauling heavy equipment such as jeeps and artillery, the gliders were to ferry more than a third of the 35,000-man force; the rest would drop by parachute. All the craft had to be checked out, loading space allotted, heavy equipment and cargo stowed, and troop complements prepared.

Gliders posed only a single problem in the air planning. Transports to carry paratroops and tow planes to pull the gliders must be diverted from their normal task of supplying the advancing armies and grounded in order to be readied for Market. The crews of bomber squadrons had to be alerted and briefed for missions in the Market-Garden area prior to, and during, the attack. Swarms of fighter squadrons from all over England—more than 1,500 planes—would be needed to escort the airborne force. Intricate aerial traffic patterns were of prime importance. Routes between England and Holland had to be laid out to avoid heavy enemy antiaircraft fire and the equally dangerous possibility of air collision. Air-sea rescue operations, resupply missions, even a dummy parachute drop in another area of Holland to deceive the enemy, were also planned. In all, it was estimated that almost 5,000 aircraft of all types would be involved in Market. To develop plans and ready this vast air armada would take a minimum of seventy-two hours.

The most pressing question of the conference, in Brereton's opinion, was whether the operation should be undertaken by day or by night. Previous major airborne operations had taken place in moonlight. But semidarkness had led to confusion in finding landing zones, lack of troop concentration and unnecessary casualties. The General decreed that the huge airborne assault would take place in broad daylight. It was an unprecedented decision. In the history of airborne operations, a daylight drop of such proportions had never before been made.

Brereton had other reasons than the desire to avoid confusion. The week scheduled for Operation Market was a no-moon period and night landings on a large scale were therefore impossible. Apart from that, Brereton chose a daylight attack because, for the first time in the war, it was feasible. Allied fighters held such overwhelming superiority over the battlefields that now interference from the Luftwaffe was practically nonexistent. But the Germans did have night fighters. In a night drop, against columns of slow-moving troop-carrying planes and gliders, they might prove devastatingly effective. German antiaircraft strength was another consideration: flak maps of the approaches to the Market drop areas were dotted with antiaircraft positions. The charts, based on photo-reconnaissance flights and the experience of bomber crews flying over Holland en route to Germany, looked formidable—particularly so because gliders were without protective armor, except in the cockpits, and C-47 troop-carriers and tow planes had no self-sealing gas tanks. Nevertheless, Brereton believed that enemy antiaircraft positions could be neutralized by concentrated bomber and fighter attacks preceding and during the assault. In any event, most antiaircraft was radar-directed, and therefore was as effective after dark as it was during the day. Either way, losses were to be expected. Still, unless bad weather and high winds intervened, the airborne force, by attacking in daylight, could be dropped with almost pinpoint accuracy on the landing zones, thus guaranteeing a quick concentration of troops in the corridor. "The advantages," Brereton told his commanders, "far outweigh the risks."

Brereton made his final announcement. To command the giant operation he appointed his deputy, the fastidious forty-seven-year-old Lieutenant General Frederick "Boy" Browning, head of the British I Airborne Corps. It was an excellent choice, though disappointing to Lieutenant General Matthew B. Ridgway, commander of the other corps in the airborne army—the XVIII Airborne Corps. Still, Browning had been slated to command the aborted Operation Comet, which, though smaller and utilizing only British and Polish airborne troops, was similar in concept to Market-Garden. Now, under the enlarged and innovative plan Montgomery had devised, American paratroops would serve under a British airborne commander for the first time.

To the assembled airborne commanders Browning delivered an optimistic summation. He ended his talk with the kind of picturesque confidence that had always made him a heroic figure to his men. As his chief of staff, Brigadier Gordon Walch, remembers, "General Browning was in high spirits, delighted that at last we were going. 'The object,' he told us, 'is to lay a carpet of airborne troops down over which our ground forces can pass.' He believed this single operation held the key to the duration of the war."

Browning's enthusiasm was catching. As the large meeting broke up, to be replaced by smaller staff conferences which would last throughout the night, few officers were aware that an underlying friction existed between Brereton and Browning. Originally, when the First Allied Airborne Army was formed, British hopes ran high that Browning, Britain's senior airborne authority and one of the pioneers in the use of paratroops, would be named commander. Because of the preponderance of American troops and equipment within the newly organized army, the coveted post went to an American, General Brereton.

In rank, Browning was six months Brereton's senior; and although the American was a distinguished tactical air force officer, he had never before commanded airborne forces. Additionally, there were wide personality differences between the two men. Brereton had been a World War I flyer and had served brilliantly in World War II, first in the Far and Middle East and later as commanding general of the U.S. Ninth Air Force in England. He was tenacious and single-minded, but his zeal to achieve was cloaked by a quiet, stolid demeanor. Now Brereton proceeded on the awesome assignment he had been handed with the determination and bulldozing tactics that characterized many of his fellow American career officers.

Browning, a Grenadier Guards officer, was also a perfectionist, equally determined to prove the worth of paratroops. But he had never commanded an airborne corps before. In contrast to Brereton, "Boy" Browning was a somewhat glamorous figure, elegant and impeccably groomed, with an air of easy assurance often misunderstood for arrogance, not only by Americans but by some of his own commanders. Though he was temperamental and sometimes overly impatient, his reputation as an airborne theorist was legendary among his admirers. Still, he lacked the battle experience of some other officers, such as General Richard Gale of the British 6th Airborne Division and the veteran American commanders, Generals Gavin and Taylor. And, Browning had yet to prove that he possessed the administrative genius of the most experienced of all airborne commanders, General Ridgway.

Only days before, an incident had occurred that pointed up the differences between Brereton and Browning. On September 3, Browning had protested to Brereton the dangers of trying to launch an airborne assault on just thirty-six hours' notice. Since D Day on June 6, seventeen airborne operations had been prepared and canceled. In the thirty-three days of Brereton's command, in his eagerness to get into action, plans had been processed at the rate of almost one a week. None reached the launching stage. Browning, watching the mass production of airborne schemes, was deeply concerned about the haste and the risks being run. When Operation Linnet I—a drop before the British army in Belgium—was canceled on September 2, Brereton quickly found new objectives ahead of the speeding armies and proposed Operation Linnet II, as a substitute attack to take place on the morning of September 4.

As Brereton later recalled the incident, "Browning was quite agitated about Operation Linnet II in which there was a serious shortage of information, photographs and, in particular, maps. As a result, 'Boy' claimed his troops could not be briefed properly." Airborne operations, Browning contended, "should not be attempted on such short notice." In principle Brereton had agreed, but he had told his deputy that "the disorganization of the enemy demands that chances be taken." The disagreement between the two men had ended with Browning stiffly stating that he intended to submit his protest in writing. A few hours later his letter had arrived. Because "of our sharp differences of opinion," Browning wrote, he could no longer "continue as Deputy Commander of the First Allied Airborne Army." Brereton, unintimidated, had begun at once to consider the problem of Browning's replacement. He had alerted General Ridgway to "stand by to take over." The delicate problem was solved when Operation Linnet II was canceled; the following day Brereton had persuaded Browning to withdraw his letter of resignation.

Now, their differences set aside, both men faced the huge, complex task of preparing Market. Whatever reservations Browning entertained were now secondary to the job ahead.

There was one decision Brereton could not make at the initial meeting: exactly how the airborne troops comprising the carpet were to be carried to the targets. The airborne commanders could not make detailed plans until this greatest of all problems was solved. The fact was that the airborne army was only as mobile as the planes that would carry it. Apart from gliders, Brereton had no transports of his own. To achieve complete surprise, the ideal plan called for the three and one-half divisions in Market to be delivered to landing zones on the same day at the same hour. But the immense size of the operation ruled out this possibility. There was an acute shortage of both aircraft and gliders; the planes would have to make more than one trip. Other factors also forced a different approach. Each division had separate combat requirements. For example, it was essential that the transport for General Taylor's 101st Airborne carry more men than equipment when the attack began so that the division could carry out its assigned task of achieving a link-up with the Garden forces within the first few hours. Also, Taylor's men had to join quickly with the 82nd Airborne on the corridor north of them. There, General Gavin's troops not only had to secure the formidable bridges across the Maas and the Waal but also hold the Groesbeek ridge to the southeast, terrain which had to be denied the Germans because it dominated the countryside. Gavin's special assignment also imposed special requirements. Because the 82nd Airborne would have to fight longer than the 101st before the link-up occurred, Gavin needed not only troops but artillery.

Farther north, the problems of the British 1st Airborne under General Urquhart were different still. The British 1st was to hold the Arnhem bridge until relieved. With luck, German reaction would be sluggish enough so that ground forces could reach the lightly armed British troopers before any real enemy strength developed. But until Horrocks' tanks arrived, Urquhart's men would have to hang on. Urquhart could not dissipate his strength by sending units south to link up with Gavin. Lying at the farthest end of the airborne carpet, the British 1st Airborne would have to hold longer than anyone else. For this reason, Urquhart's force was the largest, his division bolstered by the addition of Polish paratroops, plus the 52nd Lowland Division, which was to be flown in as soon as air strips could be located and prepared in the Arnhem area.

On the morning of the eleventh, after a hectic night of assessing and analyzing aircraft availability for the attack, Major General Paul L. Williams, commander of the U.S. IX Troop Carrier Command, and in charge of all Market air operations, gave his estimate to Brereton. There was such a shortage of gliders and planes, he reported, that even with an all-out effort, at best only half the troop strength of Browning's total force could be flown in on D Day. Essential items such as artillery, jeeps and other heavy cargo scheduled for the gliders could be included only on a strict priority basis. Brereton urged his air commander to explore the possibility of two D-Day airlifts but the suggestion was found impractical. "Owing to the reduced hours of daylight and the distances involved, it would not be possible to consider more than one lift per day," General Williams said. It was too risky. There would be no time for maintenance or battle-damage repair, he pointed out, and almost certainly "casualties would result from pilot and crew fatigue."

Hamstrung by the shortage of aircraft and the time limit, Brereton made some general assessments. A full day would be required to take aerial-reconnaissance photographs of the Dutch bridges and terrain; two days must go into the preparation and distribution of maps of the areas; intelligence had to be gathered and analyzed; detailed battle plans must be prepared. The most crucial decision of all: Brereton was forced to tailor the Market plan to suit the existing airlift capability. He must transport his force in installments, flying the three and one half divisions to their targets over a period of three days. The risks were great: German reinforcements might reach the Market-Garden area faster than anyone anticipated; antiaircraft fire could intensify; and there was always the possibility of bad weather. Fog, high winds, a sudden storm—all likely at this time of the year—could cause disaster.

Worse, once on the ground, the paratroopers and glider-borne infantry, arriving without heavy artillery or tanks, would be highly vulnerable. General Horrocks' XXX Corps tank columns, using one narrow highway, could not make the 64-mile dash to Arnhem and beyond unless Brereton's men seized the bridges and held open the advance route. Conversely, the airborne army had to be relieved at top speed. Cut off far behind enemy lines and dependent on supplies by air, the airborne forces could expect German reinforcements to increase with each passing day. At best the beleaguered troopers might hold out in their "airheads" for only a few days. If the British armored drive was held up or failed to move fast enough, the airborne troops would inevitably be overrun and destroyed.

More could go wrong. If General Taylor's "Screaming Eagles" failed to secure the bridges directly ahead of the British Second Army's tank spearheads, it would make little difference whether or not the men under General Gavin's or General Urquhart's command secured their objectives in Nijmegen and Arnhem. Their forces would be isolated.

Certain classic airborne risks had to be accepted: divisions might be dropped or landed by gliders in the wrong areas; crossings might be destroyed by the enemy even as the attack began; bad weather could make air resupply impossible; and even if all the bridges were seized, the corridor might be cut at any point. These were but a few of the imponderables. The planners were gambling on speed, boldness, accuracy and surprise—all deriving from a precise synchronized land-and-airborne plan that, in its turn, gambled on German disorganization and inadequate strength. Each link in Market-Garden was interlocked with the next. If one gave way, disaster might result for all.

In Brereton's opinion, such risks had to be accepted. The opportunity might never arise again. Additionally, on the basis of the latest information of enemy strength, from Montgomery's 21st Army Group, Allied Airborne headquarters still felt that Brereton's forces would meet an "ill-organized enemy of varying standards." It was not expected that "any mobile force larger than a brigade group [about 3,000 men] with very few tanks and guns could be concentrated against the airborne troops before relief by the ground forces." It was expected "that the flight and landings would be hazardous, that the capture intact of the bridge objectives was more a matter of surprise and confusion than hard fighting." There was nothing here that the planners had not already taken under consideration. The last words of the intelligence summation seemed almost superfluous—"the advance of the ground forces would be very swift if the airborne operations were successful."

Major Brian Urquhart was deeply disturbed by the optimism permeating General Browning's British I Airborne Corps headquarters. The twenty-five-year-old intelligence chief felt that he was probably the only one on the staff with any doubts about Market-Garden. Urquhart (no relation to the British 1st Airborne Division commander, Major General Robert Urquhart) did not believe the optimistic estimates on enemy strength which arrived almost daily from Montgomery's 21st Army command. By the morning of Tuesday, September 12, with D Day only five days away, his doubts about Market-Garden amounted to near-panic.

His feeling had been triggered by a cautious message from General Dempsey's British Second Army headquarters. Quoting a Dutch report, Dempsey's intelligence staff warned of an increase in German strength in the Market-Garden area and spoke of the presence of "battered panzer formations believed to be in Holland to refit." Admittedly, the information was vague. Lacking any kind of confirmation, Dempsey's report was not included in the latest intelligence summaries of either Montgomery's or Eisenhower's headquarters. Urquhart could not understand why. He had been receiving similar disquieting news from Dutch liaison officers at Corps headquarters itself. And, like General Dempsey's staff, he believed them. Adding his own information to that received from Dempsey's command, Major Urquhart felt reasonably certain that elements of at least two panzer divisions were somewhere in the Arnhem area. The evidence was thin. The units were unidentified, with strength unknown, and he could not tell whether they were actually being refitted or merely passing through Arnhem. Nevertheless, Urquhart, as he later recalled, "was really very shook up."

Ever since the inception of Operation Comet and its evolution into Market-Garden, Major Urquhart's fears had been growing. Repeatedly, he had voiced his objections to the operation to "anybody who would listen on the staff." He was "quite frankly horrified by Market-Garden, because its weakness seemed to be the assumption that the Germans would put up no effective resistance." Urquhart himself was convinced that the Germans were rapidly recovering and might well have more men and equipment in Holland than anyone realized. Yet the whole essence of the scheme, as he saw it, "depended on the unbelievable notion that once the bridges were captured, XXX Corps's tanks could drive up this abominably narrow corridor—which was little more than a causeway, allowing no maneuverability—and then walk into Germany like a bride into a church. I simply did not believe that the Germans were going to roll over and surrender."

At planning conferences, Major Urquhart became increasingly alarmed at what he saw as "the desperate desire on everybody's part to get the airborne into action." There were constant comparisons between the current situation and the collapse of the Germans in 1918. Urquhart remembers that General Browning, perhaps reflecting Montgomery's views and those of "several other British commanders, was thinking about another great breakthrough." It seemed to the worried intelligence officer that everyone around him thought the war would be over by winter and "the Arnhem attack might be the airborne's last chance of getting into action." Urquhart was appalled at the lighthearted metaphor—"it was described as a 'party'"—used in reference to Market-Garden. And, in particular, he was upset by General Browning's statement that the object of the airborne attack was to "lay a carpet of airborne troops down over which our ground forces can pass." He believed that "that single cliché had the psychological effect of lulling many commanders into a passive and absolutely unimaginative state of mind in which no reaction to German resistance, apart from dogged gallantry, was envisaged." He considered the atmosphere at headquarters so unrealistic that, at one of the planning conferences, he asked "whether the 'carpet' was to consist of live airborne troops or dead ones."

"It was absolutely impossible," he said later, "to get them to face the realities of the situation; their personal longing to get into the campaign before it ended completely blinded them." But young Urquhart was convinced that General Dempsey's warning was accurate. He believed there was German armor in the vicinity of Arnhem, but he needed to substantiate the report by getting more evidence. A Spitfire fighter squadron equipped with special cameras for taking oblique pictures was stationed, Urquhart knew, at nearby Benson in Oxfordshire. The squadron was currently searching out rocket sites along the Dutch coast.

On the afternoon of September 12, Major Urquhart requested low-level R.A.F. reconnaissance sweeps of the Arnhem area. To avoid detection, enemy tanks would be hidden in forests or beneath camouflaged netting and might well escape high-altitude photographic flights. Urquhart's request was acknowledged; low-level missions would be flown over the Arnhem area, and he would get the results as fast as possible. Photographs of the tanks, if they were there, might prove to all concerned that Major Urquhart's fears were justified.

There was too little time now for airborne division commanders to check out intelligence reports firsthand. They were dependent on Corps or First Allied Airborne headquarters for the latest estimates. From experience, each commander knew that even this information would be several days old by the time he received it. Still, in the general view, there was little reason to anticipate any powerful enemy resistance. The risks involved in Market-Garden were, as a result, considered acceptable.

Once Generals Brereton and Browning had outlined the plan, determined the objectives and decided on airlift capability, each commander developed his own combat plans. The choice of drop zones and landing sites had priority. From previous operations, veteran airborne commanders knew that the best chance of success depended on how close to their objectives assaulting troops could be dropped. Ideally, they should be landed almost on their targets or within quick marching distance, especially if they were expected to seize a bridge. With the meager ground transport available, the pinpointing of these sites was vital.

Major General Maxwell D. Taylor was all too aware that his sites must be chosen for maximum effect. While Taylor would have the majority of his Screaming Eagle paratroops on D Day, his engineering units, artillery and most of the 101st transport would not arrive until D plus 1 and 2. Studying the southernmost part of the corridor where the 101st Airborne Division was to hold between Eindhoven and Veghel, Taylor quickly noted that over the fifteen-mile stretch of highway, his troops must capture two major canal crossings and no less than nine highway and railroad bridges. At Veghel, over the river Aa and the Willems Canal, there were four bridges, one a major canal crossing. Five miles south in St. Oedenrode, a bridge over the Lower Dommel had to be seized; four miles from there was the second major canal crossing, over the Wilhelmina Canal near the village of Son, and to the west a bridge near the hamlet of Best. Five miles farther south in Eindhoven, four bridges over the Upper Dommel had to be taken.

After studying the flat terrain between Eindhoven and Veghel, with its veining waterways, dikes, ditches and tree-lined roads, Taylor decided to pinpoint his major landing site almost in the center of his assault area, by the edge of a forest barely one and one half miles from Son and roughly equidistant between Eindhoven and Veghel. He would land two of his regiments, the 502nd and the 506th, on this zone. The 502nd was charged with objectives in St. Oedenrode and Best; the 506th with those in Son and Eindhoven. The third regiment, the 501st, was to land in two areas north and west of Veghel, within a few hundred yards of the vital four bridges. It was a formidable assignment for his men to accomplish on D Day without their back-up auxiliary units, but Taylor believed that "with luck, we can make it."

The task of the 82nd Airborne was more intricate. Its ten-mile sector was wider than that of the 101st. In this central segment of the corridor, the huge, nine-span, 1,500-foot-long bridge over the Maas river at Grave and at least one of four smaller railroad and highway crossings over the Maas-Waal Canal must be seized. The great bridge over the Waal river at Nijmegen, almost in the center of this city of 90,000, was also a prime objective. None of these could be called "secured" unless the Groesbeek Heights, dominating the area two miles southwest of Nijmegen, were held. Also, to the east was the great belt of forest along the German border—the Reichswald—where the Germans might assemble for attack. When General Gavin explained to his headquarters' officers what was expected of them, his chief of staff, Colonel Robert H. Wienecke, protested, "We'll need two divisions to do all that." Gavin was terse. "There it is, and we're going to do it with one."

Remembering the 82nd Airborne's attacks in Sicily and Italy, when his troops were scattered sometimes as far as thirty-five miles from their drop zone (the standard division joke was that "we always use blind pilots"), Gavin was determined to land his men this time almost on their targets. In order of priority, he decided that his objectives were: first, the Groesbeek Heights; second, the bridge at Grave; third, the crossings on the Maas-Waal Canal; and fourth, the Waal bridge at Nijmegen. "Because of probable quick enemy reaction," Gavin later recalled, "I decided to drop the largest part of my paratroops between the Groesbeek Heights and the Reichswald." He chose two landing zones in the Groesbeek vicinity less than a mile and a half from the ridge itself and three to four miles southwest of Nijmegen. There, his 508th and 505th regiments, plus the headquarters staff, would land. The third regiment, the 504th, was to drop on the western side of the Groesbeek Heights in the triangle between the

Maas river and the Maas-Waal Canal, a mile from the eastern end of the Grave bridge and two miles west of the Maas-Waal Canal bridges. To insure the capture of the vital Grave bridge, which might be prepared for demolition, an additional phase of his plan was developed in which a company of the 504th was to be dropped a half mile from the western end of the bridge. Before the enemy could retaliate, the 504th would rush the bridge from both ends.

Obviously, the great Nijmegen bridge was the most important of all his objectives and crucial to the entire Market-Garden operation. Yet Gavin was well aware that, without holding the other objectives, the Waal river crossing by itself would be useless. General Browning agreed with him. If the first bridges were not taken or if the enemy held the Groesbeek Heights, the corridor for the Garden forces would never be opened. Therefore, Browning specifically directed, Gavin was not to attempt an attack on the Nijmegen bridge until the primary objectives were secured.

Although he was concerned about the wide dispersal of his troops, Gavin was satisfied with the plan. One aspect bothered him, as it had bothered Taylor. His entire division would not be organically complete until supporting units arrived on D plus 1 and 2, and he wondered how his men—who knew nothing about Market-Garden as yet—would react. Still, in the experienced 82nd, morale was high as always; many of his men had made three combat jumps already. "Jumping Jim" Gavin, at thirty-seven the youngest brigadier general in the U.S. Army, had no doubts that his "fugitives from the law of averages," as they called themselves, would do their job.

The most difficult and dangerous assignment, by far, had been given to a modest, reticent career officer, Major General Robert "Roy" Urquhart, forty-two-year-old commander of the British 1st Airborne Division and the attached Polish Brigade.

Unlike General Browning and his American colleagues, Urquhart, a highly professional soldier who had fought with great distinction in North Africa, Sicily and Italy, had no airborne warfare experience. He would be commanding an airborne division in battle for the first time. Browning had chosen him because he was "hot from battle," but Urquhart had been surprised at his appointment. He had always considered airborne units "tightly knit organizations, closed family affairs and quite exclusive." Yet Urquhart had confidence in his ability to lead the elite unit. Once the force was on the ground the basic fighting rules remained the same, and he viewed his airborne division as "very highly trained infantry troops."

Despite his long combat experience, Urquhart was bothered about one thing: he had never parachuted or been in a glider. "I was even prone to airsickness," he was later to remark. On taking command in January, 1944, nine months before, Urquhart had suggested to General Browning that perhaps, as the new division commander, he ought to have some parachute training. Browning, who impressed Urquhart as a "lithe, immaculately turned-out man who gave the appearance of a restless hawk," answered that Urquhart's job was to get his division ready for an invasion of the Continent. Looking over the six-foot, 200-pound Scotsman, Browning added, "Leave the parachuting to younger chaps. Not only are you too large, but you're getting on."°

Throughout the long months of training, Urquhart "often felt like an outsider, a kind of military landlubber." He was aware of "being watched closely; not with hostility, though some airborne officers had reservations and a few did not bother to conceal them. I was on trial; my actions were being judged. It was an unenviable position, but one I accepted." Slowly, Urquhart's confident, assured handling of the division won over his officers. And among the troopers, Urquhart was far more popular than he knew. Private James W. Sims, of the 1st Airborne Division's 1st Parachute Brigade, remembers "the General's supreme confidence and his calmness." Sergeant John Rate, of Division headquarters, had the impression that "General Urquhart did whatever job had

---

° At their first interview Urquhart was still wearing his Brigadier's badges and tight-fitting Tartan trousers (trews) and spats of the Highland Division. As the meeting broke up, Browning, pointing to Urquhart's pants, said, "You might also get yourself properly dressed and get rid of those trews."

to be done. He didn't just ask someone else to do it. The General didn't stand on ceremony." Signalman Kenneth John Pearce called him "a big wonderful fellow. He called us 'son' or used our first names if he knew them." And from Sergeant Roy Ernest Hatch, of the Glider Pilot Regiment, Urquhart earned the supreme compliment. "He was," Hatch asserted, "a bloody general who didn't mind doin' the job of a sergeant."

To Urquhart's frustration, his division had not been chosen for the Normandy invasion, and "the summer passed interminably, planning one operation after another, only to see each canceled." Now, his "Red Devils" were "hungering for a fight." They had almost given up. "We were calling ourselves 'The Stillborn Division,'" recalls Major Geoffrey S. Powell of the 4th Parachute Brigade. "We figured we were being kept in reserve for use in the victory parade." As Urquhart saw it, "there was a dangerous mixture of ennui and cynicism slowly creeping into our lives. We were trained to a fine edge and I knew that if we didn't get into battle soon, we would lose it. We were ready and willing to accept anything, with all the 'ifs.'"

Urquhart's principal target—the prize of Operation Market-Garden—was Arnhem's concrete-and-steel highway bridge over the Lower Rhine. Additionally, Urquhart's men had two secondary objectives: a nearby floating pontoon bridge and a double-track railway crossing upriver, two and a half miles west of the town.

Urquhart's assignment presented a series of problems. Two were particularly worrisome. Reports of heavy antiaircraft defenses in the area indicated that some enemy units were massing in the vicinity of the Arnhem bridge itself. And Urquhart was uneasy about the three days it would take to airlift his entire force of British and Polish paratroops to their objectives. Both these problems had a direct bearing on Urquhart's choice of landing sites. Unlike the 82nd and 101st Airborne Divisions, he could not pick zones almost on or even close to the principal target. Ideally, he should land his forces near the Arnhem bridge on both sides of the river; but Urquhart's terrain was by no means ideal.

The northern exit of the crossing ran directly into the densely populated, built-up center of Arnhem itself. Near the southern exit, low-level polder land was, according to reports, too marshy for men or gliders. "Many of my own commanders," Urquhart remembers, "were quite willing to land on the southern side, even though it was marshy. Indeed, some were ready to risk injury by parachuting on the northern side—on the town itself."

In the previous week, bomber crews returning from other missions had reported a 30 percent increase in antiaircraft fire near the Arnhem crossing and from Deelen airfield seven miles to the north. Consequently, R.A.F. commanders whose pilots were scheduled to tow Urquhart's glider-borne troops raised strong objections to landing zones close to the Arnhem bridge. If sites were located near the southern exit, tug aircraft wheeling north after releasing gliders would run into heavy flak over the airfield. Turning south was almost as bad; planes might risk collision with aircraft dropping the 82nd Airborne near Nijmegen, eleven miles away. Urquhart was confronted with a dilemma: he could insist that the R.A.F. place his troops in proximity to the bridge, or he could choose drop zones much farther away, outside Arnhem itself, with all the dangers that choice entailed—delay, loss of surprise, possible German opposition. The risks were multiplied because on D Day Urquhart would have only a part of his division. "My problem was to get enough men down on the first lift," Urquhart recalled, "not only to seize the main bridge in the town itself, but also to guard and defend the drop zones and landing areas for the succeeding lifts. To seize the main bridge on the first day my strength was reduced to just one parachute brigade."

Faced with these restrictions, Urquhart appealed to Browning for extra planes. It seemed to him, he told the Corps commander, "that the Americans are getting all they need." Browning disagreed. The allocation of aircraft, he assured Urquhart, was "entirely due to priorities and not to any high-level American pressure." The entire operation, he explained, had to be planned from south to north, "bottom to top"; objectives in the southern and central sections of the corridor must be "seized first to get the ground forces through. Otherwise, the 1st Airborne would be wiped out."

In his command caravan on the Moor Park golf course near the clubhouse that General Browning used as headquarters, Urquhart pored over his maps and pondered the situation. Some open sectors existed north of Arnhem in a national park, but these were too small and the terrain was unsuitable. At best, these spots might accommodate a small parachute force but no gliders. The only alternative was to land in some broad expanses of open heaths and pasture land bordered by pine woods, 250 feet above sea level, lying west and northwest of Arnhem. The heathlands were firm and flat, perfect for gliders and parachutists. They were ideal in every way—except one: the areas lay between six and eight miles from the Arnhem bridge. Faced with the R.A.F.'s continued opposition to a drop in the immediate vicinity of the bridge, Urquhart reluctantly decided on the distant sites. "There was nothing else to do," he recalled, "but to accept the risks and plan for them. I was left with no choice."°

By September 12, Urquhart had his plan ready. Outlined on the map were five landing and drop zones straddling the Arnhem-Amsterdam railroad in the vicinity of Wolfheze, approximately four miles northwest of Arnhem. Three sites lay north of Wolfheze and two south, the southern zones together making up an irregular box-shaped tract more than a mile square. All were at least six miles away from the bridge at Arnhem; the farthest, northwest of Wolfheze, was eight.

On D Day two brigades would go in—Brigadier Philip "Pip" Hicks's 1st Airlanding Brigade, scheduled to hold the drop zones, and Brigadier Gerald Lathbury's 1st Parachute Brigade, which would make a dash for Arnhem and its highway, railroad and pontoon bridges. Leading the way would be a motorized reconnaissance squadron of jeeps and motorcycles. Urquhart was

° Colonel George S. Chatterton, commanding the Glider Pilot Regiment, recalls that he wanted a *coup de main*, "a force of five or six gliders to land near the bridge and take it. I saw no reason why we could not do it, but apparently nobody else saw the need for it, and I distinctly remember being called a bloody murderer and assassin for suggesting it."

counting on Major C. F. H. "Freddie" Gough's highly specialized force of some 275 men in four troops—the only unit of its kind in the British army—to reach the highway bridge and hold it until the main body of the brigade arrived.

The next day, D plus 1, Brigadier John "Shan" Hackett's 4th Parachute Brigade was due to arrive, together with the remainder of the Airlanding Brigade; and on the third day, Major General Stanislaw Sosabowski's Polish 1st Parachute Brigade was to be landed. Urquhart had marked in a sixth drop zone for the Poles. Because it was anticipated that, by D plus 2, the bridge would be captured and the flak batteries knocked out, the Poles were to drop on the southern bank of the Lower Rhine near the village of Elden about one mile south of the Arnhem crossing.

Despite the risks he must accept, Urquhart felt confident. He believed he had "a reasonable operation and a good plan." Casualties, he thought, might be "somewhere in the neighborhood of 30 percent"; considering the intricate nature of the attack, he did not think the cost was too high. In the early evening of September 12, he briefed his commanders on the operation and, Urquhart remembers, "everybody seemed quite content with the plan."

One commander, however, had grave misgivings. Major General Stanislaw Sosabowski, the trim, fifty-two-year-old leader of the Polish 1st Parachute Brigade, was quite sure that "we were in for a bitter struggle." The former Polish War Academy professor had already stated his position to Generals Urquhart and Browning when he first heard about Operation Comet. At that time he had demanded that Urquhart give him his orders in writing so that "I would not be held responsible for the disaster." With Urquhart he had visited Browning and told him "this mission cannot possibly succeed." Browning asked why. As Sosabowski remembered, "I told him it would be suicide to attempt it with the forces we had and Browning answered, 'But, my dear Sosabowski, the Red Devils and the gallant Poles can do anything!' "

Now, one week later, as he listened to Urquhart, Sosabowski thought, "the British are not only grossly underestimating German strength in the Arnhem area, but they seem ignorant of the significance Arnhem has for the Fatherland." Sosabowski believed that to the Germans Arnhem represented "the gateway to Germany, and I did not expect the Germans to leave it open." He did not believe that "troops in the area were of very low caliber, with only a few battered tanks sitting around." He was appalled when Urquhart told the assembled brigade commanders that the 1st Airborne was to be dropped "at least six miles from the objective." To reach the bridge the main body of troops would have "a five-hour march; so how could surprise be achieved? Any fool of a German would immediately know our plans."

There was another part of the plan Sosabowski did not like. Heavy equipment and ammunition for his brigade was to go in by glider on an earlier lift. Thus, his stores would be on a northern landing zone when his troops landed on the southern bank. What would happen if the bridge was not taken by the time the Poles landed? As Urquhart spelled out the plan, Sosabowski learned to his astonishment that, if the bridge was still in German hands by that time, his Polish troops would be expected to take it.

Despite Sosabowski's anxieties, at the September 12 briefing he remained silent. "I remember Urquhart asking for questions and nobody raised any," he recalled. "Everyone sat nonchalantly, legs crossed, looking bored. I wanted to say something about this impossible plan, but I just couldn't. I was unpopular as it was, and anyway who would have listened?"

Later, when the entire airborne operation was reviewed for all commanders at General Browning's headquarters, others had grave misgivings about the British part of the plan but they too remained silent. Brigadier General James M. Gavin, commander of the American 82nd Airborne, was so astonished when he heard of Urquhart's choice of landing sites that he said to his operations chief, Lieutenant Colonel John Norton, "My God, he can't mean it." Norton was equally appalled. "He does," he said grimly, "but I wouldn't care to try it." In Gavin's view, it was far better to take "10 percent initial casualties by dropping either on or close to the bridge than to run the risk of landing on distant drop zones." He was "surprised that General Browning did not question Urquhart's plan." Still, Gavin said nothing "for I assumed that the British, with their extensive combat experience, knew exactly what they were doing."

✲ 2 ✲

SS STURMBANNFÜHRER (MAJOR) SEPP KRAFFT did not intend to move again if he could avoid it. In the past few weeks his understrength SS Panzer Grenadier Training and Reserve Battalion had been ordered back and forth across Holland. Now, after only five days, the unit was being ordered out of the village of Oosterbeek—and not by a superior of Krafft's, but by a Wehrmacht major.

Krafft protested vehemently. The main body of his three companies of men was billeted in the village, with the rest in Arnhem, and another 1,000 SS recruits were due to arrive momentarily for training. The Wehrmacht major was adamant. "I don't care about that," he told Krafft bluntly, "you've got to get out." Krafft fought back. The ambitious thirty-seven-year-old officer took orders only from his SS superiors. "I refuse," he said. The Wehrmacht officer was not intimidated. "Let me make things clear to you," he said. "You're moving out of Oosterbeek because Model's headquarters is moving in."

Krafft quickly calmed down. He had no wish to run afoul of Field Marshal Walter Model. Still, the order rankled. Krafft moved, but not very far. He decided to bivouac his troops in the woods and farms northwest of Oosterbeek, not far from the village of Wolfheze. The spot he happened to choose was alongside the Wolfheze road, almost between the zones marked on maps in England for the men of the British 1st Airborne Division to land, and blocking the route into Arnhem itself.

✵ *3* ✵

H ENRI KNAP, Arnhem's underground intelligence chief, felt safe in his new role. To protect his wife and two daughters from complicity in his activities, he had left home four months earlier and moved a few blocks away. His headquarters were now in the offices of a general practitioner, Dr. Leo C. Breebaart. The white-coated Knap was now the doctor's "assistant," and certain "patients" were messengers and couriers belonging to his intelligence network: forty men and women and a few teen-agers.

Knap's was a time-consuming and frustrating job. He had to evaluate the information he received and then pass it along by phone. Arnhem's resistance chief, Pieter Kruyff, had given Knap three telephone numbers, each with twelve to fifteen digits, and told him to commit them to memory. Knap never knew where or to whom he was calling. His instructions were to dial each number in turn until contact was made.*

Gathering intelligence was even more complicated. Knap's requests were passed down through the network chain, and he never knew what agent procured the information. If a report seemed dubious, Knap investigated on his own. At the moment he

---

* Knap has never learned who his contacts were except that his reports were passed on to a top-secret unit known as the "Albrecht Group." He knew the calls he made were long distance. At the time, Dutch telephone numbers consisted of four digits. A brilliant telephone technician named Nicolaas Tjalling de Bode devised a method for underground members under which, by using certain telephone numbers, they could bypass local switchboards and automatically call all over Holland.

was intrigued and puzzled by several reports that had reached him about enemy activity in Oosterbeek.

A German officer wearing staff insignia, Major Horst Smöckel, had visited a number of stores in Renkum, Oosterbeek and Arnhem and ordered a variety of supplies to be delivered to Oosterbeek's Tafelberg Hotel. What Knap found curious were the requisitions; among them were hard-to-find foods and other specialty items which the Dutch population rarely saw anymore, such as *Genever* gin.

Additionally, German signalmen had been busy laying a welter of telephone cables to a number of hotels in the suburbs, including the Tafelberg. The conclusion, Knap felt, was obvious: a high-ranking headquarters was moving into Oosterbeek. But which one? Who was the general? And had he arrived?

It was even more important for Knap to keep abreast of the enemy strength in and around the Arnhem region. He knew there were other intelligence men sending back information in each town and that he was "only a small cog in a vast collection system." As a result, there was probably "much duplication of effort." Nevertheless, everything was important, for "what one cell might miss, we might pick up."

Two weeks before, as he later recalled, "there was almost no German strength in the Arnhem region." Since then, the military picture had changed dramatically. Now, Knap was alarmed at the German buildup. From his network sources, over the previous seven days, Knap had reported that "the remains of several divisions, including panzer units, were in the process of reorganizing in and around Arnhem or were moving into Germany." By now, more specific news had come. His sources reported the presence of tanks north and northeast of Arnhem. Knap believed that "parts of at least one or even two panzer divisions" were in the area, but their identity and exact location were, so far, not known.

Knap wanted details quickly. Urgently, he passed the word to his network. He demanded more exact information on the panzer activity and he wanted to know immediately the identity of the "new occupant" in the Tafelberg Hotel.

Twenty-five-year-old Wouter van de Kraats had never heard of Henri Knap. His contact in the underground was a man he knew only as "Jansen" who lived somewhere in Arnhem. Jansen had a new assignment for him—the Tafelberg Hotel. A high-ranking German officer had arrived, he was told, and Van de Kraats was to see if any of the staff cars outside "carried an identifying pennant or flag." If so, he was to report the colors and symbols on the standard.

Van de Kraats had noticed an influx of German activity around the hotel. German military police and sentries had moved into the area. His problem was how to get through the sentries along the road—the Pietersbergweg—running past the Tafelberg. He decided to bluff his way through.

As he made for the hotel, he was immediately stopped by a sentry. "But I must get through," Van de Kraats told the German. "I work at the petrol station up the street." The German let him pass. Three other sentries gave him only a cursory glance. Then, as Van de Kraats passed the Tafelberg, he quickly looked at the entrance and the driveway. None of the parked cars had any identifying markings, but near the front door of the hotel stood a checkerboard black, red and white metal pennant—the insignia of a German army group commander.

On the afternoon of Thursday, September 14, Henri Knap heard from his network. Several sources reported large formations of panzer troops, tanks and armored vehicles encamped in a semicircle to the north of Arnhem. There were units at Beekbergen, Epse and along the Ijssel River. There was even a startling report of "20 to 30 Tiger tanks." Exactly how many units were involved, he was unable to ascertain. He was able to clearly identify only one, and that by a fluke. One of his agents noted "strange markings—reverse *F*'s with a ball at the foot of them"—on some tanks. Checking through a special German manual, Knap was able to identify the unit. He immediately called his telephone contact and reported the presence of the 9th SS Panzer Division Hohenstaufen. From the agent's report, Knap located its position as lying approximately to the north between Arnhem and Apeldoorn and from there, eastward to Zutphen.

Shortly afterward he received word about the Tafelberg Hotel. He passed this report on, too. The significant black, red and white checkerboard pennant told its own story. There was only one German army group commander in this part of the western front. Although Knap reported the news as hearsay, it seemed to him the officer had to be Field Marshal Walter Model.

✧ 4 ✧

TWENTY-FIVE MILES EAST of Oosterbeek at his II SS Panzer Corps headquarters in a small castle on the outskirts of Doetinchem, General Wilhelm Bittrich held a meeting with his two remaining division commanders. Bittrich was in a bad mood, barely able to contain his temper. The outlook for his battered panzer corps was now far worse than it had been a week earlier. Impatiently Bittrich had awaited replacements in men, armor and equipment. None had arrived. On the contrary, his force had been whittled down even more. He had been ordered to send two combat groups to the front. One was with the German Seventh Army trying to hold the Americans near Aachen; the other was dispatched to bolster General Kurt Student's First Parachute Army after British tanks successfully breached the Albert Canal line, crossed the Meuse-Escaut Canal and grabbed a bridgehead at Neerpelt almost on the Dutch border. Now, at a time when the British were massing to renew their offensive—an attack that the intelligence chief at Army Group B called "imminent"—Bittrich had received through Field Marshal Model a "crazy directive from the fools in Berlin." One of his shattered divisions was to be cannibalized and pulled back into Germany.

A once-ardent Nazi, Bittrich denounced the order acridly. He "was sick and tired of Berlin's orders and the sycophants around Hitler who were indulging in all kinds of gimmickry." Courageous and able, Bittrich had spent most of his adult life in uniform. In World War I, he had served as a lieutenant in the German air force and had been twice wounded. Later, for a few years, he worked in a stockbroker's office. Then, rejoining the armed forces, Bittrich became a member of a secret German air-force team and for eight years taught flying to the Russians. When Hitler came to power, Bittrich joined the newly formed Luftwaffe but in the mid-thirties he switched to the Waffen SS, where promotion was faster.°

In Normandy, Bittrich's faith in Hitler's leadership began to waver. He sided with Field Marshal Rommel against Hitler's "insane fight-to-the-last-man" philosophy. Once he confided to Rommel that "we are being so badly led from above that I can no longer carry out senseless orders. I have never been a robot and don't intend to become one." After the July 20 plot, when he learned that his former commander Colonel General Eric Hoepner, as a conspirator, had been condemned to death by hanging, Bittrich raged to his staff that "this is the blackest day for the German army." Bittrich's outspoken criticism of Hitler's military leadership soon reached Berlin. As Bittrich later recalled, "my

° As a suspected war criminal, Bittrich spent eight years in prison after World War II; on June 22, 1953, he was found innocent and released. Waffen SS commanders are difficult to locate and interview, but Bittrich and his officers were extremely helpful to me in setting the record straight on many hitherto unknown events in the Arnhem battle. Bittrich wanted me to clarify one minor matter relating to his personal life. In various British accounts "I have been described as a musician who hoped to be a conductor," he told me. "But the authors have confused me with my brother, Dr. Gerhard Bittrich, an extremely talented pianist and conductor."

remarks were reported to the chief of the SS, Reichsführer Heinrich Himmler, and the name Bittrich was no longer mentioned around Hitler's headquarters." Only the near-collapse of the German front in the west, a situation demanding Bittrich's kind of expertise, and the attitude of sympathetic commanders had saved him from being recalled. Even so, Himmler was still "eager for me to return to Germany for a little talk." Bittrich had no illusions about Himmler's invitation. Nor had Model; he was determined to keep Bittrich in the west and flatly refused to entertain Himmler's repeated requests to send Bittrich home.

Now the outraged Bittrich outlined Berlin's latest plan to the commanders of his divisions—SS Brigadeführer (Brigadier General) Heinz Harmel of the 10th Frundsberg Division and SS Obersturmbannführer (Lieutenant Colonel) Walter Harzer of the 9th Hohenstaufen Division. Bittrich told Harzer—who had already learned something about the plan from Model's chief of staff, Lieutenant General Hans Krebs—that his 9th Hohenstaufen Division was to entrain immediately for Germany, where it would be located near Siegen, northeast of Koblenz. Harmel's 10th Division was to remain in Holland. It would be refitted and brought up to strength in its present location east and southeast of Arnhem, ready to be committed again.

The thirty-eight-year-old Harmel, whose bluff heartiness had earned him the affectionate nickname of *der alte Frundsberg* from his men, was not pleased with the decision. It seemed to him that "Bittrich was, as usual, showing preference for the Hohenstaufen Division, perhaps because it had been his own before he became corps commander and perhaps, too, because Harzer had been his chief of staff." Although he did not think "Bittrich was consciously unfair, it always seemed to work out that the Hohenstaufen got the cushy jobs."

His younger counterpart, thirty-two-year-old Walter Harzer, was elated at the news, even though he thought "the likelihood of getting Berlin leave seemed doubtful." Ideally, after refitting he expected to have a "brand-new Hohenstaufen Division." Privately, too, the tough Harzer, his face marked by a saber scar, had high hopes now of achieving his ambition: to be promoted to the rank befitting an SS division commander—brigadier general. Still, as Bittrich outlined the entire plan, one segment was not to Harzer's liking.

Although badly depleted, his division was still stronger than Harmel's. Instead of the usual 9,000 men, the Hohenstaufen had barely 6,000, the Frundsberg about 3,500. Harzer had close to twenty Mark V Panther tanks, but not all were serviceable. He did, however, have a considerable number of armored vehicles: self-propelled guns, armored cars and forty armored personnel carriers, all with heavy machine guns, some mounted with artillery pieces. Harmel's Frundsberg Division had almost no tanks and was desperately short of all kinds of armored vehicles. Both divisions still had formidable artillery, mortar and antiaircraft units. To build up the Frundsberg Division, which would remain behind, Bittrich said, Harzer was to transfer as much of his transportation and equipment as he could to Harmel. Harzer was skeptical. "In my heart," Harzer later recalled, "I knew damn well that if I gave over my few tanks or the armored personnel carriers to Harmel, they'd never be replaced." Harzer did not protest the decision, but he had no intention of giving up all his vehicles.

Harzer had long ago learned to husband his division's resources. He had more vehicles than even Bittrich realized—including American jeeps he had captured during the long retreat from France. He decided to ignore the order by "some paper maneuvering." By removing caterpillar tracks, wheels or guns from his vehicles, he could make them temporarily unserviceable until he reached Germany. In the meantime they would be listed on his armored strength returns as disabled.

Even with the extra men and vehicles from Harzer's cannibalized division, Bittrich continued, the Frundsberg would still be understrength. There was only one way to stress the urgency of the situation to Berlin: by presenting the facts directly to SS operational headquarters. Maybe then, replacements and reinforcements would be forthcoming. But Bittrich had no intention of visiting Berlin; Harmel was made the emissary, to his surprise.

"I don't know why he chose me rather than Harzer," Harmel remembers. "But we urgently needed men and armor, and perhaps Bittrich thought a general might carry more weight. The whole matter was to be kept secret from Field Marshal Model. So, as we were not expecting any trouble in the Arnhem area, it was decided that I would leave for Berlin on the evening of September 16."

The exchange of equipment between Harzer and Harmel and the move of the cannibalized Hohenstaufen Division to Germany, Bittrich ordered, was to begin immediately. While the operation was in process, he added, Field Marshal Model wanted small mobile attack groups to be readied as *Alarmeinheiten* ("alarm units") which could be committed in case of emergency. As a result, Harzer privately decided that his "best units would be entrained last." Bittrich expected the entire equipment transfer and move completed by September 22. Because six trains a day left for Germany, Harzer thought the task could be completed much earlier. He believed his last and best units could leave for the Fatherland in just three more days—probably on the afternoon of September 17.

A demoralizing rumor was making the rounds. By September 14, several senior German officers in Holland were saying that an airborne drop would take place.

The talk originated from a conversation between Hitler's operations chief, Colonel General Alfred Jodl, and the Commander in Chief, West, Field Marshal von Rundstedt. Jodl was concerned that the Allies might invade Holland from the sea. If Eisenhower followed his usual tactics, Jodl said, airborne troops would be dropped as a prelude to the seaborne attack. Von Rundstedt, though skeptical of the suggestion (he, by contrast, was convinced that paratroopers would be dropped in conjunction with an attack on the Ruhr), passed the information on to Army Group B's commander, Field Marshal Model. Model's view was the same as Von Rundstedt's. Nevertheless, he could not ignore Jodl's warning. He ordered the German armed forces commander in Holland, the jittery Luftwaffe general, Friedrich Christiansen, to dispatch units of his meager grab bag of army, navy, Luftwaffe and Dutch Waffen SS personnel to the coast.

Since Jodl's call on September 11, the scare had traveled down the various echelons of command, particularly through Luftwaffe channels. Although the invasion had so far failed to materialize, the fear of an airborne drop was still mounting. Everyone was speculating on possible sites. From their maps, some Luftwaffe commanders saw the large open areas between the north coast and Arnhem as possible landing zones. Others, nervously awaiting the renewal of the British offensive into Holland from the bridgehead over the Meuse-Escaut Canal at Neerpelt, wondered if paratroopers might be used in conjunction with that attack and dropped into the area of Nijmegen.

On September 13, Luftwaffe Colonel General Otto Dessloch, commander of the 3rd Air Fleet, heard about Berlin's fears at Von Rundstedt's headquarters in Koblenz. Dessloch was so concerned that he telephoned Field Marshal Model the following day. Model, he recalls, thought Berlin's invasion scare was "nonsense." The Field Marshal was so unconcerned "that he invited me to dinner at his new headquarters in the Tafelberg Hotel in Oosterbeek." Dessloch refused. "I have no intention of being made a prisoner," he told Model. Just before he hung up, Dessloch added: "If I were you, I would get out of that area." Model, Dessloch remembers, merely laughed.

At Deelen airfield north of Arnhem word of a possible airborne attack reached Luftwaffe fighter commander Major General Walter Grabmann. He drove to Oosterbeek for a conference with Model's chief of staff, Lieutenant General Hans Krebs. When Grabmann expressed the Luftwaffe's fears, Krebs said, "For God's sake, don't talk about such things. Anyway, where would they land?" Grabmann went to a map and, pointing to areas west of Arnhem, said, "Anywhere here. The heath is perfect for paratroopers." Krebs, Grabmann later recalled, "laughed and warned me that if I continued to talk this way, I'd make myself look ridiculous."

Holland's notorious police chief, SS Lieutenant General Hanns Albin Rauter, heard the rumor too, possibly from his superior General Christiansen. Rauter was convinced that anything was possible, including an airborne attack. Rauter, chief architect of Nazi terror in the Netherlands, expected the Dutch underground to attack and the population to rise at any moment. He was determined to stamp out any kind of insurrection by the simple expedient of executing three Dutch nationals for each Nazi killed. Rauter had declared an "emergency" immediately after the German retreat and the stampede of Dutch Nazis to Germany two weeks before. His police had taken bitter revenge against anyone even remotely involved with the Dutch resistance. Men and women were arrested, shot or sent off into concentration camps. Ordinary citizens fared little better. All travel between provinces was forbidden. More restrictive rules were imposed. Anyone found on the streets during curfew risked being fired on without warning. All over southern Holland, in anticipation of the British offensive, the Dutch were pressed into service as laborers digging trenches for the Wehrmacht. In Nijmegen, Rauter filled his workforce quota by threatening to throw entire families into concentration camps. Gatherings of any kind were forbidden. "Where more than five persons are seen together," one of Rauter's posters warned, "they will be fired on by the Wehrmacht, SS or police troops."

Now, with the British attack from the south imminent and Berlin's warning of a possible air and sea attack in the north, Rauter's world was beginning to come apart. He was terrified.°

° In the safety of his prison cell after the war, Rauter admitted to Dutch interrogators that "at the time I was very nervous. . . . I had to paralyze the resistance." Rauter was found guilty by a Dutch court on January 12, 1949, of a wide range of offenses, including "persecution of the Jews, deportation of inhabitants for slave labor, pillage, confiscation of property, illegal arrests, detentions . . . and the kill-

Learning that Model was in Holland, Rauter decided to seek reassurance and set out for the Tafelberg Hotel. On the evening of September 14, Rauter met with Model and his chief of staff, General Krebs. He was "convinced," Rauter told them, "that the Allies would now use airborne forces in southern Holland." He felt that it was the right psychological moment. Model and Krebs disagreed. Elite airborne formations, Model said, were too "precious, their training too costly" for indiscriminate use. The Field Marshal did indeed expect Montgomery to attack into Holland from Neerpelt, but the situation was not critical enough to justify the use of airborne troops. Also, since assault forces would be separated by three broad rivers to the south, he did not think that a British attack toward Arnhem was possible. Both Nijmegen and Arnhem were too far from the British forces. Besides, Model continued, Montgomery was "tactically a very cautious man. He would never use airborne forces in a reckless adventure."

By the time the prisoner reached Major Friedrich Kieswetter's headquarters in the village of Driebergen, west of Oosterbeek, on September 15, the deputy chief of Wehrmacht counterintelligence in Holland knew a great deal about him. There was an ample file on slow-witted, twenty-eight-year-old Christiaan Antonius Lindemans, better known, because of his huge size (6'3", 260 lbs.), as "King Kong." Lindemans had been captured by a patrol near the Dutch-Belgian border, in the no man's land between the British and German lines. At first, because of his British battle dress, Lindemans was taken for a soldier but, at the battalion command post near Valkenswaard, to the amazement of his interrogators, he demanded to see Lieutenant Colonel Hermann Giskes—German spy chief in Holland and Kieswetter's superior. After a series of phone calls, Lindemans' captors were

---

ings of innocent civilians as reprisals for offenses . . . against the occupying authorities." He was executed on March 25, 1949.

even more astonished to receive orders to drive the prisoner immediately to Driebergen. Lindemans alone displayed no surprise. Some of his compatriots thought him to be a stanch member of the Dutch underground; but the Germans knew him in another capacity—as a spy. King Kong was a double agent.

Lindemans had turned traitor in 1943. At that time he offered to work for Giskes in return for the release of his current mistress and younger brother, Henk, arrested by the Gestapo as a member of the underground and said to be awaiting execution. Giskes had readily agreed; and ever since, Lindemans had served the Germans well. His perfidy had resulted in the penetration of many underground cells and the arrest and execution of numerous Dutch and Belgian patriots. Although he was crude and boastful, given to wild, drunken excesses and possessed of an insatiable appetite for women, Lindemans had so far miraculously escaped exposure. However, many resistance leaders considered him a dangerous risk, unlike certain Allied officers in Brussels who were so impressed by King Kong that Lindemans now worked for a British intelligence unit under the command of a Canadian captain.

In Giskes' absence, Kieswetter dealt with Lindemans for the first time. He found the towering braggart, who introduced himself to everyone in the office as the "great King Kong," disgusting. Lindemans told the major of his latest mission. The Canadian intelligence officer had sent him to warn underground leaders in Eindhoven that downed Allied pilots were no longer to be sent through the "escape line" into Belgium. Because the British were due to break out from the Neerpelt bridgehead toward Eindhoven, the pilots were to be kept hidden. Lindemans, who had spent five days coming through the lines, was able to give Kieswetter some details on the British buildup. The attack, he said flatly, would take place on September 17.

The imminence of the British move was hardly news. Kieswetter, like everyone else, had been expecting it momentarily. Lindemans also informed Kieswetter of another development: coincidental with the British attack, he reported, a paratroop

drop was planned beyond Eindhoven to help capture the town.°
The revelation made no sense to Kieswetter. Why use paratroopers when the British army could easily reach Eindhoven by
itself? Perhaps because Lindemans' information seemed unrealistic or more likely because of his antipathy toward King Kong,
Kieswetter told Lindemans to continue on with his mission and
then return to the British lines. Kieswetter took no immediate
action. He thought so little of Lindemans' information that he did
not pass it on directly to Wehrmacht headquarters. He sent it,
instead, through the Sicherheitsdienst (SS security and intelligence service). He also dictated a brief memorandum of his
conversation with Lindemans for Giskes, at the moment away on
another assignment. Giskes, who had always considered King
Kong reliable, would not receive it until the afternoon of September 17.

° After the war, some British newspapers charged that it was because Lindemans
pinpointed Arnhem as the main airborne objective that the panzer divisions were
waiting. Obviously this is not so. Bittrich's corps reached its positions before Eisenhower and Montgomery met on September 10 and decided on Market-Garden.
Neither could Lindemans have known anything about the Arnhem attack or the
massive dimensions of the operation. Again, Allied decisions on dates, placement of
drop zones, etc. were made long after Lindemans left Brussels to cross the German
lines. A second often-repeated story is that Lindemans was taken to Colonel
General Kurt Student's headquarters at Vught for questioning, and it has been
suggested that the airborne expert correctly evaluated the report and gave the
alert. Student flatly denies this allegation. "It is a large fat lie," he told me. "I
never met Lindemans. Indeed, I first heard of the whole affair in a prison camp
after the war." Student adds, "The truth is, nobody in the German command knew
anything about the attack until it happened." Shortly after Market-Garden, sus-
picion fell on Lindemans and he was arrested by the Dutch. King Kong, the great
Lothario, lived up to his reputation to the very end. In July, 1946, forty-eight
hours before his trial, Lindemans, in a prison hospital, was found unconscious with
a prison nurse nearby. Both of them, in a bizarre "love pact," had taken over-
doses of sleeping pills. Lindemans died, the girl survived.

✵ 5 ✵

OPERATION MARKET-GARDEN was now less than forty-eight hours away. In his office Lieutenant General Walter Bedell Smith, Eisenhower's chief of staff, listened to SHAEF's intelligence chief, British Major General Kenneth W. Strong, disclose his latest news with growing alarm. Beyond doubt, Strong said, there was German armor in the Market-Garden area.

For days, Strong and his staff had been sifting and assessing every intelligence report in an effort to determine the whereabouts of the 9th and 10th SS Panzer divisions. Since the first week in September there had been no contact with the units. Both were badly cut up, but it was considered unlikely that they had been completely destroyed. One theory held that the units might have been ordered back into Germany. Now Dutch underground messages told a different story. The lost divisions had been spotted.

The 9th and, presumably, the 10th SS Panzer divisions were in Holland, Strong reported to Smith, "in all probability to be refitted with tanks." Exactly what remained of the units or their fighting capability no one could say, but there was no longer any doubt about their location, Strong reported. They were definitely in the vicinity of Arnhem.

Deeply concerned about Market-Garden and, in his own words, "alarmed over the possibility of failure," Smith immediately conferred with the Supreme Commander. The British 1st Airborne Division, due to land at Arnhem, "could not hold out against two armored divisions," Smith told Eisenhower. To be sure, there was a question—a big question—about the strength of the units, but to be on the safe side Smith thought that Market-Garden should be reinforced. He believed two airborne divisions would be required in the Arnhem area. (Presumably, Smith had in mind as the additional unit the veteran British 6th Airborne Division, commanded by Major General Richard Gale, which had been used successfully during the Normandy invasion, but was not included in Market-Garden.) Otherwise, Smith told Eisenhower, the plan must be revised. "My feeling," he later said, "was that if we could not drop the equivalent of another division in the area, then we should shift one of the American airborne divisions, which were to form the 'carpet' further north, to reinforce the British."

Eisenhower considered the problem and its risks. On the basis of this intelligence report and almost on the eve of the attack, he was being urged to override Monty's plan—one that Eisenhower himself had approved. It meant challenging Montgomery's generalship and upsetting an already delicate command situation. As Supreme Commander, he had another option open: Market-Garden could be canceled; but the only grounds for such a decision would be this single piece of intelligence. Eisenhower had obviously to assume that Montgomery was the best judge of enemy strength before him and that he would plan accordingly. As Eisenhower explained to Smith, "I cannot tell Monty how to dispose of his troops," nor could he "call off the operation, since I have already given Monty the green light." If changes were to be made, Montgomery would have to make them. Still, Eisenhower was prepared to let Smith "fly to 21st Army Group headquarters and argue it out with Montgomery."

Bedell Smith set out immediately for Brussels. He found Montgomery confident and enthusiastic. Smith explained his fears about the panzer units in the Arnhem area and strongly suggested that the plan might need revision. Montgomery "ridiculed the idea. Monty felt the greatest opposition would come more from terrain difficulties than from the Germans. All would go well, he kept repeating, if we at SHAEF would help him surmount his logistical difficulties. He was not worried about the German armor. He thought Market-Garden would go all right as set." The conference was fruitless. "At least I tried to stop him," Smith said, "but I got nowhere. Montgomery simply waved my objections airily aside."*

Even as Montgomery and Smith conferred, across the Channel startling evidence reached British I Airborne Corps headquarters. Earlier in the day, fighters of the R.A.F.'s specially equipped photo-reconnaissance squadron returning from The Hague had made a low-level sweep over the Arnhem area. Now, in his office, intelligence officer Major Brian Urquhart took up a magnifying glass and examined five oblique-angle pictures—an "end of the run" strip from one of the fighters. Hundreds of aerial photographs of the Market-Garden area had been taken and evaluated in the previous seventy-two hours, but only these five shots showed what Urquhart had long feared—the unmistakable presence of German armor. "It was the straw that broke the camel's back," Urquhart later recalled. "There, in the photos, I could clearly see tanks—if not on the very Arnhem landing and drop zones, then certainly close to them."

Major Urquhart rushed to General Browning's office with the photographic confirmation. Browning saw him immediately. Placing the pictures on the desk before Browning, Urquhart said, "Take a look at these." The General studied them one by one. Although Urquhart no longer remembers the exact wording, to the best of his recollection, Browning said, "I wouldn't trouble myself about these if I were you." Then, referring to the tanks in the photos, he continued, "They're probably not serviceable at any rate." Urquhart was stunned. Helplessly he pointed out that the armor, "whether serviceable or not, were still tanks and they

* I have based this entire section on information supplied to me by General S. L. A. Marshall, Chief Historian for the European Theatre of Operations during World War II, who kindly allowed me to see his various monographs on Market-Garden and also his 1945 interview with General Bedell Smith on the meeting with Eisenhower and later Montgomery.

had guns." Looking back, Urquhart feels that "perhaps because of information I knew nothing about, General Browning was not prepared to accept my evaluation of the photos. My feeling remained the same—that everyone was so *gung-ho* to go that nothing could stop them."

Urquhart was unaware that some members of Browning's staff considered the young intelligence officer almost too zealous. The show was about to begin, and most officers were anxious and eager to get on with it. Urquhart's pessimistic warnings irritated them. As one senior staff officer put it, "His views were colored by nervous exhaustion. He was inclined to be a bit hysterical, no doubt brought on by overwork."

Shortly after his meeting with Browning, Urquhart was visited by the corps medical officer. "I was told," Urquhart recalls, "that I was exhausted—who wasn't?—and that perhaps I should take a rest and go on leave. I was out. I had become such a pain around headquarters that on the very eve of the attack I was being removed from the scene. I was told to go home. There was nothing I could say. Although I disagreed with the plan and feared the worst, still, this was going to be the big show and, curiously, I did not want to be left behind."

❈ 6 ❈

By noon on Saturday, September 16, the German proclamation was plastered on bulletin boards all over Arnhem.

By order of the Security Police, the following is announced:
During the night an attack with explosives was made on the railroad viaduct at Schaapsdrift.

The population is called upon to cooperate in tracing the culprits of this attack.

If they have not been found before 12 o'clock noon on Sunday, September 17, 1944, a number of hostages will be shot.

I appeal to the cooperation of all of you in order that needless victims be spared.

The acting Burgomaster,

LIERA

In a cellar, leading members of the Arnhem underground met in an emergency meeting. The sabotage of the railroad viaduct had been badly botched. Henri Knap, the Arnhem intelligence chief, had not been happy about the mission from its inception. He felt that, "at best, we are all rank amateurs when it comes to sabotage." In his view, "it is far better to concentrate on feeding intelligence to the Allies and to leave demolition jobs to men who know what they are doing." The chief of the Arnhem underground, thirty-eight-year-old Pieter Kruyff, asked for the others' opinions. Nicolaas Tjalling de Bode voted that the members give themselves up. Knap remembers thinking "this was a very steep price to pay—the lives of the hostages, innocent people—for a small hole in a bridge." Gijsbert Jan Numan was conscience-stricken. He had been involved along with Harry Montfroy, Albert Deuss, Toon van Daalen and others in procuring the materials for the explosives and in planning the sabotage, and no one wanted innocent men to suffer. Yet what was to be done? Kruyff heard everyone out, then he made his decision. "The organization must stay intact even though innocent people may be shot," he decreed. Looking around at the assembled leaders, as Nicolaas de Bode remembers, Kruyff told them, "No one will give himself up to the Germans. That's my order." Henri Knap had a feeling of dread. He knew that if the Germans followed their usual procedure, ten or twelve leading citizens—doctors, lawyers and teachers among them—would be publicly executed in an Arnhem square at noon on Sunday.

☆ 7 ☆

ALL DOWN THE ALLIED LINE of command the evaluation of intelligence on the panzers in the Arnhem area was magnificently bungled. SHAEF's Intelligence Summary No. 26 issued on September 16, the eve of Market-Garden—containing the ominous warning that had caused General Bedell Smith's alarm—was disregarded. In part, it read, "9th SS Panzer Division, and presumably the 10th, has been reported withdrawing to the Arnhem area in Holland; there, they will probably collect new tanks from a depot reported in the area of Cleves."

The information, already discredited by Montgomery at his meeting with Smith, was now discounted by General Dempsey's British Second Army headquarters—the same headquarters that had originally noted the presence in Holland of "battered panzer formations" on September 10. In the most serious blunder of all, Dempsey's intelligence staff, on September 14, described the Germans in the Market-Garden area as "weak, demoralized and likely to collapse entirely if confronted with a large airborne attack." Now, in a complete reversal of their original position, they dismissed the presence of the panzers, *because Dempsey's staff officers were unable to spot enemy armor on any reconnaissance photos.*

At First Allied Airborne Army headquarters, General Brereton's chief intelligence officer, British Lieutenant Colonel Anthony Tasker, was not prepared to accept SHAEF's report either. Reviewing all the information available, he decided there was no direct evidence that the Arnhem area contained "much more than the considerable flak defenses already known to exist."

Everyone, it seemed, accepted the optimistic outlook of Mont-gomery's headquarters. As the British I Airborne Corps's chief of staff, Brigadier Gordon Walch, remembers, "21st Army Group headquarters was the principal source of our intelligence, and we took what they gave us to be true." General Urquhart, com-mander of the British 1st Airborne Division, put it another way. "Nothing," he said, "was allowed to mar the optimism prevailing across the Channel."

Yet, besides SHAEF's report on the "missing" panzers, there was other evidence of German buildup, again almost cursorily noted. At the front, ahead of General Horrocks' XXX Corps Garden forces, it was plain that an increasing number of German units were moving into the line. Now the strategic error at Antwerp ten days before was beginning to build and threaten the grand design of Operation Market-Garden. The German troops filling out General Student's front were none other than units of the splintered divisions that had escaped across the mouth of the Schelde—the battered men of Von Zangen's Fifteenth Army, the army the Allies had practically written off. Intelligence officers did note that, though the Germans had increased in number, the new units in the line were "believed to be in no fit state to resist any determined advance." Any British Tommy along the Belgium-Dutch frontier could have told them otherwise. °

The cobblestone streets of the dingy mining town of Leopolds-burg in northern Belgium, barely ten miles from the front, were

° British Major General Hubert Essame (retired) in his excellent book *The Battle for Germany* (p. 13), writes: "In misappreciation of the actual situation at the end of August and the first half of September, Allied intelligence staffs sank to a level only reached by Brigadier John Charteris, Haig's Chief Intelligence Officer at the time of the Passchendaele Battles in 1917." At that time the wartime Prime Minister David Lloyd George alleged that Charteris "selected only those figures and facts which suited his fancy and then issued hopeful reports accordingly." At various times during the 1917 Flanders campaign Charteris reported the enemy as "cracking," "mangled," "with few reserves," and even "on the run." In the dread-ful battles that ensued around Passchendaele between July 31 and November 12, casualties, according to the official British history, totaled a staggering 244,897.

choked with jeeps and scout cars. All roads seemed to lead to a cinema opposite the railway station—and never before had the nondescript theater held such an audience. Officers of Lieutenant General Horrocks' XXX Corps—the Garden forces that would drive north through Holland to link up with the paratroopers—crowded the street and milled around the entrance as their credentials were inspected by red-capped military police. It was a colorful, exuberant group and it reminded Brigadier Hubert Essame, commanding officer of the 214th Brigade, 43rd Wessex Infantry Division, of "an army assembly at a point-to-point race or a demonstration on Salisbury Plain in time of peace." He was fascinated by the colorful dress of the commanders. There was a striking variety of headgear. No one had a steel helmet, but berets of many colors bore the proud badges of famous regiments, among them the Irish, Grenadier, Coldstream, Scotch, Welsh and Royal Horse Guards, the Royal Army Service Corps and Royal Artillery. There was a regal casualness about everyone's attire. Essame noted that most commanders were dressed in "sniper's smocks, parachutists' jackets and jeep coats over brightly colored slacks, corduroys, riding britches or even jodhpurs." Instead of ties many sported ascots or "scarves of various colors."*

The renowned Lieutenant Colonel J.O.E. ("Joe") Vandeleur, the solidly built, ruddy-faced, six-foot commander of the Irish Guards Armored Group, personified the kind of devil-may-care elegance of the Guards' officers. The forty-one-year-old Vandeleur was wearing his usual combat garb: black beret, a multi-colored camouflaged parachutist's jacket, and corduroy trousers above high rubber boots. Additionally, Vandeleur wore, as always, a .45 Colt automatic strapped to his hip and, tucked into his jacket, what had become a symbol for his tankers, a flamboyant emerald-green scarf. The fastidious General "Boy" Browning, back in England, would have winced. Even Horrocks had

---

* In his history of *The 43rd Wessex Division at War* (p. 115), Essame writes: "Sartorial disciplinarians of the future" might remember "that when the morale of the British Army was as high as at any time in its history, officers wore the clothing they found most suitable to the conditions under which they had to live and fight."

once dryly admonished Vandeleur. "If the Germans ever get you, Joe," he said, "they'll think they've captured a peasant." But on this September 16 even Horrocks lacked the usual elegance of the impeccably dressed British staff officer. Instead of a shirt he wore a ribbed polo sweater and, over his battle dress, a sleeveless leather jerkin reminiscent of a British yeoman's dress.

As the popular Horrocks made his way down the aisle of the crowded theater he was greeted on all sides. The meeting he had called had sparked high excitement. Men were eager to get going again. From the Seine to Antwerp, Horrocks' tanks had often averaged fifty miles in a single day, but ever since the disastrous three-day halt on September 4 to "refit, refuel and rest," the going had been rough. With the British momentum gone, the enemy had quickly recovered. In the two vital weeks since, the British advance had been reduced to a crawl. It had taken four days for the Guards Armored Division—led by Joe Vandeleur's Irish Guards Group—to advance ten miles and capture the vital bridge over the Meuse-Escaut Canal near Neerpelt, from which the attack into Holland would begin the next day. Horrocks had no illusions about the German opposition, but he was confident that his forces could break through the enemy crust.

At precisely 11 A.M. Horrocks stepped onto the stage. All those assembled knew that the British offensive was about to be renewed, but so great was the security surrounding Montgomery's plan that only a few general officers present knew the details. With D Day for Operation Market-Garden barely twenty-four hours away, the Field Marshal's commanders now learned of the attack for the first time.

Attached to the cinema screen was a huge map of Holland. Colored tape snaked north along a single highway, crossing the great river obstacles and passing through the towns of Valkenswaard, Eindhoven, Veghel, Uden, Nijmegen and thence to Arnhem, a distance of some sixty-four miles. From there the tape continued for another thirty-odd miles to the Zuider Zee. Horrocks took a long pointer and began the briefing. "This is a tale you will tell your grandchildren," he told his audience. Then he paused and, much to the delight of the assembled officers, added: "And mightily bored they'll be."

In the audience, Lieutenant Colonel Curtis D. Renfro, liaison officer from the 101st Airborne Division and one of the few Americans present, was impressed by the Corps commander's enthusiasm and confidence. He talked for an hour, Curtis recorded, "with only an occasional reference to notes."

Step by step Horrocks explained the complexities of Market-Garden. The airborne army would go in first, he said. Its objectives: to capture the bridges in front of XXX Corps. Horrocks would give the word for the attack to begin. Depending on the weather, zero hour for the ground forces was expected to be 2 P.M. At that moment 350 guns would open fire and lay down a massive artillery barrage that would last thirty-five minutes. Then, at 2:35 P.M., led by waves of rocket-firing Typhoons, XXX Corps tanks would break out of their bridgehead and "blast down the main road." The Guards Armored Division would have the honor of leading the attack. They would be followed by the 43rd Wessex and 50th Northumberland divisions, and then by the 8th Armored Brigade and the Dutch Princess Irene Brigade.

There was to be "no pause, no stop," Horrocks emphasized. The Guards Armored was "to keep going like hell" all the way to Arnhem. The breakout from the bridgehead, Horrocks believed, would be "almost immediate." He expected the first Guards tanks to be in Eindhoven within two or three hours. If the enemy reacted fast enough to blow all the bridges before the airborne troops could secure them, then the 43rd Wessex Infantry Division engineers, coming up behind, would rush forward with men and bridging equipment. This massive engineering operation, should it be required, Horrocks explained, could involve 9,000 engineers and some 2,277 vehicles already in the Leopoldsburg area. The entire XXX Corps armored column was to be fed up the main road with the vehicles two abreast, thirty-five vehicles per mile. Traffic would be one way, and Horrocks expected "to pass 20,000 vehicles over the highway to Arnhem in sixty hours."

General Allan Adair, the forty-six-year-old commander of the famed Guards Armored Division, listening to Horrocks, thought Market-Garden was a bold plan, but he also believed "it might be tricky." He expected the worst moment to be the breakout from the Meuse-Escaut Canal bridgehead. Once through that, although he fully expected German resistance, he thought the going would "not be difficult." Besides, he had every faith in the unit that would lead off the attack—Lieutenant Colonel Joe Vandeleur's Irish Guards Group.

Joe Vandeleur, as he learned that his tanks would spearhead the breakout, remembers thinking to himself, "Oh, Christ! Not us again." Vandeleur was proud that his veteran unit had been chosen, yet he knew his troops were tired and his units understrength. Since the breakout from Normandy he had received very few replacements in either men or tanks; furthermore, "they weren't allowing a hell of a lot of time for planning." But then he thought, how much time do you really need to plan for a straight bash through the German lines? Next to him, his cousin, thirty-three-year-old Lieutenant Colonel Giles Vandeleur, who commanded the 2nd Battalion under Joe, was "struck with horror at the plan to blast through the German resistance on a one-tank front." To him, it was not proper armored warfare. But he recalls "swallowing whatever misgivings I had and succumbing to a strange, tense excitement, like being at the pole at the start of a horse race."

To three men in the theater, the announcement produced deep personal feelings. The senior officers of the Dutch Princess Irene Brigade had led their men in battle all the way from Normandy. First they had fought alongside the Canadians; then, after the fall of Brussels, they were transferred to the British Second Army. Now they would be coming home. Much as they looked forward to the liberation of Holland, the commander, Colonel Albert "Steve" de Ruyter van Steveninck; his second in command, Lieutenant Colonel Charles Pahud de Mortanges; and the chief of staff, Major Jonkheer Jan Beelaerts van Blokland, had grave misgivings about the manner in which it was to be accomplished.

Steveninck considered the entire plan risky. Mortanges' impression was that the British were more offhand about what lay ahead than the facts justified. As he put it, "It was made to seem quite elementary. First, we'll take this bridge; then that one and hop this river. . . . The terrain ahead with its rivers, marshes, dikes and lowlands, was extremely difficult—as the British well knew from our many presentations." The thirty-three-year-old chief of staff, Beelaerts van Blokland, could not help thinking of past military history. "We seemed to be violating Napoleon's maxim about never fighting unless you are at least 75 percent sure of success. Then, the other 25 percent can be left to chance. The British were reversing the process; we were leaving 75 percent to chance. We had only forty-eight hours to get to Arnhem, and if the slightest thing went wrong—a bridge blown, stiffer German resistance than anticipated—we'd be off schedule." Blokland had a private worry, too. His parents lived in the village of Oosterbeek, just two and a half miles from the Arnhem bridge.

One of the few officers below the rank of brigade major who heard the briefing was twenty-one-year-old Lieutenant John Gorman of the Irish Guards. He was stimulated by the whole affair and thought Horrocks was "at his finest." The Corps commander, Gorman later recalled, "called into play all his wit and humor, interspersing the more dramatic or technical points with humorous little asides. He really was quite a showman." Gorman was particularly pleased with Operation Garden because "the Guards were to lead out and obviously their role would be tremendously dramatic."

When the meeting had ended and commanders headed out to brief their troops, young Gorman felt his first "private doubts about the chances of success." Lingering in front of a map, he remembers thinking that Market-Garden was "a feasible operation—but only just feasible." There were simply "too many bridges." Nor was he enthusiastic about the terrain itself. He thought it was poor tank country and advancing on "a one-tank front, we would be very vulnerable." But the promise of support from rocket-firing Typhoons was reassuring. So was another promise of sorts. Gorman remembered the day, months before, when he had received the Military Cross for bravery from Montgomery himself.[*] At the investiture, Monty had said, "If I were a betting man I should say it would be an even bet that the war will be over by Christmas." And Horrocks, Gorman recalls, had "told us that this attack could end the war." The only alternative Gorman could find to "going north seemed to be a long dreary winter camped on or near the Escaut Canal." Monty's plan, he believed, "had just the right amount of dash and daring to work. If there was a chance to win the war by Christmas, then I was for pushing on."

Now, in the flat, gray Belgian countryside with its coal fields and slag heaps which reminded so many of Wales, the men who would lead the way for General Dempsey's British Second Army heard of the plan and the promise of Arnhem. Along side roads, in bivouac areas and in encampments, soldiers gathered around their officers to learn the part they would play in Operation Market-Garden. When Lieutenant Colonel Giles Vandeleur told his officers that the Irish would be leading out, twenty-nine-year-old Major Edward G. Tyler remembers that a "half moan" went up from the assembled officers. "We figured," he recalls, "that we deserved a bit of a break after taking the bridge over the Escaut Canal, which we named 'Joe's bridge' after Joe Vandeleur. But our commanding officer told us that it was a great honor for us to be chosen." Despite his desire for a reprieve, Tyler thought so too. "We were used to one-tank fronts," he remembers, "and in this case we were trusting to speed and support. No one seemed worried."

But Lieutenant Barry Quinan, who had just turned twenty-one, was "filled with trepidation." He was going into action for the first time with the lead Guards Armored tank squadron under Captain Mick O'Cock. Quinan's infantry would travel on the backs of the tanks, Russian-style. To him, "the number of rivers ahead seemed

[*] Gorman won his Military Cross during the fighting at Caen, Normandy. Leading a trio of Sherman tanks, he was suddenly confronted by four German tanks, one a 60-ton Tiger. His men dispatched the German armor and Gorman rammed the huge Tiger tank, destroyed its gun and killed its crew as they tried to escape.

ominous. We were not amphibious." Yet Quinan felt proud that his men would be "leading the entire British Second Army."

Lieutenant Rupert Mahaffey, also twenty-one, vividly remembers being told that "if the operation was a success the wives and children at home would be relieved from the threat of the Germans' V-2 rockets." Mahaffey's mother lived in London, which by that time was under intense bombardment. Although he was excited at the prospect of the attack, the single road leading all the way up to Arnhem was, he thought, "an awfully long way to go."

Captain Roland S. Langton, twenty-three, just returned from five days in a field hospital after receiving shrapnel wounds, learned that he was no longer adjutant of the 2nd Irish Guards Battalion. Instead, he was assigned as second in command of Captain Mick O'Cock's breakout squadron. He was jubilant about the assignment. The breakout seemed to Langton a straightforward thing. Garden could not be anything but a success. It was "obvious to all that the Germans were disorganized and shaken, lacking cohesion, and capable only of fighting in small pockets."

Not everyone was so confident. As Lieutenant A. G. C. "Tony" Jones, twenty-one, of the Royal Engineers, listened to the plan, he thought it was "clearly going to be very difficult." The bridges were the key to the entire operation and, as one officer remarked, "The drive of the XXX Corps will be like threading seven needles with one piece of cotton and we only have to miss one to be in trouble." To veteran Guardsman Tim Smith, twenty-four, the attack was "just another battle." On this day his greatest concern was the famed St. Leger race at Newmarket. He had a tip that a horse called Tehran, to be ridden by the famous jockey Gordon Richards, was "a sure thing." He placed every penny he had on Tehran with a lance corporal at battalion headquarters. If Market-Garden was the operation that would win the war, this was just the day to win the St. Leger. To his amazement, Tehran won. He was quite sure now that Market-Garden would succeed.

One man was "decidedly uncomfortable." Flight Lieutenant Donald Love, twenty-eight, an R.A.F. fighter-reconnaissance pilot, felt completely out of place among the officers of the Guards Armored. He was part of the air liaison team which would call in the rocket-firing Typhoon fighters from the ground when the breakout began. His lightly armored vehicle (code-named "Winecup"), with its canvas roof and its maze of communications equipment, would be up front close to Lieutenant Colonel Joe Vandeleur's command car. Love felt naked and defenseless: the only weapons the R.A.F. team possessed were revolvers. As he listened to Vandeleur talking about "a rolling barrage that would move forward at a speed of 200 yards per minute" and heard the burly Irishman describe Love's little scout car as an "armored signal tender for direct communication with pilots in the sky," Love's concern mounted. "I got the distinct impression that I would be the one responsible for calling in the 'cab rank' of Typhoons overhead." The thought was not reassuring. Love knew very little about the radio setup, and he had never before acted as a ground-to-air tactical officer. Then, to his acute relief, he learned that an expert, Squadron Leader Max Sutherland, would join him the following day to handle the communications for the initial breakout. Thereafter, Love would be in charge. Love began to wonder whether he should have volunteered in the first place. He had only taken the job "because I thought it might be a nice change of pace."

A change of a different sort bothered the commander of the Irish Guards. During the capture of the bridgehead over the Escaut Canal, Joe Vandeleur had lost "a close and distinguished friend." His broadcasting van, with its huge trumpetlike loudspeaker on the roof, had been destroyed by a German shell. All through training back in England and in the great advance from Normandy, Joe had used the van to broadcast to his troops and after each session, being a lover of classical music, he had always put on a record or two—selections that didn't always please the Guardsmen. The van had been blown to pieces and shards of the classical records—along with Vandeleur's favorite popular tune—had showered down over the countryside. Joe was saddened by his loss; not so, his Irish Guardsmen. They thought the drive to

Arnhem would be arduous enough without having to listen to Joe's loudspeaker blaring out his current theme song, "Praise the Lord and Pass the Ammunition."

Meanwhile, in England the paratroopers and glider-borne infantry of the First Allied Airborne Army were even now in marshaling areas, ready for the moment of takeoff. Over the previous forty-eight hours, using maps, photographs and scale models, officers had briefed and rebriefed their men. The preparations were immense and meticulous. At twenty-four air bases (8 British, 16 American), vast fleets of troop-carrying aircraft, tow planes and gliders were checked out, fueled and loaded with equipment ranging from artillery to jeeps. Some ninety miles north of London, Brigadier General James M. Gavin's "All-American" 82nd Airborne Division was already shut off from the outside world at a cluster of airfields around Grantham in Lincolnshire. So were part of General Roy Urquhart's Red Devils, the British 1st Airborne Division, and Major General Stanislaw Sosabowski's Polish 1st Parachute Brigade. To the south around Newbury, roughly eighty miles west of London, Major General Maxwell D. Taylor's Screaming Eagles, the 101st Airborne Division, were also "sealed in." In the same area, and stretching as far down as Dorsetshire, was the remainder of Urquhart's division. The majority of his units would not move to the airfields until the morning of the seventeenth, but in hamlets, villages and bivouac areas close to the departure points, they too made ready. Everywhere now, the airborne forces of Market-Garden waited out the time until takeoff and the historic invasion of Holland from the sky.

Some men felt more concern at being sealed in than about the mission itself. At an airfield near the village of Ramsbury, the security precautions made Corporal Hansford Vest, of the 101st Division's 502nd Regiment, distinctly uneasy. Aircraft and gliders "were parked for miles all over the countryside and there were guards everywhere." He noted that the airfield was surrounded by a barbed-wire fence with "British guards on the outside and our own guards on the inside." Vest had the "feeling that our freedom was gone." Private James Allardyce of the 508th Regiment, in his crowded tent city, tried to ignore the barbed wire and guards. He checked and rechecked his equipment "until it was almost worn out." Allardyce could not shake off the feeling that "we were like condemned men waiting to be led off."

Other men worried principally about their chances of going on the mission. So many previous operations had been canceled that one new recruit, nineteen-year-old Private Melvin Isenekev, of the 506th Regiment (he had arrived from the States on June 6, the day the 101st had jumped into Normandy), still didn't believe they would go when they reached the marshaling area. Isenekev felt he had trained "long and hard for this and I didn't want to be held back." Yet he almost was. Trying to light a makeshift oil burner used for heating water, he threw a lighted match into an oil drum. When nothing happened, Isenekev "put my head over it to look in and it exploded." Temporarily blinded, he instantly thought, "Now I've done it. They won't let me go." However within a few minutes his eyes stopped burning and he could see again. But he believes he was the only member of the 101st jumping into Holland with no eyebrows.

First Sergeant Daniel Zapalski, twenty-four, of the 502nd, "sweated out the jump; hoping the chute was packed right; hoping the field was soft; and hoping I didn't land in a tree." He was eager to go. Although he had not fully recovered from a Normandy leg wound, Zapalski believed his injury "was not serious enough to keep me from doing my normal duty." His battalion commander, the popular Lieutenant Colonel Robert G. Cole, disagreed. He had turned down Zapalski's pleas. Undeterred, Zapalski had bypassed Cole and obtained a written release certifying his combat readiness from the regimental surgeon. Though Zapalski and Cole had fought together in Normandy, the sergeant now got a "typical Cole chewing out. He called me 'a fatheaded Polack, impractical, burdensome and unreasonable.' " But he let Zapalski go.

Captain Raymond S. Hall, the 502nd's regimental chaplain, had a somewhat similar problem. He was "most anxious to return to action and to be with my men." But he too had been wounded in Normandy. Now the doctors would not let him jump. He was finally told that he could go in by glider. The chaplain was horrified. A veteran paratrooper, he considered gliders distinctly unsafe.

Fear of death or of failure to perform well disturbed others. Captain LeGrand Johnson, twenty-two-year-old company commander, remembering "the horrors and narrow escapes" during the 101st's night airborne attack preceding the Normandy invasion, was fatalistically "resigned." He was convinced that he would not return from this mission. Still, the young officer "fully intended to raise as much hell as I could." Johnson was not sure he liked the idea of a daylight drop. It might produce more casualties. On the other hand, this time "we would be able to see the enemy." To hide his nervousness, Johnson made bets with his fellow troopers on who would get the first Dutch beer. One of Johnson's staff sergeants, Charles Dohun, was "almost numb" with worry. He did "not know how to compare this daylight jump with Normandy or what to expect." Within forty-eight hours, his numbness forgotten, Staff Sergeant Dohun would heroically save the life of the fatalistic Captain Johnson.

Technical Sergeant Marshall Copas, twenty-two, had perhaps more reason than most for anxiety. He was one of the "pathfinders" who would jump first to mark the drop zones for the 101st. In the Normandy drop, Copas recalled, "we had forty-five minutes before the main body of troopers began jumping—now we had only twelve minutes." Copas and his friend Sergeant John Rudolph Brandt, twenty-nine, had one concern in common: both would have felt better "had General Patton's Third Army been on the ground below us, rather than the British. We had never fought with the Tommies before."

In the Grantham area, Private John Garzia, a veteran of three combat jumps with the 82nd Airborne Division, was stunned. To him, Market-Garden "was sheer insanity." He thought "Ike had transferred to the German side."

Now that Operation Market-Garden was actually on, Lieutenant Colonel Louis Mendez, battalion commander of the 82nd's 508th Regiment, had no hesitation in speaking out on one particular subject. With the nighttime experiences of his regiment in Normandy still painfully clear in his mind, Colonel Mendez delivered a scathing warning to the pilots who would carry his battalion into action the next day. "Gentlemen," Mendez said coldly, "my officers know this map of Holland and the drop zones by heart and we're ready to go. When I brought my battalion to the briefing prior to Normandy, I had the finest combat-ready force of its size that will ever be known. By the time I gathered them together in Normandy, half were gone. I charge you: put us down in Holland or put us down in hell, but put us all down together in one place."

Private First Class John Allen, twenty-four, a three-jump veteran and still recovering from wounds sustained in Normandy, was philosophical about the operation: "They never got me in a night jump," he solemnly told his buddies, "so now they'll be able to see me and get off a good shot." Staff Sergeant Russell O'Neal, with three night combat jumps behind him, was convinced that his "Irish luck was about to run out." When he heard the 82nd was to jump in daylight, he composed a letter he never sent—"You can hang a gold star in your window tonight, Mother. The Germans have a good chance to hit us before we even land." To lighten the atmosphere—though in doing so he may have made it worse—Private Philip H. Nadler, of the 504th Regiment, spread a few rumors. The one he liked best was that a large German camp of SS men were bivouacked on one of the 82nd drop zones.

Nadler had not been overly impressed by the briefing of the platoon. One of the 504th's objectives was the bridge at Grave. Gathering the men around him, the briefing lieutenant threw back the cover on a sandtable model and said, "Men, this is your destination." He rested a pointer on the bridge which bore the single word "Grave." Nadler was the first to comment. "Yeah, we know that, Lieutenant," he said, "but what country are we droppin' on?"

Major Edward Wellems, of the 504th's 2nd Battalion, thought

175

the name of the bridge was rather ominous, too, despite the fact that the officers who briefed his group suddenly began to change the pronunciation, referring to it as the "gravey bridge."

The briefings caused mixed reactions. Nineteen-year-old Corporal Jack Bommer thought that "six or eight weeks would see us home and then they'd send us on to the Pacific." Private Leo Hart, twenty-one, did not believe they were going at all. He had heard—probably as a result of Private Nadler's rumor—that there were 4,000 SS troops in the general jump area.

Major Edwin Bedell, thirty-eight, remembers that one private's sole concern was the safety of a live hare that he had won in a local village raffle. The private was fearful that his pet, which was so tame that it followed him everywhere, would not survive the jump, and that if it did it might still wind up in a stew pot.

Near Spanhoe airfield in the Grantham area, Lieutenant "Pat" Glover of the British 1st Airborne Division's 4th Parachute Brigade worried about Myrtle, a reddish-brown chicken that had been Glover's special pet since early summer. With parachute wings fastened to an elastic band around her neck, Myrtle "the parachick" had made six training jumps. At first she rode in a small zippered canvas bag attached to Glover's left shoulder. Later, he released her at fifty feet above the ground. By now Myrtle was an expert, and Glover could free her at three hundred feet. With a frenzied flutter of wings and raucous squawking, Myrtle gracelessly floated down to earth. There, Glover recalls, "this rather gentle pet would wait patiently on the ground for me to land and collect her." Myrtle the parachick was going to Arnhem. It would be her first combat jump. But Glover did not intend to tempt fate. He planned to keep Myrtle in her bag until he hit the ground in Holland.

Lance Corporal Sydney Nunn, twenty-three, of the 1st Airlanding Brigade, based in the south near Keevil, was only too glad to get away from his "pet." He thought the camp was "a nightmare." Nunn couldn't wait to get to Arnhem or anyplace else, so long as it was far enough away from the persistent mole who kept burrowing into his mattress.

For the men of the British 1st Airborne Division, now standing by in bases stretching from the Midlands south to Dorsetshire, the prevailing mood was one of relief that, at last, they were going into action. Besides, briefing officers stressed the fact that Market-Garden could shorten the war. For the British, fighting since 1939, the news was heady. Sergeant Ron Kent, of the 21st Independent Parachute Company, heard that "the success of the operation might even give us Berlin" and that ground opposition in Arnhem "would consist mainly of Hitler Youth and old men on bicycles." Sergeant Walter Inglis, of the 1st Parachute Brigade, was equally confident. The attack, he thought, would be "a piece of cake." All the Red Devils had to do was "hang on to the Arnhem bridge for forty-eight hours until XXX Corps tanks arrived; then the war would be practically over." Inglis expected to be back home in England in a week. Lance Corporal Gordon Spicer, of the 1st Parachute Brigade, offhandedly considered the operation "a fairly simple affair with a few backstage Germans recoiling in horror at our approach"; while Lance Bombardier Percy Parkes, of the 1st Airlanding Brigade, felt, after his briefing, that "all we would encounter at Arnhem was a mixed bag of Jerry cooks and clerks." The presence of tanks, Parkes says, was "mentioned only in passing, and we were told our air cover would be so strong that it would darken the sky above us." Confidence was such that Medic Geoffrey Stanners expected only "a couple of hernia battalions" and Signalman Victor Read was "looking forward to seeing German WAAF's who," he thought, "would be the only Germans defending Arnhem."

Some men who could legitimately remain behind were eager to go. Sergeant Alfred Roullier, of the 1st Airlanding Brigade's Artillery, was one of these. The thirty-one-year-old trooper discovered that he was not slated for the Arnhem operation. Although Roullier had been trained as an artilleryman, he was currently the acting mess sergeant at his battalion headquarters. Because of his culinary expertise, it appeared that he might spend the remainder of the war in the job. Twice, Alf Roullier had appealed to Sergeant Major John Siely to be included in the attack, but each time he was turned down. For the third time Alf pressed his case. "I know this operation can shorten the war," he told Siely. "I've got a wife and two children, but if this attack will get me home quicker and guarantee them a better future, then I want to go." Siely pulled a few strings. Alf Roullier's name was added to the list of those who would go to Arnhem—where, within the next week, the assistant mess sergeant would become something of a legend.

In the prevailing high mood before the onset of Market-Garden, there were undercurrents of doubt among some officers and enlisted men. They were troubled for a variety of reasons, although most took care to hide their feelings. Corporal Daniel Morgans, of the 1st Parachute Brigade, considered "Market a snorter of an operation." Still, "to drop six or seven miles from the objective and then to fight through a city to get there, was really asking for trouble." Regimental Sergeant Major J. C. Lord, with a lifetime in the army behind him, thought so, too. "The plan was a bit dicey," he felt. Nor did Lord give much credence to the talk of an understrength, worn-out enemy. He knew that "the German is no fool and a mighty warrior." Still, J. C. Lord, whose demeanor could intimidate even the veterans in his charge (almost in awe, some called him "Jesus Christ" behind his back), did not reveal his uneasiness, because "it would have been catastrophic to morale."

Captain Eric Mackay, whose engineers were, among other tasks, to race to the main road bridge in Arnhem and remove expected German charges, was suspicious of the entire operation. He thought the division "might just as well be dropped a hundred miles away from the objective as eight." The advantage of surprise and "a quick lightning stroke" would surely be lost. Mackay quietly ordered his men to double the amount of ammunition and grenades each would carry and personally briefed everyone in the troop on escape techniques.*

* One of the most accurate accounts of the First British Airborne's activities on the Arnhem bridge is to be found in "The Battle of Arnhem Bridge" by Eric Mackay, *Blackwood's* Magazine, October 1945.

Major Anthony Deane-Drummond, twenty-seven, second in command of 1st Airborne Division Signals, was particularly concerned about his communications. Apart from the main command units, he was worried about the smaller "22" sets that would be used between Urquhart and the various brigades during the Arnhem attack. The "22's" could best transmit and receive within a diameter of three to five miles. With drop zones seven to eight miles from the objective, performance was expected to be erratic. Worse, the sets must also contact General Browning's Airborne Corps headquarters, planned for Nijmegen, from the drop zones approximately fifteen miles to the south. Adding to the problem was the terrain. Between the main road bridge at Arnhem and the landing areas was the town itself, plus heavily wooded sections and suburban developments. On the other hand, an independent fact-gathering liaison unit, called "Phantom"—organized to collect and pass on intelligence estimates and immediate reports to each commander in the field, in this case General Browning of Airborne Corps—was not worried about the range of its own "22's." Twenty-five-year-old Lieutenant Neville Hay, in charge of the Phantom team's highly trained specialists, was even a "little disdainful of the Royal Corps of Signals," whom his group was inclined to treat "as poor cousins." By using a special kind of antenna, Hay and his operators had been able to transmit at distances of over one hundred miles on a "22."

Even with Hay's success and although various forms of communications* would be used in the event of emergency, Deane-Drummond was uneasy. He mentioned to his superior, Lieutenant Colonel Tom Stephenson, that "the likelihood of the sets working satisfactorily in the initial phases of the operation is very doubtful." Stephenson agreed. Still, it would hardly matter. In the surprise assault, troops were expected to close up on the Arnhem bridge very quickly. Therefore, it was believed that units would not be out of touch with headquarters for more than one or

* Included in the communications setup were 82 pigeons provided from R.A.F. sources. The lofts for these birds were situated in the London area—meaning that the birds, if they survived the airborne landing and the Germans, would have to fly approximately 240 miles to deliver a message.

two hours, by which time, Deane-Drummond heard, "things would have sorted themselves out and Urquhart's command post would be with the 1st Parachute Brigade on the bridge itself." Although not entirely reassured, Deane-Drummond recalled that, "like almost everyone else, I was swept along with the prevailing attitude: 'Don't be negative; and for God's sake, don't rock the boat; let's get on with the attack.' "

Now the final word depended not on men but on the weather. From Supreme Command headquarters down, senior officers anxiously awaited meteorological reports. Given less than seven days to meet Montgomery's deadline, Market-Garden was as ready as it would ever be, but a minimum forecast of three full days of fair weather was needed. In the early evening of September 16, the weather experts issued their findings: apart from some early morning fog, the weather for the next three days would be fair, with little cloud and virtually no winds. At First Allied Airborne Army headquarters Lieutenant General Brereton quickly made his decision. The coded teleprinter message that went out to his commanders at 7:45 P.M. read, "CONFIRM MARKET SUNDAY 17TH. ACKNOWLEDGE." In his diary, Brereton recorded, "At last we are going into action." He thought he would sleep well this night for, as he told his staff, "Now that I've made the decision, I've quit worrying."

In crowded hangars, cities of tents and Nissen huts, the waiting men were given the news. On a large mirror over the fireplace in the sergeants' mess of the British 1st Airborne Division Signals near Grantham, someone chalked up "14 hours to go . . . no cancellation." Sergeant Horace "Hocker" Spivey noted that, as each hour passed, the number was rechalked. To Spivey, tired of being briefed for operations that never came off, the ever-diminishing number on the mirror was the best proof yet that this time "we were definitely going."

On all their bases the men of the First Allied Airborne Army made last-minute preparations. They had been fully briefed, their weapons had been checked and their currency exchanged for Dutch guilders, and there was little now for the isolated troopers to do but wait. Some spent the time writing letters, "celebrating" their departure the following morning, packing personal belongings, sleeping or participating in marathon card games ranging from blackjack and poker to bridge. Twenty-year-old Sergeant Francis Moncur, of the 1st Parachute Brigade's 2nd Battalion, played blackjack hour after hour. To his surprise, he won steadily. Looking at the ever-growing pile of guilders before him, Moncur felt like a millionaire. He expected to have a "whale of a time in Arnhem after the battle," which, in his opinion, would "last only forty-eight hours." That would be long enough for the sergeant to settle a score with the Germans. Seventy-two hours earlier, Moncur's brother, a seventeen-year-old R.A.F. flight sergeant, had been killed in an attempt to jump from his disabled bomber at 200 feet. His parachute had failed to open completely.

South of Grantham at a base in Cottesmore, Sergeant "Joe" Sunley of the 4th Parachute Brigade was on security patrol, making sure that "no paratroopers had slipped off base into the village." Returning to the airdrome, Sunley saw Sergeant "Ginger" Green, a physical-training instructor and a "gentle giant of a man," tossing a deflated football up in the air. Green deftly caught the ball and threw it to Sunley. "What the hell are you doing with this?" Sunley asked. Ginger explained that he was taking the deflated ball to Arnhem, "so we can have a little game on the drop zone after we're finished."

At Manston, Kent, Staff Sergeant George Baylis of the Glider Pilot Regiment was also looking forward to some recreation. He had heard that the Dutch liked to dance; so George carefully packed his dancing pumps. Signalman Stanley G. Copley of the 1st Parachute Brigade Signals bought extra film for his camera. As little opposition was expected he thought it was "a perfect chance to get some pictures of the Dutch countryside and towns."

One man was taking presents that he had bought in London a few days earlier. When the Netherlands was overrun, thirty-two-year-old Lieutenant Commander Arnoldus Wolters of the Dutch navy had escaped in his minesweeper and sailed to England. Since that time, he had been attached to the Netherlands government in exile, holding a variety of desk jobs dealing with information and intelligence. A few days earlier, Wolters had been asked to go to Holland as part of the military government and civil affairs team attached to General Urquhart's headquarters. It was proposed that Wolters become military commissioner of the Netherlands territories to be liberated by the airborne forces. "It was a startling suggestion—going from a desk chair to a glider," he recalled. He was attached to a unit under Colonel Hilary Barlow, second in command of the 1st Airlanding Brigade, who was designated to become the town commandant in Arnhem after its capture. Wolters would be his assistant. Now, excited about the prospect of returning to Holland, Wolters "was struck by the optimism, and I believed everything I was told. I really did not expect the operation to be very difficult. It seemed that the war was virtually over and the attack dead easy. I expected to land on Sunday and be home on Tuesday with my wife and child at Hilversum." For his wife, Maria, Wolters had bought a watch, and for his daughter, whom he had last seen as a baby four years before, he had a two-foot Teddy bear. He hoped nobody would mind if he took it in the glider.

Lieutenant Colonel John Frost, thirty-one, who was to lead the battalion assigned to capture the Arnhem bridge, packed his copper fox-hunting horn with the rest of his battle gear. It had been presented to him by the members of the Royal Exodus Hunt, of which he was Master in 1939–40. During training, Frost had used the horn to rally his men. He would do so on this operation. Frost had no qualms about a daylight jump. From the information given at briefings, "we were made to feel that the Germans were weak and demoralized and German troops in the area were of a decidedly low category and badly equipped." Frost did have misgivings about the drop zones. He had been told that the "polder on the southern side of the bridge was unsuitable for parachutists and gliders." Why then, he wondered, were the Poles to drop on the southern side of the bridge "if it was so unsuitable?"

Though he was anxious to get into action, Frost "hated to leave for Holland." Secretly, he hoped for a last-minute cancellation or postponement. He had enjoyed the area of Stoke Rochford in Lincolnshire and wished for "perhaps another day or two just doing all the pleasant things I had done in the past." But with these thoughts were others, "telling me that we had been here long enough and it was time to get away." Frost slept soundly on September 16. Although he wasn't naïve enough to think the battle of Arnhem would be "much of a lark," he did tell his batman, Wicks, to pack his gun, cartridges, golf clubs and dinner jacket in the staff car that would follow.

On the mirror above the fireplace in the sergeants' mess, now empty, there was one last notation, scrawled before men became too busy to bother. It read: "2 hours to go . . . no cancellation."

Part Three

THE ATTACK

❊ 1 ❊

THE THUNDER OF THE HUGE FORMATIONS was earsplitting. Around British glider bases in Oxfordshire and Gloucestershire, horses and cattle panicked and bolted in the fields. In southern and eastern England thousands of people watched in amazement. In some villages and towns road traffic jammed and came to a halt. Passengers in speeding trains crowded one another to stare out of windows. Everywhere people gaped, dumfounded, at a spectacle no one had ever seen before. The mightiest airborne force in history was off the ground and heading for its targets.

By coincidence on this bright Sunday morning, September 17, 1944, special services were being held all over England to commemorate "the valiant few," the handful of R.A.F. pilots who had boldly challenged Hitler's Luftwaffe four years before and fought them to a standstill. As worshipers knelt in prayer, the steady, overpowering drone of propellers completely drowned out some services. In London's great Westminster Cathedral the soaring organ tones of the solemn Magnificat could not be heard. In twos and threes, people left their pews to join the crowds already gathered in the streets. There, Londoners stared upward, overwhelmed by the din as formation after formation of aircraft passed overhead at low altitude. In north London, a Salvation Army band overpowered by the noise gave up, but the bass drummer, his eyes on the sky, thumped out a symbolic beat: three dots and a dash—in Morse code, V for *victory*.

To the onlookers, the nature of the attack was clearly revealed by the great streams of planes towing gliders. But it would be six more hours before the British people learned that they had witnessed the opening phase of the most momentous airborne offensive ever conceived. A Red Cross worker, Angela Hawkings, may have best summed up the reactions of those who saw the vast armada pass. From the window of a train, she stared up, astonished, as wave after wave of planes flew over like "droves of starlings." She was convinced that "this attack, wherever bound, must surely bring about the end of the war."

The men of the First Allied Airborne Army were as unprepared as the civilians on the ground for the awesome spectacle of their own departure. The paratroopers, glider-borne infantry and pilots who set out for Holland were staggered by the size and majesty of the air fleets. Captain Arie D. Bestebreurtje, a Dutch officer attached to the 82nd Airborne, thought the sight was "unbelievable. Every plane the Allies possessed must have been engaged in this single scheme." In fact, some 4,700 aircraft were involved—the greatest number ever used on a single airborne mission.

The operation had begun in the predawn hours and continued on throughout the morning. First, more than 1,400 Allied bombers had taken off from British airfields and had pounded German antiaircraft positions and troop concentrations in the Market-Garden area. Then, at 9:45 A.M. and for two and one quarter hours more, 2,023 troop-carrying planes, gliders and their tugs swarmed into the air from twenty-four U.S. and British bases.° C-47's carrying paratroopers flew in long 45-plane formations. More C-47's and British bombers—Halifaxes, Stirlings and Albemarles—pulled 478 gliders. In seemingly endless sky trains, these huge equipment- and troop-carrying gliders bounced behind their tow planes at the end of 300-foot-long ropes. Swaying among the smaller Horsa and Waco gliders were massive slab-

° Many official accounts give 10:25 A.M. as the time when the first Market aircraft left the ground. Perhaps they had in mind the departure of the pathfinders, who arrived first. From an examination of log books and air controllers' time schedules, it is clear that the airlift began at 9:45 A.M.

sided Hamilcars, each with a cargo capacity of eight tons; they could hold a small tank or two 3-ton trucks with artillery or ammunition. Above, below and on the flanks, protecting these huge formations, were almost 1,500 Allied fighters and fighter-bombers—British Spitfires, rocket-firing Typhoons, Tempests and Mosquitoes; U.S. Thunderbolts, Lightnings, Mustangs and low-level dive bombers. There were so many planes in the air that Captain Neil Sweeney of the 101st Airborne Division remembered that "it looked like we could get out on the wings and walk all the way to Holland."

The British glider forces were the first to take off. Farther north on the Market-Garden corridor than the Americans and with different requirements, General Urquhart needed the maximum in men, equipment and artillery—especially antitank guns—in the first lift, to capture and hold his objectives until the land forces could link up. Therefore, the bulk of his division was glider-borne; 320 gliders carried the men, transport and artillery of Brigadier Philip "Pips" Hicks's 1st Airlanding Brigade. They would reach landing zones west of Arnhem a little after 1 P.M. Thirty minutes later, Brigadier Gerald Lathbury's 1st Parachute Brigade, in 145 troop-carrying planes, would begin dropping. Because the unwieldy gliders and tugs were slower—120 miles per hour versus 140 for the paratroop-carrier planes—these immense "sky trains"—or serials, as the airborne called them—had to be launched first. From eight bases in Gloucestershire and Oxfordshire, gliders and tugs rolled down runways and rose in the air at a launch rate never before attempted: one combination per minute. Forming up was especially intricate and dangerous. Climbing slowly to altitude, the planes headed west over the Bristol Channel. Then, speeds synchronized, the tugs and gliders echeloned to the right in pairs, turned back, flew over the takeoff bases and headed for a marshaling point above the town of Hatfield, north of London.

Even as the first British glider serials were forming up above the Bristol Channel, twelve British Stirling bombers and six U.S.

C-47's began taking off at 10:25 A.M. for Holland. In them were U.S. and British pathfinders—the men who would land first to mark landing and drop zones for the Market forces.

Simultaneously, the men of the U.S. 82nd Airborne and the paratroop elements of the British First Division took off from bases around Grantham, Lincolnshire, in 625 troop-carrier planes and 50 C-47's towing gliders. With astonishing precision, the planes of the IX Troop Carrier Command left the ground at five- to twenty-second intervals. In wave after wave they rendezvoused above the town of March, Cambridgeshire, and from there set out in three parallel streams to cross the coast at Aldeburgh.

At the same time, from southern airfields around Greenham Common, the 101st Airborne took to the air, in 424 C-47's plus 70 gliders and tugs. Forming up, they too passed over the traffic control point at Hatfield and flew east to cross the coast at Bradwell Bay.

In immense triple columns, together at least ten miles across and approximately a hundred miles long, the vast armada swept over the English countryside. The 82nd Airborne and British 1st Division, enroute to Nijmegen and Arnhem, flew along the northern track. A special serial of 38 gliders carrying General Browning's Corps headquarters, bound for Nijmegen, traveled with them. On the southern route, passing over Bradwell Bay, the 101st Airborne headed for its drop zones slightly north of Eindhoven. By 11:55 A.M., the entire force—more than 20,000 troops, 511 vehicles, 330 artillery pieces and 590 tons of equipment—was off the ground. First Lieutenant James J. Coyle of the 82nd Airborne, looking down on the English countryside from an altitude of only 1,500 feet, saw nuns waving from the courtyard of a convent. He thought "the beautiful day and the nuns made a picture that had the quality of an oil painting." Waving back, he wondered "if they could possibly know who we were and where we were going."

For the majority of the airborne troops, the mood of the initial part of the journey, across England, was lighthearted. To Private Roy Edwards of the 1st Parachute Brigade, "everything was so serene it was like going on a bus outing to the seaside." Private A. G. Warrender remembers that "this was a perfect Sunday; a morning for a walk down a country lane and a pint at the local."

The commanding officer of the Glider Pilot Regiment, Colonel George S. Chatterton, piloting the glider carrying General Browning, described the Sunday as "an extremely fine day. It did not seem possible that we were taking off for one of the greatest battles in history." Chatterton was struck by Browning's entourage and equipment. With the General were his batman, headquarters' medical officer, cook, as well as his tent and personal jeep. Browning sat on an empty Worthington Beer crate between the pilot and copilot, and Chatterton noted that he was "immaculately dressed in a Barathea battle dress, with a highly polished Sam Browne belt, knife-edge-creased trousers, leather holster gleaming like glass, a swagger stick and spotless gray kid gloves." The General, says Chatterton, "was in tremendous form, because he realized he had reached one of the climaxes of his career. There was an air of immense gaiety."

In another glider serial, the quiet Scot with the most difficult Market-Garden assignment, the 1st Airborne Division's General Roy Urquhart, thought it was "difficult not to feel excited that we were off at last." Yet the popular officer's mind, as always, was on his men and the job that lay ahead. Like Browning, he had an entourage. Now, looking down the length of the Horsa glider—which was carrying his aide Roberts, batman Hancock, the Reverend G. A. Pare, padre of the Glider Pilot Regiment, a signaler, two military police, their motorcycles and the General's jeep—Urquhart felt a pang of conscience. He thought of his paratroopers, laden down with packs, guns and equipment, crowded into heavy transport planes. Urquhart carried only a small shoulder pack, two hand grenades, a map case and a notebook. He was bothered by his own comfort.

Almost up to the moment of takeoff Urquhart had been called

on to make difficult decisions. Some hours before leaving, his chief of staff, Colonel Charles Mackenzie, had received a telephone call from a senior American air force officer. Was the mental asylum at Wolfheze to be bombed? The American, Mackenzie had reported, "wanted a personal assurance from Urquhart that there were Germans in it and not lunatics; otherwise the Americans could not accept responsibility." The asylum was dangerously close to the division's assembly point, and Urquhart's staff believed it to be held by the Germans. Mackenzie had accepted responsibility. "On your head be it," the American had replied. Urquhart had approved his chief of staff's action. "I meant to be as prepared as possible and that's all there was to it," he remembered.

As Mackenzie was about to leave for his own glider, Urquhart had taken him privately aside. "Look, Charles," he had told Mackenzie, "if anything happens to me the succession of command should be as follows: first, Lathbury, then Hicks and Hackett in that order." Urquhart's choice was based on experience. "Everyone knew that Lathbury was my deputy," he later recalled. "Hackett was senior in rank to Hicks, but he was much younger and I was quite convinced that Hicks had more experience in handling infantry. My decision was no reflection on Hackett's ability to command." Perhaps, Urquhart reflected, he should have informed each of his brigadiers of his decision earlier, but he had "frankly considered the whole question quite academic." The chance of the division losing both Urquhart and Lathbury was remote.

Now, all decisions made, Urquhart idly watched "squadrons of fighters flashing past the glider trains." This was his first operational trip in a glider, and earlier he had taken a couple of airsickness pills. His throat was dry and he had difficulty swallowing. He was conscious, too, that "Hancock, my batman, was watching me, a look of concern on his face. Like everyone else, he expected me to be airsick." Urquhart did not oblige. "We were in a huge stream of aircraft and I concentrated on impressions. We were committed. We had made a good plan. I still wished we

AIRBORNE INVASION ROUTES
SEPT. 17, 1944

GERMANY

HOLLAND

ZUIDER ZEE

Amsterdam

1ST BR. AIRBORNE DIV. AND POLES
ARNHEM

U.S. 82ND AIRBORNE DIV.
NIJMEGEN

LOWER RHINE
WAAL R.
MAAS R.

Rotterdam

U.S. 101ST AIRBORNE DIV.
EINDHOVEN

RHINE R.

FRONT LINE
SEPT. 17/44

LUX.

MEUSE R.

0   50
Miles

SCHOUWEN

Antwerp

BELGIUM

Ghent

NORTH SEA

NORTHERN ROUTE

RESCUE SHIPS

SOUTHERN ROUTE

RESCUE SHIPS

FRANCE

MARCH

Burtham

Chipping Ongar

HATFIELD

LONDON

ENGLAND

Balderton
Fulbeck
Langar
Barkston Heath
Saltby
Cottesmore
Folkingham
Spanhoe

Broadwell
Fairford
Down Ampney
Blackwell
Keevil
Membury
Ramsbury
Welford
Aldermaston
Chilbolton
Greatham Common
Tarrant Rushton

Brize Norton
Chalgrove

ENGLISH CHANNEL

N

palacios

could have gotten closer to the bridge, but I did not brood on it."

In spite of the operational efficiency displayed in launching the giant armada, mishaps occurred almost immediately. Just before takeoff, the port wing of one glider was chewed off by the propeller of a Stirling bomber. No one was hurt. As the glider carrying Lieutenant Alan Harvey Cox of the Airlanding Brigade lumbered into the air, it ran into trouble. Low clouds obstructed the glider pilot's view and he was unable to line up with the tail of his tug. The glider went in one direction, the plane in another, the tow rope threatening to loop the glider's wing and overturn it. Unable to realign with his tug, the glider pilot grabbed for the red-topped release lever and cast off. Cox's glider landed without damage in a hay field at Sandford-on-Thames. A more bizarre incident occurred in a C-47 carrying the men of the 82nd Airborne, who sat facing each other on opposite sides of the plane. Five minutes after takeoff, Corporal Jack Bommer saw "the cargo hatch directly behind the men facing me spring open." The force of air almost sucked the men through the hatchway into space. As they desperately hung on, recalls Bommer, "the pilot did a beautiful tail flip and the hatch slammed shut."

Lance Corporal Sydney Nunn, who was so anxious to leave his base near Keevil and the activities of the mole in his mattress, now felt lucky to be alive. After more than an hour of uneventful flight, his glider ran into cloud. Emerging from the cloud bank, the glider pilot saw that the tow rope had twisted itself around the port wing. Over the intercom to his tug, Nunn heard the glider pilot say, "I'm in trouble! I'm in trouble!" The next instant, he cast off. "We seemed to come to a dead stop in the air," Nunn remembers. "Then the glider's nose dropped and we careened earthward with the tow rope streaming alongside like a broken kite string." Nunn sat "petrified," listening to the wind screaming along the fuselage, "hoping that the chains holding a jeep in the glider would take the strain." Then he heard the pilot warn them to "Brace up, blokes. Here we come." The glider hit the ground, bounced, hit once more, and came slowly to a stop. In the sudden silence, Nunn heard the pilot ask, "Are you blokes all right?" Everyone was, and the men were returned to Keevil to fly out in the second lift on September 18.

Others were not so fortunate. Tragedy struck one glider serial over Wiltshire. R.A.F. Sergeant Walter Simpson, sitting in the plexiglass turret of a Stirling bomber, was watching the Horsa glider trailing along behind. Suddenly, "The glider just seemed to part in the middle; it looked as if the back end just dropped off the front." Horrified, Simpson shouted to the captain, "My God, the glider's coming apart!" The tow rope broke and the front of the glider sank "like a rock falling to earth." The Stirling left formation, gradually lost height, and turned back to locate the wreckage. The front half was spotted in a field. The tail was nowhere to be seen. Marking the spot, the crew returned to Keevil and drove by jeep to the crash location. There, Simpson saw what appeared "like a match box that had been stepped on." The bodies of the men had remained inside. Simpson had no way of estimating how many dead there were—"it was just a mass of arms, legs and bodies."

By the time the last serials reached the English coast—the northern streams passing over the checkpoint at Aldeburgh, the southern columns flying over Bradwell Bay—thirty troop- and equipment-carrying gliders were down. Tug engine failure, broken tow ropes, and, in places, heavy clouds had caused the abortions. Although by military standards the operation had begun with eminent success—casualties were light, and many of the men and most of the downed cargo would be flown in on later lifts—the losses were sure to hurt. On this vital day when every man, vehicle and piece of equipment was important to General Urquhart, twenty-three of his glider loads were already lost. Not until the Arnhem force reached its drop and landing zones would commanders discover just how crucial these losses would be.

Now, as the long sky trains swarmed out over the English Channel and the land fell behind, a new kind of expectancy began to permeate the armada. The "Sunday outing" mood was fast disappearing. As American serials passed over the seaside resort of Margate, Private Melvin Isenekev of the 101st Airborne saw the white cliffs of Dover off to the right. From the distance, they looked like the wintry hillsides of the Adirondacks near his home in upper New York State. Corporal D. Thomas of the 1st British Airborne, staring out through an open plane door until his country's coastline disappeared, felt his eyes fill with tears.

From the marshaling points at March and Hatfield, the airborne columns had been aided by various navigational devices: radar beacons, special hooded lights and radio direction-finding signals. Now, beacons on ships in the North Sea began to guide the planes. Additionally, strings of launches—17 along the northern route; 10 below the southern flight path—stretched away across the water. To Flight Sergeant William Tompson, at the controls of a plane towing a four-ton Horsa glider, "there wasn't much navigating to do. The launches below us were set out like stepping stones across the Channel." But these fast naval vessels were much more than directional aids. They were part of a vast air-sea rescue operation, and they were already busy.

In the thirty-minute trip across the North Sea, men saw gliders bobbing on the gray waters as low-flying amphibious planes circled to mark their positions until rescue launches could reach the spot. Lieutenant Neville Hay, of the Phantom fact-gathering liaison unit, watched "with complete detachment two downed gliders and another ditching." He tapped his corporal on the shoulder. "Have a look down there, Hobkirk," Hay shouted. The corporal glanced down and, as Hay remembers, "I could almost see him turn green." Hay hurriedly reassured the man. "There's nothing to worry about. Look at the boats already picking them up."

Staff Sergeant Joseph Kitchener, piloting a glider, was equally impressed by the speed of the air-sea rescue launch that came alongside a floating glider he had spotted. "They picked up the men so fast I don't even think they got their feet wet," he recalls. Men in a glider piloted by Staff Sergeant Cyril Line were less fortunate—but lucky to be alive. In an aerial train of swaying black Horsas, Line observed one combination drop slowly out of position. Mesmerized, he watched the Horsa cut loose and descend almost leisurely toward the sea. A ring of white foam appeared as it hit the water. He wondered "who the poor devils were." At that moment, the starboard propellers on the Stirling pulling his glider slowed, and stopped. As the plane's speed was reduced Line found himself "in the embarrassing position of overtaking my own tug." He immediately released the tow line and his copilot called out, "Stand by for ditching!" From behind in the cabin, they could hear rifle butts crashing against the side of the glider's plywood fuselage as the frantic passengers tried to open up an escape route. Rapidly losing altitude, Line looked back and was horrified to see that the desperate troopers had "cut through the top of the glider and the sides were just beginning to go." Line screamed out, "Stop that! Strap yourselves in!" Then, with a heavy thud, the glider hit the water. When Line surfaced, he saw the wreckage floating some thirty feet away. There was no sign whatever of the cabin, but every one of his passengers was accounted for. Within minutes, all were picked up.

In all, eight gliders ditched safely during this first lift; once they were on the water, the air-sea rescue service, in a spectacular performance, saved nearly all crews and passengers. Once again, however, it was Urquhart's force that was whittled down. Of the eight gliders, five were Arnhem-bound.

Apart from some long-range inaccurate shelling of a downed glider, there was no serious enemy opposition during the Channel crossing. The 101st Airborne Division, following the southern route, which would bring it over Allied-held Belgium, was experiencing an almost perfect flight. But as the Dutch coastline appeared in the distance, the 82nd and the British troopers in the northern columns began to see the ominous telltale gray and black puffs of flak—German antiaircraft fire. As they flew on, at an altitude of only 1,500 feet, enemy guns firing from the outer Dutch isles of Walcheren, North Beveland and Schouwen were clearly visible. So were flak ships and barges around the mouth of the Schelde.

Escorting fighters began peeling out of formation, engaging the gun positions. In the planes men could hear spent shrapnel scraping against the metal sides of the C-47's. Veteran paratrooper Private Leo Hart of the 82nd heard a rookie aboard his plane ask, "Are these bucket seats bullet proof?" Hart just glowered at him; the light metal seats wouldn't have offered protection against a well-thrown stone. Private Harold Brockley, in another C-47, remembers one replacement wondering, "Hey, what are all those little black and gray puffs below?" Before anyone could answer, a piece of shrapnel came through the bottom of the ship and pinged harmlessly against a mess kit.

Veteran troopers hid their fears in different ways. When Staff Sergeant Paul Nunan saw the "familiar golf balls of red tracer bullets weaving up toward us" he pretended to doze off. Tracers barely missed Private Kenneth Truax's plane. "No one said anything," he recalls. "There was only a weak smile or two." Sergeant Bill Tucker, who had gone through antiaircraft fire in Normandy, was haunted by a "horrible fear of getting hit from underneath." He felt "less naked" sitting on three air-force flak jackets. And Private Rudolph Kos remembers that he felt "like sitting on my helmet, but I knew I would need it on my head."

One man was more concerned with the danger within than that without. Copilot Sergeant Bill Oakes, struggling to hold his Horsa glider steady in the air, looked back to see how his passengers were faring. To his horror, three troopers were "calmly sitting on the floor brewing up a mess tin of tea over a small cooker. Five others were standing around with their mugs, waiting to be served." Oakes was galvanized into action. He handed the controls over to the pilot and hurried aft, expecting the glider's plywood floor to catch fire at any minute. "Or, worse still, the mortar bombs in the trailer we were carrying could explode. The heat from that little field stove was terrific." He was livid with anger. "We're just having a little brew up," one of the troopers told him soothingly. Oakes hurried back to the cockpit and reported the matter to the pilot, Staff Sergeant Bert Watkins. The pilot smiled. "Tell 'em not to forget us when the tea's ready," he said. Oakes sank into his seat and buried his head in his hands.

Although the escort fighters silenced most of the coastal flak positions, some planes were damaged and one tug, its glider and a troop-carrier C-47 were shot down over Schouwen Island. The tug crash-landed, and its crew was killed. The glider, an 82nd Airborne Waco, broke up in mid-air and may have been seen by Major Dennis Munford, flying in a British column nearby. He watched, aghast, as the Waco disintegrated and "men and equipment spilt out of it like toys from a Christmas cracker." Others saw the troop-carrier go down. Equipment bundles attached beneath the C-47 were set on fire by tracer bullets. "Yellow and red streamers of flame appeared in the black smoke," recalls Captain Arthur Ferguson, who was flying in a nearby plane. Within minutes the C-47 was blazing. First Lieutenant Virgil Carmichael, standing in the door of his plane, watched as paratroopers jumped from the stricken aircraft. "As our men were using camouflaged chutes, I was able to count them as they left and saw that all had escaped safely."

The pilot, although the aircraft was engulfed in flames, somehow kept the plane steady until the paratroopers jumped. Then Carmichael saw one more figure leave. "The Air Corps used white parachutes, so I figured he had to be the crew chief." He was the last man out. Almost immediately the blazing plane nosedived and, at full throttle, plowed into a flooded area of Schouwen Island below. Carmichael remembers that, "on impact, a white chute billowed out in front of the plane, probably ejected by the force of the crash." To First Lieutenant James Megellas the sight of the downed C-47 had a "terrible effect." As jumpmaster in his plane, he had previously told his men that he would give the command "to stand up and hook up five minutes before reaching the drop zone." Now, he immediately gave the order. In many other planes, jumpmasters reacted as Megellas had and gave similar commands. To them, the battle was already joined—and, in fact, the drop and landing zones for the airborne men were now only thirty to forty minutes away.

✵ 2 ✵

INCREDIBLY, DESPITE THE NIGHT's widespread bombing, and now the aerial attacks against Arnhem, Nijmegen and Eindhoven, the Germans failed to realize what was happening. Throughout the chain of command, attention was focused on a single threat: the renewal of the British Second Army's offensive from its bridgehead over the Meuse-Escaut Canal.

"Commanders and troops, myself and my staff in particular, were so overtaxed and under such severe strain in the face of our difficulties that we thought only in terms of ground operations," recalls Colonel General Kurt Student. Germany's illustrious airborne expert was at his headquarters in a cottage near Vught, approximately twenty-one miles northwest of Eindhoven, working on "red tape—a mountain of papers that followed me even into the battlefield." Student walked out onto a balcony, watched the bombers for a few moments, then, unconcerned, returned to his paper work.

Lieutenant Colonel Walter Harzer, commanding officer of the 9th SS Panzer Division Hohenstaufen, had by now transferred as much equipment as he intended to his rival, General Heinz Harmel of the 10th SS Panzer Division Frundsberg. Harmel, on Bittrich's orders and without Model's knowledge, was by now in Berlin. The last flatcars containing Harzer's "disabled" armored personnel carriers were ready to leave on a 2 P.M. train for Germany. Having been bombed repeatedly from Normandy onward, Harzer "paid little attention to planes." He saw nothing unusual about the huge bomber formations over Holland. He and his veteran tankers knew "it was routine to see bombers traveling east to Germany and returning several times a day. My men and I were numb from constant shelling and bombing." With Major Egon Skalka, the 9th Panzer's chief medical officer, Harzer set out from his headquarters at Beekbergen for the Hoenderloo barracks, about eight miles north of Arnhem. In a ceremony before the 600-man reconnaissance battalion of the division, he would decorate its commander, Captain Paul Gräbner, with the Knight's Cross. Afterward there would be champagne and a special luncheon.

At II SS Panzer Corps headquarters at Doetinchem, Lieutenant General Wilhelm Bittrich was equally unconcerned about the air attacks. To him, "it was routine fare." Field Marshal Walter Model, in his headquarters at the Tafelberg Hotel in Oosterbeek, had been watching the bomber formations for some time. The view at headquarters was unanimous: the squadrons of Flying Fortresses were returning from their nightly bombing of Germany, and as usual, other streams of Fortresses in the never-ending bombing of Germany were enroute east heading for other targets. As for the local bombing, it was not uncommon for bombers to jettison any unused bombs over the Ruhr and often, as a result, into Holland itself. Model and his chief of staff, Lieutenant General Hans Krebs, believed the bombardment and low-level strafing were "softening-up operations"—a prelude to the opening of the British ground offensive.

One officer was mildly concerned by the increased aerial activity over Holland. At the headquarters of OB West in Aremberg near Koblenz, approximately 120 miles away, Field Marshal Gerd von Rundstedt—although he still believed that airborne forces would be used only in an attack against the Ruhr—wanted more information. In Annex 2227 of the morning report for September 17, his operations chief recorded that Von Rundstedt had asked Model to investigate the possibility that a combined sea and airborne invasion was underway against northern Holland. The notation read, "The general situation and notable increase of enemy reconnaissance activities . . . has caused the Commander in Chief, West, to again examine the possibilities of ship assault and air landing operations. . . . Results of the survey are to be reported to OKW [Hitler]."

The message reached Model's headquarters at about the time the first planes of the armada crossed the coast.

Over Arnhem at 11:30 A.M. columns of black smoke rose in the sky as fires burned throughout the city in the aftermath of a three-hour near-saturation bombing. In Wolfheze, Oosterbeek, Nijmegen and Eindhoven, whole buildings were leveled, streets were cratered and littered with debris and glass, and casualties were mounting minute by minute. Even now, low-level fighters were strafing machine-gun and antiaircraft positions all over the area. The mood of the Dutch, huddling in churches, homes, cellars and shelters or, with foolhardy courage, cycling the streets or staring from rooftops, alternated between terror and exultation. No one knew what to believe or what would happen next. To the south, eighty-three miles from Nijmegen, Maastricht, the first Dutch city to be liberated, had been entered by the U.S. First Army on September 14. Many Dutch expected American infantry to arrive at any moment in their own towns and villages. Radio Orange, broadcasting from London, fed this impression in a flurry of bulletins: "The time is nearly here. What we have been waiting for is about to happen at last. . . . Owing to the rapid advance of the Allied armies . . . it is possible that the troops will not carry Dutch money yet. If our Allies offer French or Belgian notes . . . cooperate and accept this money in payment. . . . Farmers should finish off and deliver their harvest. . . ." Prince Bernhard, in a radio message, urged the Dutch "not to show joy by offering flowers or fruit when Allied troops liberate Netherlands territory . . . in the past the enemy has concealed explosives among offerings presented to the liberators." Uppermost in the minds of most Dutchmen was the certainty that these intensive bombings were the prelude to Allied invasion—the opening of the ground offensive. Like their German conquerors, the Dutch had no inkling of the impending airborne attack.

Jan and Bertha Voskuil, taking shelter in the home of Voskuil's father-in-law in Oosterbeek, thought the bombers in their area were aiming for Model's headquarters in the Tafelberg Hotel. The bright day, Voskuil remembers, "was perfect bombing weather." Yet he found it hard to "reconcile the war that was coming with the smell of ripe beetroots and sight of hundreds of sunflowers, their stems bent under the weight of their great heads. It did not seem possible that men were dying and buildings burning." Voskuil felt strangely calm. From his father-in-law's front veranda, he watched fighters flashing overhead and was sure they were strafing the hotel. Suddenly, a German soldier appeared in the garden without helmet or rifle and dressed only in a shirt and trousers. Politely he asked Voskuil, "May I take shelter here?" Voskuil stared at the man. "Why?" he asked. "You have your trenches." The German smiled. "I know," he answered, "but they are full." The soldier came up on the porch. "It is a very heavy bombing," he told Voskuil, "but I don't think Oosterbeek is the target. They seem to be concentrating more to the east and west of the village."

From inside the house, Voskuil heard voices. A friend of the family had just arrived from the Wolfheze area. It had been heavily hit, she told them, and many people were dead. "I am afraid," she said, tremblingly, "it is our Last Supper." Voskuil looked at the German. "Perhaps they're bombing the Tafelberg because of Model," he said mildly. The German's face was impassive. "No," he told Voskuil, "I don't think so. No bombs fell there." Later, after the soldier had gone, Voskuil went out to survey the damage. Rumors abounded. He heard that Arnhem had been heavily hit and that Wolfheze was almost leveled. Surely, he thought, the Allies were now under march and would arrive at any hour. He was both elated and saddened. Caen, in Normandy, he remembered, had been reduced to rubble during the invasion. He was convinced that Oosterbeek, where he and his family had found shelter, would become a ruined village.

Around Wolfheze, German ammunition caches in the woods were exploding, and the famed mental institute had received direct hits. Four pavilions surrounding the administration building were leveled, forty-five patients were dead (the toll would increase to over eighty), and countless more were wounded. Sixty terrified inmates, mostly women, were wandering about in the adjoining woods. The electricity had failed, and Dr. Marius van der Beek, the deputy medical superintendent, could not summon help. Impatiently he awaited the arrival of doctors from Oosterbeek and Arnhem, who, he knew, would surely hear the news and come. He needed to set up two operating theaters with surgical teams as quickly as possible.

One of the "inmates," Hendrik Wijburg, was in reality a member of the underground hiding out in the asylum. "The Germans," he recalls, "were not actually inside the institute at the moment, although they did have positions nearby and artillery and ammunition stored in the woods." During the bombings when the dump was hit, Wijburg, on the veranda of one building, was knocked to the floor. "There was a huge explosion," he remembers, "and shells from the dump began whizzing into the hospital, killing and injuring many." Wijburg hastily scrambled to his feet and helped nurses, at the height of the strafing attacks, to lay out white sheets forming a huge cross on the grass. The entire area had been so badly hit that it looked to him as if "the place would soon be filled to the rafters with the dead and dying."

In Arnhem, fire brigades fought desperately to bring the spreading flames under control. Dirk Hiddink, in charge of a fifteen-man outdated fire-fighting unit (his men pushed two carts—one loaded with coiled hoses, the other with ladders), was ordered to the German-occupied Willems Barracks, which had received direct hits from low-flying Mosquitoes. Although the barracks were blazing, Hiddink's instructions from the Arnhem Fire Brigade Headquarters were unusual: let them burn down, he was told, but protect the surrounding houses. When his unit arrived, Hiddink saw that it would have been impossible to save the barracks in any case. The fires were too far advanced.

From his father's apartment at Willemsplein 28, Gerhardus Gysbers saw everything around him engulfed in flames. Not only the barracks, but the nearby high school and the Royal Restaurant, opposite, were burning. The heat was so intense that Gysbers remembers "the glass in our windows suddenly became wavy and then melted completely." The family evacuated the building immediately, scrambling over bricks and lumber into the square. Gysbers saw Germans stumbling from the blasted rubble of the barracks with blood pouring from their noses and ears. Streetcar driver Hendrik Karel reached the Willemsplein unintentionally. With the electric power cut by the bombing, Karel's pale-yellow streetcar coasted down a slight incline to reach a stop at the square. There he found a jumble of other streetcars which, like his own, had coasted into the square and were unable to leave. Through the smoke, crowds and debris, Karel saw waiters from the Royal Restaurant make their escape from the burning building. Abandoning the few diners who were heading for the doors, the waiters jumped right through the windows.

At the Municipal Gas Works just southeast of the great Arnhem bridge, technician Nicolaas Unck admired the skill of the bombardiers. Looking across the Rhine, he saw that twelve anti-aircraft positions had been knocked out. Only one gun was left but its barrels were twisted and bent. Now that the city was without electricity, Unck was faced with his own problems. The technicians could no longer make gas. After the fuel remaining in the three huge gasometers was exhausted, there would be no more. Aside from coal and firewood, Arnhem was now without electricity, heating or cooking fuels.

Thousands of people remained cloistered in their churches. In the huge Dutch Reformed "Grote Kerk" Church alone, there were 1,200 people, Sexton Jan Mijnhart remembers. "Even though we had clearly heard the bombs exploding outside," he says, "the Reverend Johan Gerritsen had calmly continued his sermon. When the power was cut off, the organ stopped. Some one of the congregation came forward and began pumping the bellows manually." Then, against a background of sirens, explosions and thundering planes, the organ pealed out and the entire congregation stood up to sing the "Wilhelmus," the Dutch national anthem.

In the nearby Calvinist church, near the Arnhem railroad station, Gijsbert Numan of the resistance listened to a sermon delivered by Dominee Both. Numan felt that even the intense bombing would not deter the Germans from carrying out their threat to execute civilian hostages sometime during the day in reprisal for the resistance's attack on the viaduct. His conscience bothered him as he listened to Dominee Both's sermon on "the responsibility for your acts toward God and your fellow man," and he decided that once the service had ended, he would give himself up to the Germans. Leaving the church, Numan made his way through the littered streets to a telephone. There, he called Pieter Kruyff and told the regional commander his decision. Kruyff was blunt and to the point. "Rejected," he told Numan. "Carry on with your work." But Kruyff's was not to be the final decision. Market-Garden would save the hostages.

In Nijmegen, eleven miles to the south, bombers had hit German antiaircraft positions with such accuracy that only one was still firing. The great, towering PGEM power station, supplying electricity for the entire province of Gelderland, had received only superficial damage, but high-tension wires were severed, cutting off power throughout the area. A rayon factory near the PGEM station was badly damaged and ablaze. Houses in many parts of the city had received direct hits. Bombs had fallen on a girls' school and a large Catholic social center. Across the Waal in the village of Lent, a factory was destroyed and ammunition dumps exploded.

In the city's air-raid command post, the staff worked by candlelight. The air-raid workers were more and more puzzled by the stream of reports piling in. Working at his desk in semidarkness, Albertus Uijen registered the incoming reports and found himself growing more confused by the moment. The widespread bombings gave no clear picture of what was happening, except that all German positions on Nijmegen's perimeter had been attacked.

The principal approaches to the city—Waalbrug, St. Annastraat and Groesbeekseweg—were now blocked off. It almost seemed that an effort had been made to isolate the city.

As in Arnhem, most people in Nijmegen sought shelter from the fighters continually strafing the streets, but Elias Broekkamp, whose house was not far from the Waal bridge, had climbed to the roof for a better look. To Broekkamp's astonishment, so had the personnel of the German Town Major's office, five houses from Broekkamp's. The Germans, Broekkamp remembers, "looked very anxious. I looked, obviously, full of delight. I even remarked that the weather was lovely."

Nurse Johanna Breman watched Germans panic during the strafing. From a second-floor window of an apartment building south of the Waal bridge, Nurse Breman looked down at "wounded German soldiers helping each other along. Some were limping quite badly and I could see many with bandages. Their tunics were open and most had not even bothered to put their helmets on. On their heels came German infantrymen. As they headed toward the bridge, they fired into the windows whenever they saw Dutch peering out." When the Germans reached the bridge approaches, they began digging foxholes. "They dug everywhere," Miss Breman remembers, "next to the street leading up to the bridge, in grassy areas nearby and beneath trees. I was sure the invasion was coming and I remember thinking, 'What a beautiful view of the battle we shall have from here.' I had a feeling of expectancy." Nurse Breman's expectations did not include her marriage some months later to Master Sergeant Charles Mason of the 82nd, who would land in Glider 13 near the Groesbeek Heights, two miles southwest of her apartment.

Some towns and villages on the edges of the major Market-Garden objectives suffered damage as severe as the principal targets and had little, if any, rescue services. Close by the hamlet of Zeelst, approximately five miles west of Eindhoven, Gerardus de Wit had taken shelter in a beet field during the bombings. There had been no air raid alarm. He had seen planes high in the sky, and suddenly bombs rained down. De Wit, on a visit to his brother in the village of Veldhoven, four miles south, had turned around, pulled off the road and dived into a ditch adjoining the field. Now, he was frantic to get back to his wife and their eleven children.

Although planes were strafing, De Wit decided to risk the trip. Raising his head to look across the field, he saw that "even the leaves were scorched." Leaving his cycle behind, he climbed out of the ditch and ran across the open field. As he neared the village, he noted that bombs presumably intended for the Welschap airfield outside Eindhoven had fallen, instead, directly on little Zeelst. De Wit could see nothing but ruins. Several houses were burning, others had collapsed; and people stood about dazed and crying. One of De Wit's acquaintances, Mrs. Van Helmont, a widow, spotted him and begged him to come with her to cover a dead boy with a sheet. Tearfully, she explained that she could not do it herself. The child had been decapitated, but De Wit recognized the body as a neighbor's son. Quickly, he covered the corpse. "I didn't look at anything more," he remembers. "I just tried to get home as quickly as possible." As he neared his own house, a neighbor who lived opposite tried to detain him. "I'm bleeding to death," the man called out. "I've been hit by a bomb splinter."

At that moment, De Wit saw his wife, Adriana, standing in the street crying. She ran to him. "I thought you'd never get here," she told him. "Come quickly. Our Tiny has been hit." De Wit went past his injured neighbor. "I never thought of anything but my son. When I got to him I saw that the whole of his right side was open and his right leg was cut almost through. He was still fully conscious and asked for water. I saw that his right arm was missing. He asked me about his arm and, to comfort him, I said, 'You're lying on it.'" As De Wit knelt by the boy, a doctor arrived. "He told me not to hope anymore," De Wit remembers, "because our son was going to die." Cradling the boy, De Wit set out for the Duc George cigar factory, where a Red Cross post had been set up. Before he reached the factory, his fourteen-year-old son died in his arms.

In all the terror, confusion and hope, few of the Dutch saw the vanguard of the Allied Airborne Army. At approximately 12:40 P.M., twelve British Stirling bombers swept in over the Arnhem area. At 12:47, four U.S. C-47's appeared over the heaths north of Eindhoven, while two others flew across the open fields southwest of Nijmegen, close to the town of Overasselt. In the planes were British and American pathfinders.

Returning to his farm bordering Renkum heath, less than a mile from Wolfheze, Jan Pennings saw planes coming from the west, flying low. He thought they had returned to bomb the railway line. He watched them warily, ready to dive for cover if bombs dropped. As the planes came over Renkum heath, the astounded Pennings saw "bundles dropped, and then parachutists coming out. I knew that in Normandy the Allies had used parachutists and I was sure this was the beginning of *our* invasion."

Minutes later, cycling up to his farm, Jan shouted to his wife, "Come out! We're free!" Then, the first paratroopers he had ever seen walked into the farmyard. Dazed and awed, Pennings shook their hands. Within half an hour, they told him, "hundreds more of us will arrive."

Chauffeur Jan Peelen too saw the pathfinders land on Renkum heath. He recalls that "they came down almost silently. They were well-disciplined and immediately began to peg out the heath." Like other pathfinders north of the railway line, they were marking out the landing and dropping zones.

Fifteen miles south, near the town of Overasselt, nineteen-year-old Theodorus Roelofs, in hiding from the Germans, was suddenly liberated by 82nd Airborne pathfinders who landed in the vicinity of the family farm. The Americans, he remembers, were "scouts, and my big fear was that this small group of braves could easily be done away with." The pathfinders wasted little time. Discovering that the young Dutchman spoke English, they quickly enlisted Roelofs to help as guide and interpreter. Confirming positions on their maps and directing them to the designated landing sites, Roelofs watched with fascination as the troopers marked the area with "colored strips and smoke stoves." Within three minutes a yellow-paneled "O" and violet smoke clearly outlined the area.

The four C-47's carrying the 101st pathfinders to zones north of Eindhoven ran into heavy antiaircraft fire. One planeload was shot down in flames. There were only four survivors. The other three planes continued on, and the pathfinders dropped accurately on the 101st's two zones. By 12:54 P.M. dropping and landing zones throughout the entire Market-Garden area were located and marked. Incredibly, the Germans still had not raised an alarm.

At Hoenderloo barracks, Lieutenant Colonel Walter Harzer, commander of the Hohenstaufen Division, toasted newly decorated Captain Paul Gräbner. A few minutes before, Harzer had seen a few parachutes fall to the west of Arnhem. He was not surprised. He thought they were bailed-out bomber crews. In Oosterbeek, at the Tafelberg Hotel, Field Marshal Model was having a preluncheon aperitif—a glass of chilled Moselle—with his chief of staff, Lieutenant General Hans Krebs, the operations officer Colonel Hans von Tempelhof and the headquarters adjutant Colonel Leodegard Freyberg. As administrations officer Lieutenant Gustav Sedelhauser remembers, "Whenever he was at the headquarters, the Field Marshal was punctual to a fault. We always sat down to luncheon at precisely 1300 hours." That time was H Hour for the Market forces.

✧ 3 ✧

Now, IN TIGHT FORMATIONS, the great procession of C-47's carrying the 101st Airborne thundered across Allied-held Belgium. Some twenty-five miles beyond Brussels, the serials swung north heading for the Dutch border. Then, men in the planes looked down and, for the first time, saw their earthbound counterpart, the Garden forces whose ground attack was to be synchronized with the air assault. It was a spectacular, unforgettable sight. The vast panoply of General Horrocks' XXX Corps spread out over every field, trail and road. Massed columns of tanks, half-tracks, armored cars and personnel carriers and line after line of guns stood poised for the breakout. On tank antennas pennants fluttered in the wind, and thousands of Britishers standing on vehicles and crowding the fields waved up to the men of the airborne. Orange smoke billowing into the air marked the British front line. Beyond was the enemy.

Skimming the ground, fighter-bombers led the way to the drop zones, attempting to clear everything ahead of the formations. Even though the intense bombing that preceded the airborne assault had leveled many antiaircraft batteries, camouflaged nettings suddenly swung back to reveal hidden enemy positions. Some men remember seeing the tops of haystacks open to disclose nests of 88 and 20 mm. guns. Despite the thoroughness of the fighter-plane attacks, it was impossible to silence all enemy opposition. Just seven minutes away from their drop zones north of Eindhoven, the men of the 101st ran into intense flak.

Pfc. John Cipolla was dozing when he was suddenly awakto Nijmegen

AA R.

WILLEMS CANAL

1 ST BATTALION 501 REGT.

Uden

MARSH

501 REGT. LESS 1ST. BATTALION

Veghel

MARSH

Glider with Market-Garden plans lands and is captured near Student's Hq.

DOMMEL R.

AA R.

WILLEMS CANAL

St. Oedenrode

1ST BATTALION

502 REGT.

DIV. HQ., SIG. CO., MED. CO., RECON. PLAT. & TRANSP. LANDED BY PARACHUTE & GLIDER

506 REGT.

CO. H

Best

FOREST

Son

BRIDGE BLOWN

WILHELMINA CANAL

N

EINDHOVEN

DOMMEL R.

ASSAULT AREA U.S. 101st AIRBORNE DIV.

SEPT. 17, 1944

palacios

0   Miles   4

ened by "the sharp crack of antiaircraft guns, and shrapnel ripped through our plane." Like everyone else, Cipolla was so weighted down by equipment that he could hardly move. Besides his rifle, knapsack, raincoat and blanket, he had ammunition belts draping his shoulders, pockets full of hand grenades, rations and his main parachute plus reserve. In addition, in his plane, each man carried a land mine. As he recalls, " a C-47 on our left flank burst into flames, then another, and I thought 'My God, we are next! How will I ever get out of this plane!' "

His C-47 was shuddering and everyone seemed to be yelling at the same time, "Let's get out! We've been hit!" The jumpmaster gave the order to "Stand up and hook up." Then he calmly began an equipment check. Cipolla could hear the men as they called out, "One O.K. Two O.K. Three O.K." It seemed hours before Cipolla, the last man of the stick, was able to shout, "Twenty-one O.K." Then the green light went on and, in a rush, the men were out and falling, parachutes blossoming above them. Looking up to check his canopy, Cipolla saw that the C-47 he had just left was blazing. As he watched, the plane went down in flames.

Despite the bursting shells that engulfed the planes, the formations did not waver. The pilots of the IX Troop Carrier Command held to their courses without deviating. Second Lieutenant Robert O'Connell remembers that his formation flew so tight, "I thought our pilot was going to stick his wing into the ear of the pilot flying on our left." O'Connell's plane was on fire. The red prejump warning light was on, and "so much smoke was fogging the aisle that I could not see back to the end of my stick." Men were coughing and yelling to get out. O'Connell "braced himself against the door to keep them in." The pilots flew on steadily, without taking evasive action, and O'Connell saw that the formation was gradually losing altitude and slowing down, preparatory to the jump. O'Connell hoped that "if the pilot thought the ship was going down, he would give us the green in time for the troops to get out." Calmly, the pilot held his flaming plane on course until he was right over the drop zone. Then the green light went on and O'Connell and his men jumped safely. O'Connell learned later that the plane crash-landed but the crew survived.

In total disregard for their own safety, troop-carrier pilots brought their planes through the flak and over the drop zones. "Don't worry about me," Second Lieutenant Herbert E. Shulman, the pilot of one burning C-47, radioed his flight commander. "I'm going to drop these troops right on the DZ." He did. Paratroopers left the plane safely. Moments later, it crashed in flames. Staff Sergeant Charles A. Mitchell watched in horror as the plane to his left streamed flame from its port engine. As the pilot held it steady on course, Mitchell saw the entire stick of paratroopers jump right through the fire.

Tragedies did not end there. Pfc. Paul Johnson was forward next to the pilot's cabin when his plane was hit dead center and both fuel tanks caught fire. Of the sixteen paratroopers, pilot and copilot, only Johnson and two other troopers got out. They had to climb over the dead in the plane to make their jumps. Each survivor was badly burned and Johnson's hair was completely seared away. The three came down in a German tank-bivouac area. For half an hour they fought off the enemy from a ditch. Then, all three injured, they were overwhelmed and taken prisoner.

Just as the green light went on in another plane, the lead paratrooper, standing in the door, was killed. He fell back on Corporal John Altomare. His body was quickly moved aside and the rest of the group jumped. And, as another stick of troopers floated to the ground, a C-47 out of control hit two of them, its propellers chopping them to pieces.

Typically, the Americans found humor even in the terrifying approach to the drop zones. Just after Captain Cecil Lee stood to hook up, his plane was hit. Shrapnel ripped a hole through the seat he had just vacated. Nearby, a trooper shouted disgustedly, "*Now* they give us a latrine!" In another plane, Second Lieutenant Anthony Borrelli was sure he was paralyzed. The red light went on and everyone hooked up—except Borrelli, who couldn't move. An officer for only two weeks and on his first combat mission, Borrelli, who was Number 1 in the stick, was conscious of all eyes on him. To his embarrassment, he discovered he had hooked his belt to the seat. Private Robert Boyce made the trip despite the good intentions of the division dentist, who had marked him "L.O.B." (Left Out of Battle) because of his dental problems. With the intervention of his company commander, Boyce, a Normandy veteran, was permitted to go. Besides a bad tooth, he had other worries. Several new paratroop innovations— leg packs for machine guns, quick-release harness on some chutes and combat instead of jump boots—made him and many other men nervous. In particular, the troopers were concerned that their shroud lines might catch on the buckles of their new combat boots. As his plane flew low in its approach, Boyce saw Dutch civilians below holding up two fingers in the V-for-victory salute. That was all Boyce needed. "Hey, look," he called to the others, "they're giving us two to one we don't make it."

The odds against their ever reaching their drop zones seemed at least that high to many. Colonel Robert F. Sink, commander of the 506th Regiment, saw "a tremendous volume of flak coming up to greet us." As he was looking out the door, the plane shuddered violently and Sink saw a part of the wing tear and dangle. He turned to the men in his stick and said, "Well, there goes the wing." To Sink's relief, "nobody seemed to think much about it. They figured by this time we were practically in."

In plane Number 2, Sink's executive officer, Lieutenant Colonel Charles Chase, saw that their left wing was afire. Captain Thomas Mulvey remembers that Chase stared at it for a minute and then remarked mildly, "I guess they're catching up on us. We'd better go." As the green light went on in both planes, the men jumped safely. The plane in which Chase was traveling burned on the ground. Sink's plane, with its damaged wing, is thought to have made the journey back to England safely.

Similar intense flak engulfed the serials of the 502nd Regiment, and planes of two groups almost collided. One serial, slightly off course, strayed into the path of a second group, causing the latter to climb for altitude and its troopers to make a higher jump than had been planned. In the lead plane of one of the serials was the division commander, General Maxwell D. Taylor, and the 502nd's 1st Battalion commander, Lieutenant Colonel Patrick Cassidy. Standing in the doorway, Cassidy saw one of the planes in the group burst into flames. He counted only seven parachutes. Then fire broke out in another C-47 just off to the left. All the paratroopers jumped from it. Mesmerized by the blazing plane, Cassidy failed to notice that the green light was on. General Taylor, standing behind him, said quietly, "Cassidy, the light's on." Automatically Cassidy answered, "Yes, sir. I know it," and jumped. Taylor was right behind him.

To General Taylor, the 101st jump was "unusually successful; almost like an exercise." In the initial planning, Taylor's staff had anticipated casualties as high as 30 percent. Of the 6,695 paratroopers who enplaned in England, 6,669 actually jumped. Despite the intense flak, the bravery of the C-47 and fighter pilots gave the 101st an almost perfect jump. Although some units were dropped from one to three miles north of the drop zones, they landed so close together that assembly was quick. Only two planes failed to reach the drop zone, and the IX Troop Carrier Command took the brunt of all casualties by their heroic determination to get the troopers to their targets. Of the 424 C-47's carrying the 101st, every fourth plane was damaged, and sixteen went down, killing their crews.

Glider losses were heavy, too. Later, as these serials began to come in, only 53 of the original 70 would arrive without mishap on the landing zone near Son. Still, despite abortions, enemy flak and crash-landings, the gliders would eventually deliver nearly 80 percent of the men and 75 percent of the jeeps and trailers they carried.* Now, Taylor's Screaming Eagles began to move on their

---

* Because Market-Garden was considered an all-British operation, few American correspondents were accredited to cover the attack. None was at Arnhem. One of the Americans attached to the 101st was a United Press reporter named Walter Cronkite, who landed by glider. Cronkite recalls that "I thought the wheels of the glider were for landing. Imagine my surprise when we skidded along the ground and the wheels came up through the floor. I got another shock. Our helmets, which we all swore were hooked, came flying off on impact and seemed more dangerous than the incoming shells. After landing I grabbed the first helmet I saw, my trusty musette bag with the Olivetti typewriter inside and began crawling toward the canal which was the rendezvous point. When I looked back, I found a half dozen

objectives—the bridges and crossings over the vital fifteen-mile stretch of corridor ahead of the British ground forces.

☼ 4 ☼

COLONEL GENERAL KURT STUDENT and his chief of staff, Colonel Reinhard, stood on the balcony of the General's cottage near Vught and "simply stared, stunned, like fools." Student remembers clearly that "everywhere we looked, we saw chains of planes—fighters, troop carriers and cargo planes—flying over us. We climbed onto the roof of the house to get a better idea of just where these units were going." Streams of planes seemed to be heading in the direction of Grave and Nijmegen and, only a few miles to the south near Eindhoven and Son, he could clearly see troop carriers—one after the other—coming in and dropping paratroopers and equipment. Some aircraft flew so low that Student and Reinhard instinctively ducked. "On the grounds of the headquarters, our clerks, quartermasters, drivers and signalmen were out in the open, firing with all sorts of weapons. As usual, there was no sign of our own fighter planes." Student was completely baffled. "I could not tell what was happening or where these airborne units were going. In these moments, I never once thought of the danger of our own position." But Student, the paratroop expert, was filled with admiration and envy. "This mighty spectacle deeply impressed me. I thought with reflection and longing of our own airborne operations and I said to Reinhard, 'Oh, if ever I'd had such means at my disposal. Just once, to have this many planes!'" Rein-

---

guys crawling after me. It seems that I had grabbed the wrong helmet. The one I wore had two neat stripes down the back indicating that I was a lieutenant."

hard's feelings were very much in the present. "Herr General," he told Student, "we've got to *do* something!" They left the roof and went back to Student's office.

Only the previous evening, Student, in his daily report, had warned, "Heavy columns of traffic south of the Maas-Schelde Canal indicate an impending attack." The problem was: had it already begun? If so, then these airborne units were after the bridges around Eindhoven, Grave and Nijmegen. All the spans were prepared for demolition and protected by special engineer parties and security detachments. A bridge commander had been assigned to each crossing with strict orders to destroy the bridge in case of attack. "The obvious move for the Allies," it occurred to Student, "was to use airborne troops in this situation to seize the bridges before we could destroy them." At this time, Student did not even think of the importance of the Lower Rhine bridge at Arnhem. "Get me Model," he told Reinhard.

Reinhard picked up the phone to discover that the telephone lines were out. The headquarters was already cut off.

In Oosterbeek, some thirty-seven miles away, at the Tafelberg Hotel, Lieutenant Gustav Sedelhauser, Model's administration officer, was angry. "Are you hung over from last night?" he shouted into a field phone. Unteroffizier Youppinger, one of the 250-man company which, under Sedelhauser, was assigned to protect Model, repeated what he had said. At Wolfheze, "gliders are landing in our laps," he insisted. Sedelhauser slammed down the phone and rushed into the operations office, where he reported the message to a startled lieutenant colonel. Together, they hurried to the dining room, where Model and his chief of staff General Krebs were at lunch. "I've just had news that gliders are landing at Wolfheze," the colonel said. The operations officer, Colonel Tempelhof, stared; the monocle fell out of Krebs's eye. "Well, now we're for it," Tempelhof said.

Model jumped to his feet and issued a flurry of orders to evacuate the headquarters. As he headed out of the dining room to collect his own belongings, he shouted back over his shoulder, "They're after me and this headquarters!" Moments later, carrying only a small case, Model rushed through the Tafelberg's entrance. On the sidewalk he dropped the case, which flew open, spilling his linens and toilet articles.

Krebs followed Model outside in such haste that, Sedelhauser saw, "he had even forgotten his cap, pistol and belt." Tempelhof had not even had time to remove the war maps in the operations office. Colonel Freyberg, the headquarters adjutant, was equally rushed. As he passed Sedelhauser, he shouted, "Don't forget my cigars." At his car, Model told his driver, Frombeck, "Quick! Doetinchem! Bittrich's headquarters!"

Sedelhauser waited until the car drove off and then returned to the hotel. In the operations office, he saw the war maps—showing positions all the way from Holland to Switzerland—still on a table. He rolled them up and took them with him. Then he ordered the Hartenstein Hotel and the Tafelberg immediately evacuated; all transport, he said, "every car, truck and motorbike, is to leave here immediately." The last report he received before leaving for Doetinchem was that the British were less than two miles away. In all the confusion he completely forgot Freyberg's cigars.

❈ 5 ❈

Surrounded by ground haze and the smoke and fire of burning buildings, the mighty British glider fleet was landing. Already the areas marked by orange and crimson nylon strips were beginning

4TH PARACHUTE
BRIGADE
(HACKETT)
SEPT. 18

URQUHART
1ST BRITISH
AIRBORNE DIV.
1ST AIR LANDING BRIGADE
(HICKS)
1ST PARACHUTE BRIGADE
(LATHBURY)
4TH PARACHUTE BRIGADE
(HACKETT)
1ST POLISH BRIGADE
(SOSABOWSKI)

1ST
PARACHUTE
BRIGADE
(LATHBURY)
SEPT. 17

EDE-ARNHEM HIGHWAY

DOBIE'S 1ST BATTALION (LEOPARD)

SUPPLIES
DROP ZONE

WOLFHEZE

1ST. AIR LANDING
BRIGADE (HICKS)
&
1ST PARACHUTE
BRIGADE (LATHBURY)
SEPT. 17

KRAFFT'S SS BATTALION

FITCH'S 3RD BATTALION (TIGER)

FROST'S 2ND BATTALION (LION)

HARTENS
HOTEL

RENKUM

HEELSUM

SECONDARY ROAD

FERRY

← LOWER RHINE

DRIEL

palacios

ARNHEM
THE ATTACK
D·DAY SEPT. 17, 1944

0   Miles   1

N

BITTRICH
II SS PANZER CORPS

SUPPLIES
DROP ZONE

9TH SS PANZER

HARZER
"HOHENSTAUFEN" DIV.

UTRECHT-ARNHEM
HIGHWAY

10TH SS PANZER "FRUNDSBERG" DIV.

HARMEL

OSTERBEEK

ARNHEM

PONTOON
BRIDGE

ARNHEM
BRIDGE

SS PANZER
GRENADIERS

RAILWAY
BRIDGE

ELDEN

GRÄBNER'S
RECONNAISSANCE
UNIT

POLISH 1ST BRIGADE
(SOSABOWSKI)

to Nijmegen

to look like vast aircraft parking lots. Blue smoke eddied up from the two landing zones—"Reyers Camp Farm" to the north and "Renkum Heath" to the southwest—near Wolfheze. From these zones, in chain after chain, tugs and gliders stretched back almost twenty miles to their approach point near the town of s'Hertogenbosch, southwest of Nijmegen. Swarms of fighters protected these ponderous columns. Traffic was so dense that pilots were reminded of the rush-hour congestion around London's busy Piccadilly Circus.

The serials—each group separated from the next by a four-minute interval—flew slowly over the flat, water-veined Dutch countryside. The landmarks pilots had been briefed to recognize now began to pass beneath them: the great wide rivers Maas and Waal and up ahead, the Lower Rhine. Then, as each formation began its descent, men saw Arnhem off to the right and their vital objectives: the rail and highway bridges. Incredibly, despite the R.A.F. prediction of intense antiaircraft fire, the immense glider cavalcade encountered virtually no resistance. The preassault bombings had been far more effective around Arnhem than in the Eindhoven area. Not a single tug or glider was shot down in making the approach.

With clocklike precision, the skilled pilots of the R.A.F. and the Glider Pilot Regiment came over the zones. As gliders cast off, their tugs made climbing turns to free air space for the combinations coming up behind. These intricate maneuvers and the heavy traffic were causing problems of their own. Sergeant Pilot Bryan Tomblin remembers chaotic congestion over the landing zones. "There were gliders, tugs, ropes and all sorts of things in the sky," he recalls. "You had to be on the lookout all the time."

Staff Sergeant Victor Miller, piloting a Horsa, recalls coming in over the Lower Rhine and finding it "unbelievably calm." Beyond, he suddenly spotted his landing zone, with its "triangular-shaped woods and little farm nestling in the far corner." Seconds later, Miller heard the voice of his Stirling tug's navigator. "O.K. Number 2. When you're ready." Miller acknowledged. "Good luck, Number 2," the navigator told him. Miller immediately cast off. His tug disappeared, the tow rope flapping in its wake. It would be dropped, Miller knew, "on the enemy as a parting gift before the Stirling turned onto its homeward course."

The glider's air speed fell off and the field loomed nearer. Miller called for half-flaps and his copilot, Sergeant Tom Hollingsworth, instantly pushed a lever. For a moment the glider bucked, "as the great flaps descending from underneath each wing braked against our speed." The landing zone, Miller estimated, was now less than a mile away. "I reminded Tom to look out for gliders on his side. One slid across and above us less than fifty yards away," and, to Miller's amazement, "swung in on the same course. Another glider seemed to be drifting into us from starboard. I don't think the pilot even saw us, he was so intent on getting down in the field." To avoid collision, Miller deliberately dived under the incoming glider. "A great black shape flashed over our cockpit, too close for my liking. I was concentrating so hard to set down in one piece that I never wondered if the enemy was firing at us—not that we could have done much about it."

Miller continued his descent with "tree tops leaping toward our floor boards and past the wings. As the ground rushed up, another glider came alongside. I pulled back on the wheel, leveled, we hit once, bounced about three feet, and came down to stay. Tom had slammed on the brakes and we careened across the plowed field. Then the wheels sank into soft soil and we ground to a halt fifty yards short of a heavy-looking line of trees." In the silence, after the continuous deafening roar of the slip stream, Miller heard the distant crackle of small-arms fire, "but my one thought was to get out of the glider before another crashed or landed on us. I was the last man out. I didn't even pause, but jumped straight through the ramp door and hit the ground of Holland, four feet below, rather hard."

The glider in which Signalman Graham Marples was riding circled and came back over its landing zone because of the congestion. "But, by then, we had run out of wind," Marples remembers. "I saw trees coming through the glider floor. They just ripped the floor to pieces, and the next thing I knew, we nosed over and came down. I could hear everything breaking, like dry twigs snapping. We landed squarely on our nose but no one was hurt except for a few scratches and bruises." Later, the pilot told Marples he had pulled up to avoid collision with another glider.

Many gliders, having surmounted all the problems of the long trip, touched down to disaster. Staff Sergeant George Davis stood near his empty Horsa and watched other gliders come in. One of the first to land, Davis had brought in thirty-two men of the 1st Airlanding Brigade. He saw two gliders "almost side by side bump across the landing zone and into the trees. The wings of both were sheared off." Seconds later, another Horsa rumbled in. Its speed was such that Davis knew it would never be able to stop in time. The glider plowed into the trees. No one got out. With his copilot, Staff Sergeant Williams, Davis ran to the glider and looked into the plexiglass-covered cockpit. Everyone inside was dead. A 75 mm. howitzer had broken from its chain mooring, crushing the gun crew and decapitating the pilot and copilot.

Lieutenant Michael Dauncey had just landed his glider—carrying a jeep, trailer and six gunners from an artillery battery—when he saw a huge eight-ton Hamilcar touch down. "The field was soft," he recalls, "and I saw the nose of the Hamilcar digging up earth in front of it." Weight and ground speed drove it deeper until the huge tail rose up in the air and the Hamilcar flipped over on its back. Dauncey knew "it was useless to try to dig them out. A Horsa's flat on top but a Hamilcar's got a hump where the pilots sit, and we knew the pilots were finished."

Making his approach in another Hamilcar, Staff Sergeant Gordon Jenks saw the same crash and immediately deduced that the ground ahead was too soft. Instantly, he decided against landing in the field. "I reckoned if we went into a dive right then," he remembers, "we would have enough speed for me to hold her off the deck until we had cleared the fence and got safely into the next field." Jenks pushed the control column forward, dived, then leveled out a few feet above the ground. Easing the huge aircraft gently over the fence, Jenks "put her down in the far field as lightly as a feather."

All over the landing zones now the tails of gliders were being unbolted and swung back, and artillery pieces, equipment, stores, jeeps and trailers were being unloaded. The men in Lance Corporal Henry Brook's glider, like many others, found that the unloading maneuver was fine in theory but more difficult in practice. "There were eight pins with a protective wire holding the glider tail on," Brook explained. "Back in England in practice exercises, you could always get the tail off and jeep and trailer out in two minutes flat. In action, it was different. We cut the wire and got the pins out but the tail wouldn't budge." Brook and the other troopers finally chopped it off. Lance Bombardier J. W. Crook was similarly frustrated, but a nearby jeep came to the aid of his men and, with its hawser, yanked off the tail.

All over the two zones men were beginning to salvage cargo from wrecked gliders. The crash of two giant Hamilcars was a serious loss. They contained a pair of 17-pound artillery pieces plus three-ton trucks and ammunition trailers. But all of the fifteen 75 mm. pack howitzers of the 1st Airlanding Light Regiment artillery arrived safely.

Most men who came in by glider recall a strange, almost eerie silence immediately after landing. Then, from the assembly point, men heard the skirl of bagpipes playing "Blue Bonnets." At about the same time, soldiers on the edge of Renkum Heath saw Dutch civilians wandering aimlessly through the woods or hiding in fright. Lieutenant Neville Hay of the Phantom unit remembers that "it was a sobering sight. Some were in white hospital gowns and seemed to be herded along by attendants. Men and women capered about, waving, laughing and jabbering. They were obviously quite mad." Glider Pilot Victor Miller was startled by voices in the woods. Then, "groups of weird white-clothed men and women filed past." It was only later that the troopers learned the strangely behaved civilians were inmates from the bombed Wolfheze Psychiatric Institute.

General Urquhart had landed at Renkum Heath. He too was struck by the stillness. "It was," he recalls, "incredibly quiet. Unreal." While his chief of staff, Colonel Charles Mackenzie, set up the division's tactical headquarters at the edge of the woods, Urquhart headed for the parachute dropping zones, four hundred yards away. It was nearly time for Brigadier Lathbury's 1st Parachute Brigade to arrive. From the distance came the drone of approaching aircraft. The bustle and activity all over the glider zones paused as men looked up to see the long lines of C-47's. Small-arms and antiaircraft fire during the paratroop drop was as limited and spasmodic as during the glider landings. At exactly 1:53 P.M., and for the next fifteen minutes, the sky was filled with brilliant-colored parachutes as the 1st Brigade began jumping. Some 650 parapacks with bright-yellow, red and brown chutes—carrying guns, ammunition and equipment—fell rapidly through the streams of troopers. Other supply chutes, pushed out of the planes before the men jumped, floated down with a variety of cargo, including miniature foldable motorcycles. Many already overburdened paratroopers also jumped with large kitbags. In theory, these were to be lowered by a cord just before the men touched ground. Scores of the packs broke away from troopers and smashed on the zones. Several contained precious radio sets.

British Private Harry Wright jumped from an American C-47. As he fell through the air, he lost both his helmet and kitbag. He hit the ground very hard. Regimental Quartermaster Sergeant Robertson came running up. Wright's forehead was streaming blood. "Were you hit by flak?" Robertson asked. Wright slowly shook his head. "No, sarge," he said. "It was that bloody Yank. We were going too fast when we jumped." Robertson applied a dressing and then, to Wright's surprise, offered the injured man a pork pie from his haversack. "I nearly died right then of the shock," Wright recalls. "First, Robertson was a Scot, and then, as a quartermaster, he never offered anyone anything."

Odd things seemed to be happening all over the drop zones. The first person Sergeant Norman Swift saw when he landed was Sergeant Major Les Ellis, who was passing by holding a dead partridge. The amazed Swift asked where the bird had come from. "I landed on it," Ellis explained. "Who knows? It'll be a bit of all right later on, in case we're hungry."

Sapper Ronald Emery had just slipped out of his chute when an elderly Dutch lady scuttled across the field, grabbed it up and raced away, leaving the startled Emery staring after her. In another part of the field, Corporal Geoffrey Stanners, loaded down with equipment, landed on the top of a glider wing. Like a trampoline, the wing sprang up, flipping Stanners back into the air. He landed with both feet on the ground.

Dazed after a hard fall, Lieutenant Robin Vlasto lay still for a few moments, trying to orient himself. He was conscious of "an incredible number of bodies and containers coming down all around me and planes continued to pour out paratroopers." Vlasto decided to get off the drop zone quickly. As he struggled to get out of his harness, he heard a weird sound. Looking around, he saw Lieutenant Colonel John Frost, the 2nd Battalion's commander, walking past, blowing his copper hunting horn.

Frost was also observed by Private James W. Sims. Sims had already gone through quite a day even before he landed. Having always flown with the R.A.F.—whose attitude, Sims recalls, was: "Don't worry, lads, whatever it's like, we'll get you through"— Sims received quite a shock on seeing his American pilot. "He was a lieutenant colonel with one of those soft hats. His flying jacket was hanging open and he was smoking a big cigar. Our lieutenant saluted him quite smartly and asked if the men should move up to the front of the plane on takeoff." The American grinned. "Why, hell, no, lieutenant," Sims remembers him saying. "I'll get this goddam crate off the ground if I have to drag its ass halfway down the runway." Sims's officer was too startled to speak. Now, although he was fond of his colonel, Sims, watching Frost go by, had reached the limit of his patience. Surrounded by his equipment, he sat on the ground and muttered, "There goes old Johnny Frost, a .45 in one hand and that bloody horn in the other."

All over the drop and landing zones, where 5,191 men of the division had arrived safely, units were assembling, forming up and moving out. General Urquhart "couldn't have been more pleased. Everything appeared to be going splendidly." The same thought occurred to Sergeant Major John C. Lord. The veteran paratrooper recalls that "this was one of the best exercises I'd ever been on. Everyone was calm and businesslike." But the reservations he'd had before takeoff still bothered Lord. As he looked about, seeing the men assembling rapidly, with no enemy to contend with, he remembers thinking, "It's all too good to be true." Others had the same thought. As one group prepared to move off, Lieutenant Peter Stainforth heard Lieutenant Dennis Simpson say quietly, "Everything is going too well for my liking."

The man with the most urgent task on landing was forty-three-year-old Major Freddie Gough of the 1st Airborne Division reconnaissance unit. Leading a four-troop squadron in heavily armed jeeps, Gough was to make a dash for the bridge before Colonel John Frost's marching battalion reached it. Gough and his men parachuted in, and then sought their ground transport, which was being flown in by glider. Quickly Gough located his second in command, Captain David Allsop, on the landing zone and received some bad news. The entire transport for one of the four units—approximately twenty-two vehicles—had failed to arrive, Allsop reported. Thirty-six of the 320 gliders scheduled for Arnhem had been lost, and with them were lost the jeeps of Gough's A troop. Nevertheless, both Gough and Allsop believed that there were enough vehicles to race for the Arnhem bridge. Gough gave the order to move out. With his force whittled down, everything now depended on the reaction of the Germans.

✲ 6 ✲

I N ALL THE PANIC and confusion, the first German senior officer
to raise the alert was General Wilhelm Bittrich, commander of the
II SS Panzer Corps. At 1:30 P.M., Bittrich received his first report
from the Luftwaffe communications net that airborne troops were
landing in the Arnhem vicinity. A second report, arriving minutes
later, gave the assault area as Arnhem and Nijmegen. Bittrich
could not raise anybody at Field Marshal Model's headquarters at
the Tafelberg in Oosterbeek. Nor was he able to contact either the
town commander of Arnhem or General Student at his headquarters in Vught. Although the situation was obscure, Bittrich immediately thought of General Von Zangen's Fifteenth Army, most
of which had escaped across the mouth of the Schelde and into
Holland. "My first thought was that this airborne attack was designed to contain Von Zangen's army and prevent it from joining
with the remainder of our forces. Then, probably, the objective
would be a drive by the British Army across the Rhine and into
Germany." If his reasoning was correct, Bittrich believed that the
key to such an operation would be the Arnhem-Nijmegen bridges.
Immediately he alerted the 9th Hohenstaufen and the 10th
Frundsberg SS Panzer divisions.

Lieutenant Colonel Walter Harzer, commander of the Hohenstaufen, attending the luncheon following the decoration of Captain Paul Gräbner, was "in the middle of my soup" when Bittrich's call reached him. Tersely, Bittrich explained the situation
and ordered Harzer to "reconnoiter in the direction of Arnhem
and Nijmegen." The Hohenstaufen was to move out immediately,

hold the Arnhem area and destroy airborne troops west of Arnhem near Oosterbeek. Bittrich warned Harzer that "quick action
is imperative. The taking and securing of the Arnhem bridge is of
decisive importance." At the same time, Bittrich ordered the
Frundsberg Division—whose commander, General Harmel, was
in Berlin—to move toward Nijmegen, "to take, hold and defend
the city's bridges."

Harzer was now faced with the problem of unloading the last
Hohenstaufen units, due to leave by train for Germany in less
than an hour—including the "disabled" tanks, half-tracks and
armored personnel carriers he had been determined to keep from
Harmel. Harzer looked at Gräbner. "Now what are we going to
do?" he asked. "The vehicles are dismantled and on the train." Of
these, forty vehicles belonged to Gräbner's reconnaissance battalion. "How soon can you have the tracks and guns put back?"
Harzer demanded. Gräbner immediately called his engineers.
"We'll be ready to move within three to five hours," he told
Harzer. "Get it done in three," Harzer snapped as he headed for
his headquarters.

Although he had guessed right for the wrong reasons, General
Bittrich had set in motion the panzer divisions that Montgomery's
intelligence officers had totally dismissed.

The officer who had been ordered out of Oosterbeek to make
way for Field Marshal Model's headquarters found himself and
his men based almost on the British landing zones. SS Major Sepp
Krafft, commander of the Panzer Grenadier Training and Reserve
Battalion, was "sick to my stomach" with fright. His latest headquarters, in the Wolfheze Hotel, was less than one mile from
Renkum Heath. Bivouacked nearby were two of his companies; a
third was in reserve in Arnhem. From the hotel, Krafft could see
the heath "jammed with gliders and troops, some only a few
hundred yards away." He had always believed that it took hours
for airborne troops to organize, but as he watched "the English

were assembling everywhere and moving off ready to fight." He could not understand why such a force would land in this area. "The only military objective I could think of with any importance was the Arnhem bridge."

The terrified commander knew of no German infantry close by, other than his own understrength battalion. Until help could arrive, Krafft decided that "it was up to me to stop them from getting to the bridge—if that's where they were going." His companies were positioned in a rough triangle, its base—the Wolfheze road—almost bordering Renkum Heath. North of Krafft's headquarters was the main Ede–Arnhem road and the Amsterdam–Utrecht–Arnhem railway line; to the south, the Utrecht road ran via Renkum and Oosterbeek into Arnhem. Because he lacked the strength to maintain a line from one road to the other, Krafft decided to hold positions roughly from the railroad on the north to the Utrecht–Arnhem road to the south. Hurriedly, he ordered his reserve company out of Arnhem to join the rest of the battalion at Wolfheze. Machine-gun platoons were dispatched to hold each end of his line while the remainder of his troops fanned out in the woods.

Although lacking men, Krafft had a new experimental weapon at his disposal: a multibarreled, rocket-propelled launcher capable of throwing oversized mortar shells.* Several of these units had been left with him for training purposes. Now he planned to use them to confuse the British and give an impression of greater strength; at the same time, he ordered twenty-five-man attack groups to make sharp forays which might throw the paratroops off balance.

As Krafft was issuing his directions, a staff car roared up to his headquarters and Major General Kussin, Arnhem's town commander, hurried inside. Kussin had driven out of Arnhem at

---

* This weapon should not be confused with the smaller German mortar thrower, *Nebelwerfer.* Krafft maintains that there were only four of these experimental launchers in existence. I have not been able to check this fact, but I can find no record of a similar weapon on the western front. There is no doubt that it was used with devastating effect against the British. Countless witnesses describe the scream and impact of the oversized mortars, but, inexplicably, there is no discussion of the weapon in any of the British after-action reports.

breakneck speed to see at first-hand what was happening. On the way he had met Field Marshal Model heading east toward Doetinchem. Stopping briefly on the road, Model had instructed Kussin to raise the alert and to inform Berlin of the developments. Now, looking across the heath, Kussin was flabbergasted at the sight of the vast British drop. Almost desperately he told Krafft that somehow he would get reinforcements to the area by 6 P.M. As Kussin started out to make the drive back to Arnhem, Krafft warned him not to take the Utrecht–Arnhem road. Already he had received a report that British troopers were moving along it. "Take the side roads," Krafft told Kussin. "The main road may already be blocked." Kussin was grim-faced. "I'll get through all right," he answered. Krafft watched as the staff car raced off toward the highway.

He was convinced that Kussin's replacements would never reach him, and that it was only a matter of time before his small force would be overpowered. Even as he positioned his troops along the Wolfheze road, Krafft sent his driver, Private Wilhelm Rauh, to collect his personal possessions. "Pack them in the car and head for Germany," Krafft told Rauh. "I don't expect to get out of this alive."

At Bad Saarnow near Berlin, the commander of the 10th Frundsberg Division, General Heinz Harmel, conferred with the chief of Waffen SS Operations, Major General Hans Juttner, and outlined the plight of Bittrich's understrength II Panzer Corps. If the corps was to continue as an effective combat unit, Harmel insisted, "Bittrich's urgent request for men, armor, vehicles and guns must be honored." Juttner promised to do what he could, but he warned that "at this moment the strength of every combat unit is depleted." Everyone wanted priorities, and Juttner could not promise any immediate help. As the two men talked, Juttner's aide entered the office with a radio message. Juttner read it and wordlessly passed it to Harmel. The message read: "Airborne attack Arnhem. Return immediately. Bittrich." Harmel rushed out of the office and got into his car. Arnhem was an eleven-and-a-half-hour drive from Bad Saarnow. To his driver, Corporal Sepp Hinterholzer, Harmel said: "Back to Arnhem—and drive like the devil!"

☆ 7 ☆

Major Anthony Deane-Drummond, second in command of the British 1st Airborne Division Signals, could not understand what was wrong. At one moment his radio sets were getting perfect reception from Brigadier Lathbury's brigade as it headed for its objectives, including the Arnhem bridge. But now, as Lathbury's battalions moved closer to Arnhem, radio signals were fading by the minute. From Deane-Drummond's signalmen came a constant stream of reports that disturbed and puzzled him. They were unable to contact some jeep-borne sets at all, and the signals they received from others were so weak as to be barely audible. Yet the various battalions of Lathbury's brigade and Major Freddie Gough's reconnaissance units could scarcely be more than two to three miles away.

Of particular concern to Deane-Drummond was Lathbury's messages. They were vital to General Urquhart in his direction of the battle. Deane-Drummond decided to send out a jeep with a radio and operator to pick up Lathbury's signals and relay them back to Division. He instructed the team to set up at a point midway between Division and Lathbury's mobile communications. A short time later, Deane-Drummond heard signals from the relay team. The range of their set seemed drastically reduced—at minimum, the "22's" should have operated efficiently at least up to five miles—and the signal was faint. Either the set was not functioning properly, he reasoned, or the operator was poorly located to send. Even as he listened, the signal faded completely. Deane-Drummond was unable to raise anybody. Nor could a special team of American communications operators with two radio jeeps. Hastily assembled and rushed to British Airborne Division headquarters only a few hours before takeoff on the seventeenth, the Americans were to operate ground-to-air "very high frequency" sets to call in fighters for close support. In the first few hours of the battle, these radio jeeps might have made all the difference. Instead, they were found to be useless. Neither jeep's set had been adjusted to the frequencies necessary to call in planes. At this moment, with the battle barely begun, British radio communications had totally broken down.[*]

❊ 8 ❊

AS IF ON SIGNAL, German guns opened up as the planes carrying the 82nd Airborne Division made their approach to the drop zones. Looking down, Brigadier General James M. Gavin saw ground fire spurting from a line of trenches paralleling the Maas-Waal

---

[*] In Christopher Hibbert's *The Battle of Arnhem*, p. 96, dealing specifically with the British at Arnhem and equally critical of British communications, he claims that "American air-support parties were insufficiently trained . . . the disastrous consequence was that not until the last day of the operation . . . was any effective close air support given to the airborne troops." There appears to be no information on who erred in the allocation of the frequencies, nor are the names of the Americans known. The two teams, who found themselves in the middle of the battle with the means of perhaps changing the entire course of history on that vital day, have never been found. Yet these two combat units are the only American ones known to have been in the Arnhem battle.

Canal. In wooded areas, enemy batteries that had remained silent and hidden until now also began to fire. Watching, Gavin wondered if his battle plan for the 82nd, which had been based on a calculated risk, might founder.

Charged with holding the middle sector of the Market-Garden corridor, the division had widespread objectives, running ten miles south-to-north and twelve miles west-to-east. Besides the drop of one paratroop company near the western end of the Grave bridge, which was to be seized by a surprise *coup de main* assault, Gavin had chosen three drop areas and one large landing zone. The latter would accommodate his fifty Waco gliders and the thirty-eight Horsas and Wacos of General Frederick Browning's British I Airborne Corps headquarters. But Gavin had ordered only one drop zone, north of Overasselt, to be marked by pathfinders. The other three, lying close to the Groesbeek ridge and the German border, were deliberately left unmarked. Gavin's paratroopers and gliders would land without identifying beacons or smoke in order to confuse the enemy as to their touchdown areas. Some thirteen minutes after the 82nd was down, Browning's Corps headquarters would land.

Because Gavin's primary concern was that enemy tanks might suddenly emerge from the Reichswald along the German border east of his largest glider and drop zone, he had given two unusual orders. To protect both his division and Browning's headquarters, he had instructed paratroopers to jump close to any antiaircraft batteries they were able to spot from the air and render them useless as quickly as possible. And, for the first time in airborne history, he was parachuting in a complete battalion of field artillery, dropping it onto the large zone directly facing the forest and approximately one and one-half miles from the German border itself. Now, looking at the intense antiaircraft fire and thinking of the possibility of enemy tanks in the Reichswald, Gavin knew that while he had planned for nearly all eventualities, the men of the 82nd faced a tough task.

Gavin's Normandy veterans had never forgotten the slaughter of their own in Ste. Mère Église. Dropped by accident on that village, men had been machine-gunned by the Germans as they came down; many were killed as they hung helpless in their parachutes, from telephone lines and trees around the village square. Not until Ste. Mère Église was finally secured by Lieutenant Colonel Ben Vandervoort were the dead troopers cut down and buried. Now, as the 82nd prepared to jump over Holland, some men called out to troopers still hooked up behind them: "Remember Ste. Mère Église." Although it was a risky procedure, many troopers jumped with their guns blazing.

Captain Briand Beaudin, coming down over his drop zone near the Groesbeek Ridge, saw that he was descending directly over a German antiaircraft emplacement with guns aiming at him. Beaudin began firing with his Colt .45. "Suddenly I realized," Beaudin remembers, "how futile it was, aiming my little pea-shooter while oscillating in the air above large-caliber guns." Landing close to the flak site, Beaudin took the entire crew prisoner. He thinks the Germans "were so startled they couldn't fire a single shot."

First Lieutenant James J. Coyle thought he was heading for a landing on a German tent hospital. Suddenly, enemy troops poured out of the tent and began running for 20 mm. antiaircraft guns around the perimeter. He, too, worked his .45 from its holster but his parachute began to oscillate and Coyle drifted away from the tent. One of the Germans started to run in Coyle's direction. "I couldn't get off a shot at the Kraut," Coyle recalls. "One second I'd be pointing the pistol at the ground; the next, I'd be aiming at the sky. I did have enough sense left to put the Colt back into the holster so I wouldn't drop it or shoot myself when I hit." On the ground, even before he tried to get out of his harness, Coyle drew his pistol once more. "The Kraut was now only a few feet away, but he was acting as though he didn't know I existed. Suddenly I realized that he wasn't running toward me; he was just running away." As the German hurried past Coyle he threw away his gun and helmet, and Coyle could see "he was only a kid, about eighteen years old. I just couldn't shoot an unarmed man. The last I saw of the boy he was running for the German border."

When tracer bullets began ripping through his canopy, Private Edwin C. Raub became so enraged that he deliberately side-slipped his chute so as to land next to the antiaircraft gun. Without removing his harness, and dragging his parachute behind him, Raub rushed the Germans with his Tommy gun. He killed one, captured the others and then, with plastic explosives, destroyed the flak-gun barrels.

Although enemy opposition to the 505th and 508th regiments in the Groesbeek area was officially considered negligible, a considerable amount of antiaircraft and small-arms fire came from the woods surrounding the zones. Without waiting to assemble, 82nd troopers, individually and in small groups, swarmed over these pockets of resistance, quickly subduing them and taking prisoners. Simultaneously, fighter planes skimmed over the tree tops, machine-gunning the enemy emplacements. The Germans scored heavily against these low-level attacks. Within a matter of minutes, three fighters were hit and crashed near the woods. Staff Sergeant Michael Vuletich saw one of them. It cartwheeled across the drop zone and when it finally stopped, only the plane's fuselage was intact. Moments later, the pilot emerged unscathed and stopped by the wreckage to light a cigarette. Vuletich remembers that the downed flier remained with the company as an infantryman.

From the ground, Staff Sergeant James Jones saw a P-47 aflame at about 1,500 feet. He expected the pilot to bail out but the plane came down, skidded across the drop zone and broke apart. The tail snapped off, the motor rolled away, and the cockpit came to rest on the field. Jones was sure the pilot was dead but, as he watched, the canopy slid back and "a little tow-headed guy with no hat on and a .45 under his arm ran toward us." Jones remembers asking, "Man, why in the devil didn't you jump?" The pilot grinned. "Hell, I was afraid to," he told Jones.

Just after landing and assembling his gear, Staff Sergeant Russell O'Neal watched a P-51 fighter dive and strafe a hidden German position near his field. After the plane had made two passes over the machine-gun nest, it was hit; but the pilot was able to circle and make a safe belly landing. According to O'Neal, "this guy jumped out and ran up to me, shouting, 'Give me a gun, quick! I know right where that Kraut s.o.b. is and I'm gonna get him.'" As O'Neal stared after him, the pilot grabbed a gun and raced off toward the woods.

Within eighteen minutes, 4,511 men of the 82nd's 505th and 508th regiments, along with engineers and seventy tons of equipment, were down on or near their drop zones straddling the town of Groesbeek on the eastern side of the wooded heights. As the men assembled, cleared the zones and struck out for objectives, special pathfinder teams marked the areas for the artillery drop, the 82nd's glider force, and the British Corps headquarters. So far, General Gavin's calculated risk was succeeding. Yet, although radio contact between the regiments was established almost immediately, it was still too early for Gavin, who had jumped with the 505th, to learn what was occurring eight miles west, where the 504th Regiment had dropped north of Overasselt. Nor did he know whether the special assault against the Grave bridge was proceeding according to plan.

Like the rest of the division's planes, the 137 C-47's carrying Colonel Reuben H. Tucker's 504th Regiment ran into spasmodic antiaircraft fire as they neared the Overasselt drop zone. As in the other areas, pilots held their courses, and at 1:15 P.M., some 2,016 men began to jump. Eleven planes swung slightly west and headed for a small drop site near the vital nine-span, 1,500-foot-long bridge over the Maas river near Grave. These C-47's carried Company E of Major Edward Wellems' 2nd Battalion to the most crucial of the 82nd's immediate objectives. Their job was to rush the bridges from the western approach; the remainder of Wellems' battalion would strike out from Overasselt and head for the eastern side. If the Grave bridge was not taken quickly and intact, the tight Market-Garden schedule could not be maintained. Loss of the bridge might mean failure for the entire operation.

As E Company's planes headed for the western assault site,

platoon leader Lieutenant John S. Thompson could clearly see the Maas river, the town of Grave, the mass jump of the 504th to his right near Overasselt and then, coming up, the ditch-lined fields where the company was to drop. As Thompson watched, other men from the company were already out of their planes and falling toward the Grave bridge zone; but in the lieutenant's C-47 the green light had not yet flashed on. When it did, Thompson saw that they were directly over some buildings. He waited for a few seconds, saw fields beyond and jumped with his platoon. By a fortuitous error, he and his men came down only some five or six hundred yards from the southwestern edge of the bridge.

Thompson could hear erratic firing from the direction of Grave itself, but around the bridge everything seemed quiet. He did not know whether he should wait until the remainder of the company came up or attack with the sixteen men in his platoon. "Since this was our primary mission, I decided to attack," Thompson says. Sending Corporal Hugh H. Perry back to the company commander, Thompson gave him a laconic message to deliver: "We are proceeding toward the bridge."

Firing from the town and nearby buildings was now more intense, and Thompson led the platoon to cover in nearby drainage ditches. Working their way toward the bridge, men waded in water up to their necks. They began to receive fire from a flak tower close to the bridge and Thompson noticed enemy soldiers with bags in their arms running to and from a building near the crossing. He thought it must be a maintenance or power plant. Fearful that the Germans were carrying demolition charges to the bridge in preparation for destroying it, Thompson quickly deployed his men, encircled the building and opened fire. "We raked the area with machine guns, overran the power plant, found four dead Germans and one wounded," Thompson recalls. "Apparently they had been carrying their personal equipment and blankets." Suddenly, two trucks came racing down the highway from Grave, heading toward the bridge. One of Thompson's men killed a driver whose truck careened off the road as its load of German soldiers scrambled to get out. The second vehicle stopped immediately and the soldiers in it jumped to the ground. Thompson's men opened up, but the Germans showed no desire to fight. Without returning fire, they ran away.

Fire was still coming from the flak tower, but by now it was passing over the heads of the platoon. "The gunners were unable to depress the 20 mm. flak gun sufficiently to get us," Thompson remembers. The platoon's bazooka man, Private Robert McGraw, crawled forward and, at a range of about seventy-five yards, fired three rounds, two of them into the top of the tower, and the gun ceased firing.

Although a twin 20 mm. gun in a tower across the river near the far end of the bridge was firing, Thompson and his men nonetheless destroyed electrical equipment and cables that they suspected were hooked up to demolitions. The platoon then set up a roadblock and placed land mines across the highway at the southwestern approach to the bridge. In the flak tower they had knocked out, they found the gunner dead but his 20 mm. weapon undamaged. Thompson's men promptly began firing it at the flak tower across the river. The platoon, he knew, would soon be reinforced by the rest of E Company coming up behind and, shortly after, by Major Wellems' battalion even now rushing from Overasselt to grab the northeastern end of the bridge. But, as far as Lieutenant Thompson was concerned, the prime objective was already taken.°

By now, the remaining battalions of Tucker's 504th Regiment were moving eastward, like spokes on a wheel, for the three road crossings and the railroad bridge over the Maas-Waal Canal. Rushing toward the bridge also were units of the 505th and 508th regiments, bent on seizing the crossings from the opposite ends. Not all these objectives were essential to the Market-Garden

° The 82nd's after-action report and that of the 504th commander, Colonel Tucker, state the bridge was "taken" at 2:30 P.M. But Major Wellems' account states that because the bridge was still under harassing fire, the first men to actually cross from the northeastern end went over at 3:35 P.M. Still, the E Company platoon under Lieutenant Thompson held the bridge and prevented its demolition from 1:45 P.M. until it was described as "secure" at 5 P.M.

advance. In the surprise of the assault and the ensuing confusion, Gavin hoped to seize them all; but one, in addition to the all-important Grave bridge, would suffice.

To keep the enemy off balance, defend his positions, protect General Browning's Corps headquarters and aid his paratroopers as they moved on their objectives, Gavin was depending heavily on his howitzers; and now the guns of the 376th Parachute Field Artillery were coming in. Small artillery units had been dropped in previous operations, but they had been badly scattered and slow to assemble and fire. The unit of 544 men now approaching was hand-picked, every soldier a veteran paratrooper. Among the forty-eight planes carrying the battalion was the artillery—twelve 75 mm. howitzers, each broken down into seven pieces. The howitzers would be dropped first, followed by some 700 rounds of ammunition. Lining up, the C-47's came in and, in quick succession, the guns rolled out. Ammunition and men followed, all making a near-perfect landing.

One accident caused scarcely a pause. Lieutenant Colonel Wilbur Griffith, commanding the 376th, broke his ankle on the jump but his men quickly liberated a Dutch wheelbarrow in which to carry him. "I shall never forget the Colonel being trundled from place to place," Major Augustin Hart recalls, "and barking out orders for everybody to get assembled at top speed." When the job was complete, Griffith was wheeled over to General Gavin. There he reported: "Guns in position, sir, and ready to fire on call." In just over an hour, in the most successful drop of its kind ever made, the entire battalion was assembled and ten of its howitzers were already firing.

Fourteen minutes after the 82nd's field artillery landed, Waco gliders carrying an airborne antitank battalion, engineers, elements of Division headquarters, guns, ammunition, trailers and jeeps began to come in. Of the original fifty gliders leaving England, all but four reached Holland. Not all, however, touched down on their landing zone. Some gliders ended up a mile or two away. One, copiloted by Captain Anthony Jedrziewski, cut loose late from its tug and Jedrziewski saw with horror that "we were heading straight for Germany on a one-glider invasion." The pilot made a 180-degree turn and began to look for a place to land. As they came in, Jedrziewski remembers, "we lost one wing on a haystack, the other on a fence and ended up with the glider nose in the ground. Seeing earth up to my knees, I wasn't sure if my feet were still a part of me. Then, we heard the unwelcome sound of an 88 and, in nothing flat, we had the jeep out and were racing back toward our own area."

They were luckier than Captain John Connelly, whose pilot was killed during the approach. Connelly, who had never flown a glider before, took the controls and landed the Waco just inside the German border, six to seven miles away, near the town of Wyler. Only Connelly and one other man escaped capture. They were to hide out until darkness and finally reached their units by midmorning of September 18.

Yet, in all, the 82nd Airborne had successfully brought in 7,467 paratroopers and glider-borne men. The last elements to touch down in the area were 35 Horsas and Wacos carrying General Frederick Browning's Corps headquarters. Three gliders had been lost en route to the drop zone, two before reaching the Continent; the third, south of Vught, had crash-landed in the vicinity of General Student's headquarters. Browning's headquarters landed almost on the German frontier. "There was little flak, if any, and almost no enemy opposition," Browning's chief of staff, Brigadier Gordon Walch, remembers. "We set down about a hundred yards west of the Reichswald Forest and my glider was roughly fifty yards away from Browning's."

Colonel George S. Chatterton, commanding the Glider Pilot Regiment, was at the controls of Browning's Horsa. After clipping off a front wheel on an electric cable, Chatterton slid into a cabbage patch. "We got out," Chatterton recalls, "and Browning, looking around, said, 'By God, we're here, George!'" Nearby, Brigadier Walch saw Browning run across the landing zone toward the Reichswald. When he returned a few minutes later, he explained to Walch, "I wanted to be the first British officer to pee in Germany."

While Browning's jeep was being unloaded, a few German shells exploded nearby. Colonel Chatterton promptly threw himself into the closest ditch. "I shall never forget Browning standing above me, looking like some sort of explorer, and asking, 'George, whatever in the world are you doing down there?'" Chatterton was frank. "I'm bloody well hiding, sir," he said. "Well, you can bloody well stop hiding," Browning told him. "It's time we were going." From a pocket in his tunic, Browning took out a parcel wrapped in tissue paper. Handing it to Chatterton, he said, "Put it on my jeep." Chatterton unfolded the tissue and saw that it contained a pennant bearing a light-blue Pegasus against a maroon background, the insignia of the British Airborne.* With the pennant fluttering from the jeep's fender, the commander of the Market forces drove away.

At Renkum Heath west of Arnhem, Lieutenant Neville Hay, the highly trained specialist in charge of the fact-gathering liaison unit "Phantom," was totally baffled. His team of experts had assembled their radio set with its special antenna and expected immediate contact with General Browning's Corps headquarters. Hay's first priority on landing was to get through to Corps and give his position. Earlier, he had learned that Division communications had broken down. While he might have anticipated that problems would arise among the less experienced Royal Signal Corps operators, he was not prepared to believe that the difficulties he was having stemmed from his own men. "We were set up on the landing zone and, although it was screened by pine woods, we had got through in considerably worse country than

---

* Some accounts have stated that Browning's pennant was made by his wife, the novelist Daphne du Maurier. "I am sorry," she writes, "to disappoint the myth-makers . . . but anyone who has seen my attempts to thread a needle would know this was beyond me. It is a delightful thought, however, and would have greatly amused my husband." Actually, the pennant was made by Hobson & Sons Ltd., London, under the supervision of Miss Claire Miller, who also, at Browning's direction, hand-sewed tiny compasses into 500 shirt collars and belts just prior to Market-Garden.

this," he remembers. "We kept trying and getting absolutely nothing." Until he could discover where the trouble lay, there was no way of informing General Browning of the progress of General Urquhart's division or of relaying Browning's orders to the British 1st Airborne. Ironically, the Dutch telephone system was in full operation, including a special network owned and operated by the PGEM power station authorities at Nijmegen and connected with the entire province. Had he known, all Hay had to do, with the aid of the Dutch resistance, was to pick up a telephone.

Fifteen miles away there was already anxiety at General Browning's headquarters, now set up on the edge of the Groesbeek ridge. Both of the 82nd Airborne's large communication sets had been damaged on landing. Browning's had come through safely, and one of these was allocated to the 82nd, insuring immediate communication with General Gavin. The Corps communications section had also made radio contact with General Dempsey's British 2nd Army and Airborne Corps rear headquarters in England and Browning had radio contact with the 101st. But the signal section was unable to raise Urquhart's division. Brigadier Walch believes that Corps signals was to blame. "Before the operation was planned, we asked for a proper headquarters signals section," he says. "We were frightfully cognizant that our sets were inadequate and our headquarters signals staff weak and inexperienced." While Browning could direct and influence the movements of the 82nd, the 101st and Horrocks' XXX Corps, at this vital junction the all-important battle at Arnhem was beyond his control. As Walch says, "We had absolutely no idea what was happening in Arnhem."

A kind of creeping paralysis was already beginning to affect Montgomery's plan. But at this early stage no one knew it. Throughout the entire Market-Garden area, some 20,000 Allied soldiers were in Holland, heading out to secure the bridges and hold open the corridor for the massive Garden units whose lead tanks were expected to link up with 101st paratroopers by nightfall.

❊ 9 ❊

Fʀᴏᴍ ᴛʜᴇ ꜰʟᴀᴛ ʀᴏᴏꜰ of a large factory near the Meuse-Escaut Canal, General Brian Horrocks, commander of the British XXX Corps, watched the last of the huge airborne glider formations pass over his waiting tanks. He had been on the roof since 11 A.M., and as he put it, "I had plenty of time to think." The sight of the vast armada was "comforting, but I was under no illusion that this was going to be an easy battle," Horrocks remembers. Meticulously, he had covered every possible contingency, even to ordering his men to take as much food, gas and ammunition as they could carry, "since we were likely to be out in the blue on our own." There was one worry the General could not eliminate, but he had not discussed it with anyone—he did not like a Sunday attack. "No assault or attack in which I had taken part during the war which started on a Sunday had ever been completely successful." Bringing up his binoculars, he studied the white ribbon of road stretching away north toward Valkenswaard and Eindhoven. Satisfied that the airborne assault had now begun, Horrocks gave the order for the Garden forces to attack. At precisely 2:15 P.M., with a thunderous roar, some 350 guns opened fire.

The bombardment was devastating. Ton after ton of explosives flayed the enemy positions up ahead. The hurricane of fire, ranging five miles in depth and concentrated over a one-mile front, caused the earth to shake beneath the tanks of the Irish

Guards as they lumbered up to the start line. Behind the lead squadrons, hundreds of tanks and armored vehicles began to move slowly out of their parking positions, ready to fall into line as the first tanks moved off. And up above, a "cab rank" of rocket-firing Typhoon fighters circled endlessly, waiting on call for the commander of the Irish Guards Group, Lieutenant Colonel Joe Vandeleur, to direct them to targets up ahead. At 2:35 P.M., standing in the turret of the lead tank of No. 3 Squadron, Lieutenant Keith Heathcote shouted into his microphone, "Driver, advance!"

Slowly the tanks rumbled out of the bridgehead and moved up the road at eight miles an hour. Now, the curtain of artillery fire lifted to creep ahead of the armor at exactly the same speed. Tankers could see shells bursting barely one hundred yards in front of them. As the squadrons moved forward, engulfed in the dust of the barrage, men could not tell at times whether the tanks were safely back of their own fire.

Behind the lead squadrons came the scout cars of Lieutenant Colonel Joe Vandeleur and his cousin Giles. Standing in his car, Vandeleur could see, both in front of and behind him, infantry riding on the tanks, each tank marked with yellow streamers to identify it to the Typhoons above. "The din was unimaginable," Vandeleur remembers, "but everything was going according to plan." By now, the lead tanks had burst out of the bridgehead and were across the Dutch frontier. Captain "Mick" O'Cock, commanding No. 3 Squadron, radioed back, "Advance going well. Leading squadron has got through." Then, in seconds, the picture changed. As Vandeleur recalls, "The Germans really began to paste us."

Ensconced in well-hidden, fortified positions on both sides of the road, German gunners had not only survived the tremendous barrage but had waited until it passed over them. Holding their fire, the Germans let the first few tanks go through. Then, within two minutes three tanks of the lead squadron and six of the next were knocked out of action. Burning and disabled, they littered a half mile of road. "We had just crossed the border when we were ambushed," Lieutenant Cyril Russell recalls. "Suddenly the tanks in front either slewed across the road or burned where they stood. The awful realization dawned on me that the next one to go was the one I was sitting on. We jumped into the ditches by the roadside." As Russell went forward to see how the remainder of his platoon was faring, a machine gun opened up; he was hit in the arm and fell back into the ditch. For Russell, the war was over.

Lance Corporal James Doggart's tank was hit. "I don't remember seeing or hearing the explosion," he says. "I was suddenly flat on my back in a ditch with the tank leaning over me. I had a Bren gun across my chest and next to me was a young lad with his arm nearly severed. Nearby, another of our men was dead. The tank was on fire and I don't recall seeing any of the crew get out."

Lieutenant Barry Quinan, in the last tank of the lead squadron, remembers that his Sherman swung left into a ditch, and Quinan thought the driver was trying to bypass the burning tanks ahead. But the tank had been hit by a shell which killed both the driver and codriver. The Sherman began to burn and Quinan's gunner, "trying to scramble out of the hatch, half lifted me out of the turret before I realized we were 'brewing up.'" As the two men climbed out of the tank, Quinan saw others coming up behind. One after the other, the tanks were hit. "I actually saw the commander of one tank trying to shield his face from a sheet of flame that engulfed the entire machine."

The breakout had been stopped before it had really begun and nine disabled tanks now blocked the road. Squadrons coming up could not advance. Even if they could bypass the burning hulks, hidden German gunners would pick them off. To get the advance rolling again, Vandeleur called in the rocket-firing Typhoons and, aided by purple smoke shells fired from the tanks to indicate suspected German positions, the fighters screamed down. "It was the first time I had ever seen Typhoons in action," Vandeleur recalls, "and I was amazed at the guts of those pilots. They came in, one at a time, head to tail, flying right through our own barrage. One disintegrated right above me. It was incredible—

guns firing, the roar of planes, the shouts and curses of the men. In the middle of it all, Division asked how the battle was going. My second in command just held up the microphone and said, 'Listen.'"

As the planes swooped down on their targets, Vandeleur sent forward an armored bulldozer to push the burning tanks off the road. The bedlam of the battle now raged over several miles of highway, stretching back as far as Vandeleur's own car and the R.A.F. communications tender, which called the Typhoons down on demand. Flight Lieutenant Donald Love, the fighter reconnaissance pilot attached to the communications unit, was now convinced that he should never have volunteered for the job. While Squadron Leader Max Sutherland directed the Typhoons, Love got out to see what was happening. Black smoke billowed up from the road ahead and an antitank gun carrier, almost in front of the communications tender, was afire. As Love watched, a Bren gun carrier came back along the road carrying wounded. One man's shoulder was blown off, and his clothes were burned and charred. "I was sure we were surrounded," says Love. "I was horrified and I kept wondering why hadn't I stayed with the Air Force, where I belonged."

The waiting tankers farther back in the halted columns felt, as Captain Roland Langton describes it, "a strange sense of powerlessness. We could go neither forward nor backward." Langton watched infantry moving up to clean out the woods on either side of the road with two Bren gun carriers out in front. Langton thought the soldiers might be an advance party of the 43rd Infantry Division. "Suddenly I saw both carriers catapulted into the air," Langton remembers. "They had run over enemy land mines." When the smoke cleared, Langton saw "bodies in the trees. I don't know how many, it was impossible to tell. There were pieces of men hanging from every limb."

With the Typhoons firing only yards away from them, the British infantry men grimly began to dig out the Germans from their hidden trenches. Lance Corporal Doggart had escaped from the ditch where he landed when his tank was hit. He raced across the road and jumped into an empty enemy slit trench. "At the same moment, two Germans—one a young fellow without a jacket, the other a tough-looking bastard of about thirty—jumped in after me from the opposite direction," Doggart says. Without hesitating, Doggart kicked the older German in the face. The younger man, immediately cowed, surrendered. Covering both with his rifle, Doggart sent them marching back along the road "with streams of other Germans, all running with their hands behind their heads. Those that were too slow got a fast kick in the backside."

From the woods, in ditches, around haystacks and along the roadway, now being slowly cleared of the disabled tanks, came the stutter of Sten guns as the infantry mopped up. The Guardsmen showed no quarter, particularly toward snipers. Men remember that prisoners were made to double-time down the road, and when they slowed they were promptly prodded with bayonets. One prisoner in the now-growing lines tried to break away, but there was more than a company of infantry in the vicinity and several men recall that—in the words of one—"he was dead the second the thought entered his mind."

Joe Vandeleur watched the prisoners being marched past his scout car. As one German came along, Vandeleur caught a sudden movement. "The bastard had taken a grenade he'd concealed and lobbed it into one of our gun carriers. It went off with a tremendous explosion and I saw one of my sergeants lying in the road with his leg blown off. The German was cut down on all sides by machine guns."

At his command post, General Horrocks received word that the road was gradually being cleared and that the infantry, although suffering heavy casualties, had routed the Germans on the flanks. As he later put it, "The Micks were getting tired of being shot at, and as so often happens with these great fighters, they suddenly lost their tempers."

Perhaps no one was more enraged than Captain Eamon Fitzgerald, the 2nd Battalion's intelligence officer, who interrogated the captured crew of an antitank gun. According to Lieutenant

Colonel Giles Vandeleur, "Fitzgerald had an interesting way of extracting information. A huge giant of a man, he spoke German well, but with an atrocious accent. His normal custom was to produce his pistol, poke it into the German's belly and, standing as close as possible, shout questions in the man's face." The results, Vandeleur always thought, "were positively splendid. Within a few minutes after interrogating this crew, our tanks were picking off the German camouflaged antitank positions with creditable accuracy and the road was being sufficiently cleared to allow us to continue the advance."

Many Irish Guardsmen believe Sergeant Bertie Cowan turned the tide of the battle. Commanding a 17-pounder Sherman, Cowan had spotted a German antitank position and demolished it with a single shot. During the fight, Major Edward G. Tyler, in command of the squadron, was astonished to see that a German was standing on Cowan's tank directing operations. He saw the tank cross the road and open fire; then, busy himself, Tyler forgot the incident. Later, Tyler learned that Cowan had knocked out three German guns. "When I could take a moment, I went to congratulate him," Tyler says. "Cowan told me the Jerry on his tank had been a crew chief in the first position he'd overrun who had surrendered." He had been interrogated by Captain Fitzgerald and then returned to Cowan where he had proven "most cooperative."

The Irish Guards were on the way again, but constant fighting continued. The German crust was far tougher than anyone had anticipated. Among the prisoners were men of renowned parachute battalions and—to the complete surprise of the British— veteran infantrymen from the 9th and 10th SS Panzer divisions: elements of the combat groups General Wilhelm Bittrich had sent to bolster Student's First Parachute Army. To compound the surprise, some prisoners were discovered to belong to General von Zangen's Fifteenth Army. As the Irish Guards' war diary notes, "Our intelligence spent the day in a state of indignant surprise: one German regiment after another appeared which had no right to be there."

General Horrocks had expected that his lead tanks would drive the thirteen miles to Eindhoven "within two to three hours." Precious time had been lost, and the Irish Guards would cover only seven miles, reaching Valkenswaard by nightfall. Market-Garden was already ominously behind schedule.

In order to be as mobile as possible, General Maxwell D. Taylor's gliders had brought in mostly jeeps—no artillery. The fact that the British were late in reaching Eindhoven was a blow. Taylor had hoped for the support of the tankers' guns along the fifteen-mile stretch of corridor the Screaming Eagles must control. Taylor's Dutch liaison officers discovered the true situation—that the 101st would have to operate independently for longer than planned—almost immediately; with the aid of the resistance, they simply used the telephone to learn what was happening with the British.

With lightning speed Taylor's paratroopers took Veghel, the northernmost objective along the corridor, and its four crossings—the rail and highway bridges over the river Aa and the Willems Canal. Heavy fighting would ensue; nevertheless, these four objectives were seized within two hours. Farther south, midway between Veghel and Son, the town of St. Oedenrode and its highway crossing over the Dommel river were captured with relative ease. According to official Dutch telephone log books, Johanna Lathouwers, a loyal operator with the state telephone exchange, heard "an unmistakable American voice came on the Oed 1 (St. Oedenrode) line, at 1425 hours, asking for Valkenswaard, a connection that lasted forty minutes."°

The Americans quickly learned that the spearhead of the Garden forces had not as yet even reached Valkenswaard. It now seemed unlikely that Horrocks' tanks, already delayed, would reach Eindhoven at the southern end of the corridor before

° By Allied clocks it was actually 1525 hours; there was a one-hour difference between German and British times.

nightfall; and that would be too late to help the Americans seize and control their widespread targets. The men of the 101st had achieved spectacular success. Now, they ran into problems.

The most pressing of Taylor's objectives was the highway bridge over the Wilhelmina Canal at Son, approximately five miles north of Eindhoven. As a contingency plan in case this main traffic artery was blown, Taylor had decided to seize a bridge over the canal at Best, four miles to the west. Because the bridge was considered secondary, only a single company of the 502nd Regiment was detailed to Best, and it was thought that only a few Germans would be in the area. Taylor's intelligence was unaware that Colonel General Student's headquarters lay only ten miles northwest of the 101st drop zones and that recent arrivals of Von Zangen's Fifteenth Army were quartered at nearby Tilburg. Among these forces was Major General Walter Poppe's battered 59th Infantry Division plus a considerable amount of artillery.

Almost immediately upon approaching the bridge, H Company radioed that it had run into enemy roadblocks and was meeting strong resistance. The message signaled the beginning of a bloody battle that would last throughout the night and most of the following two days. What had begun as a single-company operation eventually involved more than an entire regiment. But already the heroic men of H Company, though taking heavy casualties, were blunting the first, unexpectedly strong, German blows.

While H Company was setting out for the bridge at Best, Colonel Robert F. Sink's 506th Regiment was going for the main highway bridge at Son. There was almost no opposition until troops reached the northern outskirts of the village. Then they were fired on by a German 88 artillery piece. In less than ten minutes, the advance party destroyed the gun emplacement with a bazooka and killed its crew. Fighting through the streets, the Americans were a bare fifty yards from the canal itself when the bridge was blown up, debris falling all around the paratroopers. For Colonel Sink, who was to take Eindhoven and its crossings by 8 P.M., the loss of the bridge was a bitter blow. Reacting quickly and still under fire, three men—Major James LaPrade, Second

Lieutenant Millford F. Weller and Sergeant John Dunning— dived into the canal and swam to the far side. Other members of the battalion followed their lead or went across in rowboats. On the southern bank, they subdued the German opposition and set up a bridgehead.

The central column of the bridge was still intact, and 101st engineers immediately began the construction of a temporary crossing. Help came from an unexpected source. Dutch civilians reported that a considerable amount of black-market lumber was being stored by a contractor in a nearby garage. Within one and a half hours the engineers, utilizing the bridge's center trestle and the liberated lumber, spanned the canal. As Colonel Sink recalled, "the bridge was unsatisfactory from every point of view, except that it did enable me to put the rest of the regiment across, single file." Until bridging equipment could be brought up, the Market-Garden corridor at Son was reduced to a single wooden footpath.

☆10☆

FIELD MARSHAL MODEL was still shaken when he reached General Bittrich's headquarters at Doetinchem. Normally, it would have taken him no longer than half an hour to cover the distance, but today, because he had made numerous stops along the way to alert area commanders to the airborne assault, the trip had lasted well over an hour. Although the Field Marshal seemed calm, Bittrich remembers "his first words to me were, 'They almost got me! They were after the headquarters. Imagine! They almost got me!' "

Bittrich immediately brought Model up to date on the latest

information received by II SS Panzer Corps. No clear picture of the Allied intent was emerging as yet, but Bittrich told Model his own theory: that the assault was aimed at containing the Fifteenth Army while the British Second Army drove for the Ruhr. That would require the Allies to capture the Nijmegen and Arnhem bridges. Model disagreed completely. The Arnhem bridge was not the objective, he said. These airborne troops would swerve and march northeast for the Ruhr. The situation, Model believed, was still too obscure for any final conclusions. He was puzzled as to why airborne forces had landed in the Nijmegen area. Nevertheless, he approved the measures Bittrich had already taken.

Bittrich still pressed the subject of the bridges. "Herr Field Marshal, I strongly urge that the bridges at Nijmegen and Arnhem be immediately destroyed," he said. Model looked at him in amazement. "They will not be destroyed," he told Bittrich firmly. "No matter what the English plan, these bridges can be defended. No. Absolutely not. The bridges are not to be blown." Then, dismissing the subject, Model said, "I'm looking for a new headquarters, Bittrich." Before Bittrich could answer, Model said again musingly, "You know, they almost got me."

At his headquarters at Vught, Colonel General Kurt Student faced a dilemma: his First Parachute Army had been split in two by the airborne assault. Without telephone communications and now solely dependent on radio, he was unable to direct his divided army. For the moment units were fighting on their own without any cohesive direction. Then, by a momentous and fantastic stroke of luck, an undamaged briefcase found in a downed Waco glider near his headquarters was rushed to him.

"It was incredible," Student says. "In the case was the complete enemy attack order for the operation." Student and his staff officers pored over the captured plans. "They showed us everything—the dropping zones, the corridor, the objectives, even the names of the divisions involved. Everything! Immediately we could see the strategic implications. They had to grab the bridges before we could destroy them. All I could think of was, 'This is retribution. Retribution! History is repeating itself.' During our airborne operation in Holland in 1940, one of my officers, against strict orders, had taken into battle papers that detailed our entire attack, and these had fallen into enemy hands. Now the wheel had turned full circle. I knew exactly what I had to do."[*]

Model, as yet, did not. Student had never felt so frustrated. Because of his communications breakdown, it would be nearly ten hours before he could place the secret of Market-Garden in Model's possession. The secret was that the Arnhem bridge was of crucial importance. The captured plans clearly showed that it was Montgomery's route into the Ruhr.

This was the kind of battle that Model liked best: one that demanded improvisation, daring and, above all, speed. From Bittrich's headquarters, Model telephoned OB West, Von Rundstedt. With characteristic abruptness, he described the situation and asked for immediate reinforcements. "The only way this airborne assault can be defeated is to strike hard within the first twenty-four hours," he told Von Rundstedt. Model asked for anti-aircraft units, self-propelled guns, tanks and infantry; and he wanted them on the move to Arnhem by nightfall. Von Rund-

[*] In the legend of Arnhem the story of the captured documents, like that of the spy Lindemans, is always included. Some accounts claim that the Market-Garden plan was found on the body of a dead American captain. I interviewed Student and examined all his documents. At no point does he confirm that the briefcase was carried by a captain. Nor is there any such mention in official British and American records. Perhaps, since Student says that the plans came from "a Waco freight glider," it was generally assumed that only American personnel were aboard. However, part of General Browning's Corps headquarters flew to Holland in Wacos; and one of these did crash-land near Student's headquarters. In any case, whether the personnel were British or American, I think it highly unlikely that the entire Market-Garden operational plan could have been in the possession of a captain. First, great care was taken in the distribution of the plan; and second, each copy was both numbered and restricted solely to officers of staff rank.

stedt told him that such reinforcements as were available would be on the way. Turning to Bittrich, Model said triumphantly, "Now, we'll get reinforcements!" Model had decided to operate from Doetinchem; but, although he was apparently recovered from the shock of his hasty departure from Oosterbeek, this time he was taking no chances of being caught unawares. He refused accommodations at the castle; he would direct the battle from the gardener's cottage on the grounds.

Bittrich's early foresight was already having its effect. Sections of Harzer's Hohenstaufen Division were heading swiftly toward the battle zone. Harmel's Frundsberg Division—Harmel himself was expected back from Germany during the night—were on the move, too. Bittrich had ordered Harzer to set up his headquarters in a high school in the northern Arnhem suburbs overlooking the city, and that transfer was underway. But Harzer was chafing with impatience. The armored vehicles that had been scheduled to leave for Germany in the early afternoon were still being refitted with tracks and guns. Harzer had already moved the units closest to the British landing and drop zones into blocking positions at points west of Arnhem. For the moment, he had only a few armored cars, several self-propelled guns, a few tanks and some infantry. Still, Harzer hoped that by employing hit-and-run tactics he could halt and confuse British troops until the bulk of his division was again battle-ready.

Curiously, Harzer did not even know that Major Sepp Krafft's SS Panzer Grenadier Training and Reserve Battalion was in the area and, at the moment, the only unit in the path of the British airborne forces. Harzer concentrated his own strength on the two major highways running into Arnhem: the Ede-Arnhem road and the Utrecht-Arnhem road. Certain that the paratroopers must use these main arteries, he placed his units in a semicircular screen across the two highways. By oversight, or perhaps because he lacked sufficient forces at the moment, Harzer failed to position any groups along a quiet secondary road running parallel to the northern bank of the Rhine. It was the single unprotected route the British could take to the Arnhem bridge.

☆ 11 ☆

I N THEIR CAMOUFLAGE BATTLE SMOCKS and distinctive crash helmets, laden with weapons and ammunition, the men of Brigadier
Lathbury's 1st Parachute Brigade were on the way to Arnhem.
Interspersed among the columns of marching troopers were jeeps
pulling artillery pieces and four-wheeled carts loaded with guns
and stores. As General Roy Urquhart watched them pass, he remembered a compliment paid him some months before by General
Horrocks. "Your men are killers," Horrocks had said admiringly.
At the time, Urquhart had considered the remark an overstate-
ment. On this Sunday, he was not so sure. As the 1st Brigade had
moved off, Urquhart had felt a surge of pride.

The plan called for the three battalions of Lathbury's brigade
to converge on Arnhem, each from a different direction. Lieutenant Colonel John Frost's 2nd Battalion was given the prime
objective: marching along a secondary road running close to the
north bank of the Rhine, Frost's men were to capture the main
highway bridge. En route, they were to take the railway and
pontoon bridges west of the great highway crossing. The 3rd
Battalion, under Lieutenant Colonel J. A. C. Fitch, would move
along the Utrecht-Arnhem road and approach the bridge from
the north, reinforcing Frost. Once these two battalions had been
successfully launched, Lieutenant Colonel D. Dobie's 1st Battalion was to advance along the main Ede-Arnhem highway—the
most northerly route—and occupy the high ground north of the
city. Lathbury had given each route a code name. Dobie's,
farthest north, was designated "Leopard"; Fitch's, in the middle,

was "Tiger"; and Frost's, the most crucial route, was "Lion." Speeding ahead of the entire brigade, the jeeps of Major Freddie Gough's reconnaissance squadron were expected to reach the bridge, seize it in a *coup de main,* and hold until Frost arrived.

So far, Urquhart thought, the initial phase was going well. He was not unduly alarmed by the breakdown of communications within the division at this time. He had experienced temporary signals disruption often in the North African desert campaigns. Since he could not raise Brigadier Hicks's 1st Airlanding Brigade, whose job it was to hold the landing and drop zones for the air lifts on the following two days, Urquhart drove to Hicks's headquarters. The Airlanding Brigade, he learned, was in position, and Hicks was for the moment away directing the disposition of his battalions. However, at Hicks's headquarters, Urquhart received news that one vital part of the plan to take the Arnhem bridge had gone wrong. He was told—erroneously—that most of Major Freddie Gough's reconnaissance vehicles had been lost in glider crashes; no one at Hicks's headquarters knew where Gough had gone. Without waiting for Hicks to return, Urquhart drove back to his own headquarters. He had to find Gough quickly and devise some alternative plan, but his greatest concern now was to warn Lathbury and, in particular, Frost, that the 2nd Battalion was on its own. Frost would have to take the main Arnhem bridge without the aid of Gough's planned surprise attack.

At Division, further bad news awaited Urquhart. "Not only was there no word of Gough," Urquhart recalls, "but apart from some short-range radio signals, headquarters communications had completely failed. The 1st Parachute Brigade and, indeed, the outside world, could not be contacted." Colonel Charles Mackenzie, Urquhart's chief of staff, watched the General pace up and down, "restive and anxious for news." Urquhart ordered his signals officer, Major Anthony Deane-Drummond, to investigate the "communications foul-up, see what had happened to the radio equipment and then set it right." Messengers were also sent out in search of Gough. As time passed without any new information, the worried Urquhart decided to wait no longer. Normally, he would have directed the battle from Division headquarters; but now, as each moment passed without communications, he was beginning to feel that this battle was anything but normal. Turning to Mackenzie, he said, "I think I'll go and have a look myself, Charles." Mackenzie did not try to stop him. "At the time," Mackenzie recalls, "since we were getting practically no information, it didn't seem a particularly bad thing to do." Taking only his driver and a signalman in his jeep, Urquhart set out after Lathbury. The time was 4:30 P.M.

Moving along the northern, Leopard route—the Ede-Arnhem road—Major Freddie Gough of the 1st Airlanding reconnaissance unit was making good time. Although the vehicles of A troop had failed to arrive, Gough had started off from the landing zone with the rest of the squadrons at 3:30 P.M. He was confident that he had sufficient jeeps for the *coup de main* attempt on the bridge. "In fact," he remembered, "I left several jeeps behind on the landing zone in reserve. We had more than enough to get to Arnhem." Gough had even detached twelve men from his unit to make their way south to join the 2nd Battalion, moving on the Lion route to the bridge. He was unaware that the loss of A troop's jeeps had raised a flurry of rumors and misinformation.[*]

From the beginning, Gough had had reservations about his recco unit's role in the Arnhem plan. Instead of a *coup de main*, Gough had urged that a screen of reconnaissance jeeps be sent ahead of each of the three battalions. "In that way," he says, "we would have quickly discovered the best and easiest way to reach the bridge." Failing that, he had asked that a troop of light tanks be brought in by glider to escort the *coup de main* force. Both requests had been turned down. Yet Gough had remained optimistic. "I wasn't the least bit concerned. There were supposed to

[*] Some accounts of the Arnhem battle claim that Gough's unit could not operate because so many of his vehicles failed to arrive by glider. "The failure, if it can be called that," Gough says, "was not due to a lack of jeeps, but to the fact that no one had warned us that the 9th and 10th SS Panzer divisions were in the area."

be only a few old, gray Germans in Arnhem and some ancient tanks and guns. I expected it to be a pushover."

Now, as they moved swiftly along Leopard, the lead jeeps of the unit were suddenly ambushed by German armored cars and 20 mm. guns. Gough's second in command, Captain David Allsop, happened to note the time. It was exactly 4 P.M. Gough pulled out to drive to the head of the column and investigate. "Just as I was on the point of going forward, I got a message saying that Urquhart wanted to see me immediately. I didn't know what the hell to do," Gough says. "I was under Lathbury, and I thought I should at least tell him I was going, but I had no idea where he was. The unit was now in a heavy fire fight and pinned down in defensive positions near the railroad tracks on the outskirts of Wolfheze. I reckoned they would be all right for a time, so I turned around and headed back to Division headquarters on the landing zone. That was at 4:30."

At the precise moment that General Urquhart set out to find Lathbury, Gough was speeding back to Division to report to Urquhart.

All along the three strategic lines of march, the men of the 1st Parachute Brigade were encountering jubilant, hysterical throngs of Dutch. Many civilians from farms and outlying hamlets had followed the paratroopers from the time they left the landing zones, and as the crowds grew, the welcome seemed almost to overwhelm the march itself. Captain Eric Mackay, traveling the southernmost, Lion route with Colonel Frost's 2nd Battalion, was disturbed by the holiday atmosphere. "We were hampered by Dutch civilians," he says. "Waving, cheering and clapping their hands, they offered us apples, pears, something to drink. But they interfered with our progress and filled me with dread that they would give our positions away." Lieutenant Robin Vlasto remembers that "the first part of our march was in the nature of a victory parade, and the civilians were quite delirious with joy. It all seemed so unbelievable that we almost expected to see Horrocks' XXX Corps tanks coming out of Arnhem to meet us. People lined the road and great trays of beer, milk and fruit were offered. We had the greatest difficulty forcing the men to keep alive to the possibility of a German attack."

Young Anje van Maanen, whose father was a doctor in Oosterbeek, recalls receiving an exuberant call from the Tromp family in Heelsum, just south of the British landing zone on Renkum Heath. "We are free. Free!" the Tromps told her. "The Tommies dropped behind our house and they are on their way to Oosterbeek. They are so nice! We are smoking Players and eating chocolate." Anje put the phone down, "crazy with joy. We all jumped and danced around. This is it! An invasion! Lovely!" Seventeen-year-old Anje could hardly wait for her father to come home. Dr. van Maanen was delivering a baby at a patient's home, and Anje thought it "very annoying, particularly now, because the husband of the woman was a Dutch Nazi." Mrs. Ida Clous, the wife of an Oosterbeek dentist and a friend of the Van Maanens, also heard that the airborne troops were on their way. She worked feverishly, hunting through boxes and sewing scraps to find every bit of orange cloth she possessed. When the British got to Oosterbeek, she intended to rush outside with her three small children and greet the deliverers with small handmade orange flags.

Jan Voskuil, hiding out in the home of his wife's parents in Oosterbeek, was torn between his own desire to head up the Utrecht road to greet the paratroopers and the need to prevent his father-in-law from coming with him. The elder man was adamant. "I'm seventy-eight years old and I've never been in a war before and I want to see it." Voskuil's father-in-law was finally persuaded to stay in the garden and Voskuil, joining streams of other civilians heading out to meet the British, was turned back by a policeman on the outskirts of Oosterbeek. "It's too dangerous," the officer told the crowds. "Go back." Voskuil walked slowly home. There he ran into the same German soldier who had asked for shelter when the bombing had begun during the morning. Now the soldier was in full uniform, with camouflage jacket, helmet and rifle. He offered Voskuil some chocolates and cigarettes. "I am going away now," he said. "The Tommies will come." Voskuil smiled. "Now, you will go back to Germany," he said. The soldier studied Voskuil for several seconds. Then he shook his head slowly. "No, sir," he told Voskuil. "We will fight." The Dutchman watched the German walk away. "It begins now," Voskuil thought, "but what can I do?" Impatiently he paced the yard. There was nothing to do but wait.

Unhampered by police restraints or warnings to stay indoors, Dutch farmers and their families lined each route of march in throngs. Sergeant Major Harry Callaghan, on the middle, Tiger route, remembers a farm woman breaking through the crowds and running toward him with a pitcher of milk. He thanked her and the woman smiled and said, "Good, Tommy. Good." But, like Eric Mackay on the lower road, Callaghan, a Dunkirk veteran, was bothered by the number of civilians surrounding the troops. "They ran along beside us wearing armbands, aprons, and little pieces of ribbon, all orange," he remembers. "Children, with little snippets of orange cloth pinned to their skirts or blouses, skipped along, shrieking with delight. Most of the men were reaching in their packs to hand them chocolate. It was such a different atmosphere that the men were behaving as if they were on an exercise. I began to be concerned about snipers."

As Callaghan had feared, the victory parade came to a sudden halt. "It all happened so quickly," he says. "One moment we were marching steadily toward Arnhem; the next, we were scattered in the ditches. Snipers had opened fire, and three dead airborne soldiers lay across the road." The veteran sergeant major wasted no time. He had spotted a burst of flame from trees about fifty yards ahead. As the Dutch scattered, Callaghan took a party of twelve men forward. He stopped short of one tree and looked up. Something flashed. Raising his Sten gun, he fired directly into the tree. A Schmeisser automatic pistol clattered to the ground and, as Callaghan sighted up along the trunk of the tree, he saw a German dangling limply from a rope.

Now, too, on the middle route, other men from Lieutenant Colonel Fitch's 3rd Battalion were suddenly engaged in an unexpected encounter. Private Frederick Bennett had just passed around some apples to other troopers when a German staff car came speeding down the road. Bennett opened up with his Sten gun. The car screeched to a stop and tried to back up. But it was too late. Everyone near Bennett began firing and the car came to an abrupt halt, riddled with bullets. As the troopers cautiously approached, they saw that the driver was hanging halfway out of the car. The body of a senior German officer had been thrown partly out another door. To Bennett "he looked like some high-ranking Jerry officer," as indeed he was. Major General Kussin, the Arnhem town commander, had disregarded the warning of SS Major Sepp Krafft to avoid the main Utrecht-Arnhem road.°

Many men recall that the first serious German opposition began after the first hour of march—around 4:30 P.M. Then two of the three battalions—Dobie's, on the northern route, and Fitch's, in the center—were unexpectedly engaged in fierce enemy hit-and-run attacks. Major Gough's reconnaissance unit, now commanded by Captain Allsop, was desperately trying to find a way to outflank the German forces and clear a path for Dobie's 1st Battalion. But, according to Allsop, "each movement we made was blunted by an enemy force in front of us." Trooper William Chandler of the reconnaissance unit remembers that as his C Troop explored the terrain, "German bullets came so close and so thick that they almost stung as they went by."

As the battalion approached Wolfheze, it was almost completely stopped. "We halted," Private Walter Boldock recalls. "Then we started off again. Then we halted and dug in. Next, we moved on again, changing direction. Our progress was dictated by the success of the lead companies. Mortar bombs and bullets

---

° Kussin, on Model's orders issued as the Field Marshal fled east that morning, had informed Hitler's headquarters of the landings and of Model's narrow escape. The Allied assault had caused Hitler hysterical concern. "If such a mess happens here," he conjectured, "here I sit with my own Supreme Command—Goering, Himmler, Ribbentrop. Well, then, this is a most worthwhile catch. That's obvious. I would not hesitate to risk two parachute divisions here if with one blow I could get my hands on the whole German command."

harassed us all the way." Beside a hedge, Boldock saw a sergeant he knew, lying seriously wounded. Farther ahead, he came upon the smoldering body of a lieutenant. He had been hit by a phosphorus bomb. To another soldier, Private Roy Edwards, "it just seemed we kept making a detour of the countryside and getting into running battles all afternoon."

The paratroopers were stunned by the ferociousness of the unanticipated enemy attacks. Private Andrew Milbourne, on the northern route, heard firing in the distance off to the south and was momentarily glad that the 1st Battalion had been given the assignment to hold the high ground north of Arnhem. Then, nearing Wolfheze, Milbourne realized that the column had swung south off the main road. He saw the railway station and, close to it, a tank. His first reaction was one of elation. "My God!" he thought, "Monty was right. The Second Army's here already!" Then, as the turret swung slowly around, Milbourne saw that a black cross was painted on the tank. Suddenly, he seemed to see Germans everywhere. He dived into a ditch and, raising his head cautiously, began looking for a good spot to position his Vickers machine gun.

Sergeant Reginald Isherwood saw the same tank. A jeep towing a light artillery piece drove up and started to turn around in order to engage it. "One of their sergeants yelled, 'We'd better fire before they do. Otherwise we've had it,'" Isherwood recalls. "The gun was swung around like lightning, but as our man yelled 'Fire!' I heard the German commander do the same. The Jerries must have got their shell off one tenth of a second sooner than us." The tank scored a direct hit. The jeep exploded and the gun crew were killed.

In the mounting confusion and the intense fire from all sides, it was now clear to Colonel Dobie that the opposition in front of him was heavier than anyone had expected. Nor did he believe it was still possible to occupy the high ground north of Arnhem. He was unable to raise Brigadier Lathbury by radio, and his casualties were mounting by the minute. Dobie decided to side-slip the battalion still farther south and attempt to join up with Frost going for the main Arnhem bridge.

The breakdown of communications and subsequent lack of direction was making it impossible for battalion commanders to know with any clarity what was happening now. In the unfamiliar countryside, with maps that often proved highly inaccurate, companies and platoons were frequently out of touch with one another. At a crossroads near the stretch of highway where men of Colonel Fitch's 3rd Battalion had killed General Kussin, the British caught the full brunt of SS Major Krafft's rocket-propelled mortars and machine guns. The marching columns broke as men scattered into the woods. The screeching mortars, exploding in air bursts above their heads, hurled deadly fragments in every direction.

Signalman Stanley Heyes remembers the intense enemy harassment vividly. He sprinted for some woods and dropped a spare radio transmitter; bending to recover it he was struck in the ankle. Heyes managed to crawl into the woods. As he sank down in the underbrush, he realized that the man alongside him was German. "He was young and as frightened as I was," Heyes says, "but he used my field dressing on my ankle. A short time later we both were wounded again by the mortar fire and we just lay there waiting for someone to pick us up." Heyes and the young German would remain together until well after dark, when British stretcher-bearers found and evacuated them.

Like the 1st Battalion, the 3rd too was pinned down. After two hours on the road, both battalions had covered a bare two and a half miles. Now, Colonel Fitch reached the same conclusion as Dobie on the upper road; he too would have to find an alternate route to the Arnhem bridge. Time was precious, and the bridge was still a good four miles away.

In the woods around Wolfheze SS Major Sepp Krafft was convinced he was surrounded. He estimated that the British outnumbered his understrength battalion by twenty to one. But, although he considered his defense "insane," he could hardly believe the success of his blocking action. The rocket-propelled mortars had created havoc among the British, and his men now reported that paratroopers moving along the Utrecht-Arnhem road were halted in some places, and at others appeared to be abandoning the main road entirely. Krafft still believed that his was the only German unit in the area, and he had no illusions about stopping the British for long. He was running out of mortar ammunition and suffering heavy casualties, and one of his lieutenants had deserted. Still, Krafft was ebullient about "the courageous impetuosity of my young lads." The ambitious Krafft, who would later write a fulsome self-serving report to Himmler on his Grenadier Training and Reserve Battalion's actions, had no idea that his "young lads" were now being bolstered by the tanks, artillery and armored cars of Lieutenant Colonel Walter Harzer's Hohenstaufen Division only a mile or two east of Krafft's own headquarters.

Major Freddie Gough was totally baffled. Urquhart's message summoning him back to Division had carried no hint of what the General had in mind. When he left the Leopard route of the 1st Battalion, Gough brought back with him four escort jeeps and troops of his reconnaissance unit. Now, at Division headquarters, Urquhart's chief of staff, Colonel Charles Mackenzie, could not enlighten him either. The General, Mackenzie said, had gone off in search of Brigadier Lathbury, whose headquarters was following Colonel Frost's battalion along the southern, Lion route. Taking his escort, Gough set out once more. Surely, someplace along the route, he would find either one officer or the other.

� 12 ✧

GENERAL URQUHART'S JEEP sped down the Utrecht-Arnhem highway and turned south off the main artery onto a side road that led him to Frost's Lion route. Within a few minutes he caught up with the rear elements of the 2nd Battalion. They were moving single file, along both sides of the road. Urquhart could hear firing in the distance, but it seemed to him "there was a lack of urgency. Everyone appeared to be moving slowly." Driving swiftly along the cobbled road, Urquhart reached Frost's headquarters company only to discover that Frost was up with the leading units, which had run into German opposition. "I tried to impart a sense of urgency that I hoped would be conveyed to Frost," Urquhart writes, "and told them about the ill-fortune of the Recco Squadron." Learning that Lathbury had gone up to the middle road to see how the 3rd Battalion was doing, Urquhart retraced his route. Once again, he and Gough would miss each other by minutes.

Reaching the rear elements of the 3rd Battalion on the Tiger route, the General was told that Lathbury had gone forward. He followed. At a crossroads on the Utrecht-Arnhem road, Urquhart found the Brigadier. The area was under devastating mortar fire. "Some of these bombs were falling with unsettling accuracy on the crossroads and in the woodland where many of the Third Battalion were under cover," Urquhart was later to write. "This was the first real evidence to come my way of the speed and determination of the German reaction."°

° Major General R. E. Urquhart, C.B., D.S.O. (with Wilfred Greatorex), *Arnhem*, p. 40.

Taking cover in a slit trench, Urquhart and Lathbury discussed the situation. Both officers were worried about the slow progress of the brigade, and now the critical lack of communications was paralyzing their own efforts to command. Lathbury was completely out of touch with the 1st Battalion and had only intermittent communication with Frost. It was apparent that both were able to direct operations only in the area where they physically happened to be. For the moment, Lathbury's concern was to get the 3rd Battalion off the crossroads, out of the surrounding woods and on the move again. Urquhart decided to try to contact Division headquarters on his jeep's radio. As he neared the vehicle, he saw it had been struck by a mortar and his signalman was badly wounded. Although the radio set seemed undamaged, Urquhart could not raise Division. "I cursed the appalling communications," Urquhart later wrote. "Lathbury dissuaded me from attempting to go back to my own headquarters. The enemy was now thick between us and the landing zones . . . I decided he was right . . . and I stayed. But it was at this point that I realized I was losing control of the situation."

The men of the 1st and 3rd battalions were engaging in constant, bitter skirmishes. Hardened and desperate Waffen SS troopers, inferior in numbers but bolstered by half-tracks, artillery and tanks, were reducing the British advance on the two upper roads to a crawl. In the confusion, men were separated from their officers and from one another as companies scattered into the woods or fought along side roads and in the back gardens of houses. The Red Devils had recovered from the initial surprise of the German armored strength and, though taking heavy casualties, individually and in small groups they were striking back tenaciously. Still, there was little chance that the 1st and 3rd battalions could reach their Arnhem objectives as planned. Now everything depended upon Colonel John Frost's 2nd Battalion, moving steadily along the lower Rhine road, the secondary route that the Germans had largely dismissed.

Although Frost's battalion had been held up briefly several

times by enemy fire, he had refused to allow his men to scatter or deploy. His spearheading A Company, commanded by Major Digby Tatham-Warter, pressed forward, leaving stragglers to join the companies coming up behind. From prisoners taken by the advance parties, Frost learned that an SS company was believed to be covering the western approaches of Arnhem. Using some captured transport as well as their own jeeps to scout ahead and to the sides, the battalion moved steadily on. A little after 6 P.M., the first of Frost's objectives, the railway bridge over the Lower Rhine slightly southeast of Oosterbeek, came into view. According to plan, Major Victor Dover's C Company peeled off and headed for the river. The bridge looked empty and undefended as they approached. Lieutenant Peter Barry, twenty-one, was ordered to take his platoon across. "It was quiet when we started out," Barry recalls. "As we ran across the fields I noticed that there were dead cattle everywhere." Barry's platoon was within 300 yards of the bridge when he saw "a German run onto the bridge from the other side. He reached the middle, knelt down, and started doing something. Immediately, I told one section to open fire and a second section to rush the bridge. By this time, the German had disappeared."

Barry recalls that they "got onto the bridge and began racing across at full speed. Suddenly, there was a tremendous explosion and the bridge went up in our faces." Captain Eric Mackay of the Royal Engineers felt the ground shake under the impact. "A yellow-orange flame punched up and then black smoke rose over the bridge. I think the second span from the south bank was blown," Mackay says. On the bridge, under cover of smoke bombs, Lieutenant Barry ordered his men off the wreckage and back to the northern bank. As the platoon began to move, Germans hidden across the river opened fire. Barry was hit in the leg and arm and two other men were wounded. Watching the troopers return through the smoke and fire, Mackay, who had been uneasy about the operation from the beginning, remembers thinking, "Well, there goes number one." Colonel Frost was more philosophical. "I knew one of the three bridges was gone, but it was the least important. I didn't realize then what a disadvantage it would be." It was now 6:30 P.M. and there were two more bridges to go.

☼ 13 ☼

IT HAD TAKEN THE Hohenstaufen Division engineers five hours to reassemble all the tanks, half-tracks and armored personnel carriers that Harzer had planned to send back to Germany. Newly decorated Captain Paul Gräbner, his forty-vehicle reconnaissance battalion ready, now set out from Hoenderloo Barracks, north of Arnhem, and drove quickly south. Harzer had instructed him to make a sweep of the area between Arnhem and Nijmegen to assess the strength of the Allied airborne troops in that area. Gräbner raced swiftly through Arnhem and, by radio, informed Hohenstaufen headquarters that the city seemed almost deserted. There was no sign of enemy troops. A little before 7 P.M., Gräbner's unit crossed over the great Arnhem highway bridge. A mile past the southern end, Gräbner stopped his car to report, "No enemy. No paratroopers." Mile after mile, his light armored cars slowly patrolling both sides of the highway, Gräbner's radio messages conveyed the same information. At Nijmegen itself the news was unchanged. On orders of Hohenstaufen headquarters, Gräbner was then instructed to further patrol the outskirts of Nijmegen and then return to headquarters.

Gräbner's unit and the forward elements of Frost's 2nd Battalion had missed each other by approximately an hour. Even as Gräbner had driven out of Arnhem, Frost's men were in the city itself and were stealthily approaching their remaining objectives. Inexplicably, despite General Bittrich's explicit instructions, Harzer had completely failed to safeguard the Arnhem bridge.

☼ 14 ☼

IT WAS GROWING DARK as Colonel Frost quickened the battalion's pace toward the next objective, the pontoon crossing less than a mile west of the Arnhem bridge. Major Digby Tatham-Warter's A Company, still in the lead, was again momentarily held up on the high ground at the western outskirts of Arnhem. Enemy armored cars and machine guns had forced the company off the road and into the back gardens of nearby houses. Coming up behind, Frost found ten Germans guarded by a lone A Company man and, as he was later to write, surmised that "Digby's back-garden maneuver had been completely successful and that the company had rushed on again." Frost returned to the battalion. In the dusk, bursts of fire sporadically swept the road but as the men moved along, they passed damaged vehicles and a number of dead and wounded Germans—clear evidence, Frost thought, of "Digby's quite satisfactory progress."

Moving rapidly through the streets of Arnhem, the battalion reached the pontoon bridge and halted, faced with their second setback. The center section of the bridge had been removed and it was useless. As Captain Mackay stood looking at the dismantled crossing, he decided that "it was typical of the whole cocked-up operation. My one thought was, 'Now we've *got* to get that other bloody bridge.' " He stared off in the distance. Barely a mile away, the great concrete-and-steel span was silhouetted against the last light.

On the 3rd Battalion's Tiger route, moving haltingly toward Arnhem, General Urquhart knew with certainty that he was stranded. In the growing darkness, with enemy forays constantly harassing the march, there was no possibility of his returning to Division headquarters. His mood was bleak. "I wished with every step that I knew what was going on elsewhere." Just before nightfall, Urquhart learned that the 3rd's leading companies had reached the outskirts of Oosterbeek "near someplace called the Hartenstein Hotel. . . . We were making little progress," Urquhart was later to write, "and Lathbury, after a discussion with Fitch, the battalion commander, called a halt."

In a large house set well back from the road, Urquhart and Lathbury prepared to spend the night. The owner of the house, a tall, middle-aged Dutchman, brushed aside the General's apologies for inconveniencing him and his wife, and gave the two officers a downstairs front room overlooking the main road. Urquhart was restless and unable to relax. "I kept checking to see if any contact had been made with either Gough or Frost, but there was nothing from my headquarters or from anyone else."

The great bridge loomed ahead. The concrete ramps alone were immense complexes unto themselves with roads running beneath them and along the river bank from west to east. On either side the rooftops of houses and factory buildings came up to the level of the ramps. In the twilight, the massive approaches and the high-arched girders spanning the Rhine looked awesome and intimidating. Here finally was the main objective—the pivot of Montgomery's audacious plan—and to reach it Frost's men had fought on the march for nearly seven hours.

Now, as lead elements of the 2nd Battalion neared the bridge, Lieutenant Robin Vlasto, in command of one of A Company's platoons, was amazed by "its incredible great height." Vlasto noted "pillboxes at each end, and even in the general air of desertion, they looked threatening." In darkness A Company quietly took up positions beneath the huge supports at the northern end. From above them came the slow rumble of traffic.

Captain Eric Mackay of the Royal Engineers, approaching the bridge through a mosaic of streets, reached a small square leading to the ramp. He remembers that "the quietness as we went through the streets was oppressive, and all around us there seemed to be soft movement. Men were beginning to feel the strain, and I wanted to get that bridge as quickly as we could." Suddenly the darkness was ripped by German fire from a side street. One of the engineers' explosives trolleys went up in flames, and the men were clearly illuminated. Instantly, Mackay ordered his men with their equipment across the square. They dashed over, defying the German fire. Within a few minutes, without losing a man, they were at the bridge. Studying the terrain below the northern ramp, Mackay saw four houses on the east side. "One of them was a school and it was on the corner of a crossroads," he remembers. "I thought that whoever held these houses held the bridge." Mackay promptly ordered his engineers into the school.

Shortly after 8 P.M., Colonel Frost and the battalion headquarters arrived. Frost had sent Major Douglas Crawley's B Company to the high ground above the nearby railway embankment with antitank guns to protect the battalion's left flank, freeing A Company to dash for the bridge.° C Company, under Major Dover, was instructed to follow the forward elements into the city and seize the German commandant's headquarters. Now, at the bridge, Frost was unable to raise either company by radio. Quickly he dispatched messengers to determine their whereabouts.

Deciding not to wait, Frost ordered A Company platoons onto

° Frost recalls that "a map I had taken from a German prisoner . . . showed the routes of an enemy armored-car patrol unit and I realized that the German strength was to my left."

the bridge. As the men began to move across, the Germans came to life. Troopers were raked with fire from the pillbox at the northern end and by a lone armored car on the southern end of the bridge itself. A platoon, aided by Eric Mackay's sappers carrying flamethrowers, began to move through the top floors of houses whose roofs and attics were at eye level with the ramp. Simultaneously, Lieutenant Vlasto's platoon worked its way through basements and cellars, going from house to house until it reached Mackay's locations. In position, they attacked the pillbox. As the flamethrowers went into action, Frost recalls that "all hell seemed to be let loose. The sky lit up, and there was the noise of machine-gun fire, a succession of explosions, the crackling of burning ammunition and the thump of a cannon. A wooden building nearby was wreathed in flames, and there were screams of agony and fear."° Now, too, Frost could hear the crash of Vlasto's Piat† bombs smashing into the pillbox. Suddenly, the brief savage battle was over. The guns in the pillbox fell silent and through the fires, Frost saw German soldiers staggering toward his men. A Company had successfully cleared the north end of the bridge and it was theirs. But now, hampering fires and exploding ammunition made it suicidal to risk a second rush to grab the southern side. Only half an hour earlier, Frost could have succeeded.‡ But now, on the south bank, a group of SS Panzer Grenadiers had taken up positions.

Frost attempted to contact Major Crawley once more. He wanted to locate boats or barges in which Crawley's company could cross the river and attack the Germans on the southern side. Again, radio communications were out. Worse, messengers could not even find the company; and, they reported, there were

---

° Several accounts state that the flamethrowers' aim was diverted and instead of hitting the pillbox, the fiery liquid hit several huts containing explosives.

† A short-range, spring-loaded British antitank gun weighing 33 pounds and capable of firing a projectile that could penetrate four inches of tempered armor plate.

‡ According to Dutch Police Sergeant Johannes van Kuijk the bridge was deserted and without guards when he came on duty at 7:30 that evening. Earlier, according to Van Kuijk, when the airborne landings began, the bridge garrison of twenty-five World War I veterans deserted their post.

no boats to be seen. As for C Company, the patrol sent out to contact them were pinned down and heavily engaged near the German commandant's headquarters.

Grimly Frost's men looked across the Arnhem bridge. How strong were the Germans holding the southern end? Even now, A Company believed there was a chance of seizing the southern end by a surprise attack across the river, if only the men and boats could be found.

But that opportunity had passed. In one of the great ironies of the Arnhem battle, the Lower Rhine could have been crossed within the first hour of landing. Exactly seven miles west, at the village of Heveadorp—through which Frost's battalion had marched en route to their objectives—a large cable ferry, capable of carrying automobiles and passengers, had operated back and forth all day on its normal passage across the Lower Rhine between Heveadorp on the north bank and Driel on the south. Frost knew nothing about the ferry. Nor was it ever listed as one of Urquhart's objectives. In the meticulous planning of Market-Garden an important key to the taking of the Arnhem bridge—the ferry at Driel—had been totally overlooked.*

Major Freddie Gough had finally overtaken Lathbury's brigade headquarters, following Frost's battalion on the Lion route. Quickly he sought out Major Tony Hibbert, the second in com-

* In the official orders issued to Urquhart, no reference to the Driel ferry as an objective seems to exist. R.A.F. reconnaissance photographs, used at briefings, show it clearly and one must assume that at some stage of the planning it was discussed. However, General Urquhart, when I interviewed him on the subject, told me "I can't recall that the ferry ever came up." When Urquhart finally learned of the ferry's existence, it was too late to be of any use. Says Urquhart, "By that time I did not have enough men to put across the river." In oral orders, however, the engineers were warned that "the seizure of all ferries, barges and tugs becomes of paramount importance to assist the subsequent advance of XXX Corps." Obviously, however, in the last-minute stages of the planning these orders apparently carried lower priority, for they were never formally issued. "No one told us about the ferry at Driel," Colonel Frost told the author, "and it could have made all the difference."

mand. "Where's the General and the Brigadier?" Gough asked. Hibbert didn't know. "They're together someplace," he told Gough, "but they've both gone off." Gough was now totally confused. "I didn't know what to do," he recalls. "I tried to contact Division without success, so I just decided to keep on going after Frost." Leaving Hibbert, Gough set out once more.

It was dark when Gough and his troopers drove into Arnhem and found Frost and his men holding positions near the northern end of the bridge. Immediately Gough asked where Urquhart was. Like Hibbert, Frost had no idea. He assumed Urquhart was back with Division. Once more Gough tried his radio. Now adding to his anxiety was the absence of any news of his own reconnaissance forces near Wolfheze. But again he could make no contact with anyone. Ordering his tired men to a building close by the bridge, Gough climbed to the roof just in time to see the whole southern end of the bridge "go up in flames" as Frost's men made their first attempt to seize the far end. "I heard this tremendous explosion and the whole end of the bridge seemed to be on fire. I remember somebody saying 'We've come all this way just to have the damn bridge burn down.'" Gough himself was momentarily alarmed. Then, through the smoke he saw that only the pillbox and some ammunition shacks were destroyed. Concerned and weary, Gough turned in for a few hours' rest. He had traveled route after route all day in search of Urquhart. Now, at the bridge, at least one problem was solved. He was where he had set out to be and there he would stay.

There was little more that Lieutenant Colonel Frost could do this night, except to guard the northern end of the bridge from enemy attacks on the southern side. He still had no contact with his missing companies and now, in a house on a corner overlooking the bridge, Frost set up battalion headquarters. Lance Corporal Harold Back of the 2nd Battalion's cipher section remembers that from the front window of the house, the headquarters personnel could look out on the ramp. "The side window of the room gave us a direct view of the bridge itself," says Back. "Our signalers stuck their antennas through the roof and moved their sets constantly, but they couldn't make contact with anybody."

Shortly after, Brigade headquarters arrived and set up in the attic of a house near Frost's. After conferring with his officers, Frost thought it was now obvious that the 1st and 3rd battalions had either been held up on the Tiger and Leopard routes or were fighting north of the bridge somewhere in Arnhem. Without communications, it was impossible to tell what had happened. But if the two battalions did not reach Arnhem during the hours of darkness, the Germans would have the precious time necessary to close the area between Frost's men and the rest of the division. Additionally, Frost was worried that the great bridge might still be blown. In the opinion of the engineers, the heat from fires had already destroyed any fuses laid from the bridge to the town and all visible cables had already been cut by sappers. Still, no one knew exactly where other cables might be hidden. And, as Frost recalls, "the fires prevented even one man from being able to get on to the bridge to remove any charges that might still be there."

But the northern end of the Arnhem bridge was in Frost's hands and he and his courageous men had no intention of giving it up. Although he worried about his missing companies and the rest of the division, he did not show his concern. Visiting various sections now billeted in several houses near the ramp, he found his men "in great heart, as they had every reason to be." As Private James Sims recalls, "We felt quite pleased with ourselves, with the Colonel making jokes and inquiring about our comfort."

At battalion headquarters, Frost himself now settled down for the first time during the day. Sipping from a large mug of tea, he thought that, all in all, the situation was not too bad. "We had come eight miles through close, difficult country, to capture our objective within seven hours of landing in Holland . . . a very fine feat of arms indeed." Although restless, Frost, like his men, was optimistic. He now had a force numbering about five hundred men of various units, and he had every faith that his own

ARNHEM BRIDGE

WEERDIES

LANG

EUSEBIL · PLEIN

RYN - KADE

LOWER RHINE

COL. JOHN FROST'S POSITION

BRITISH DEFENSE LINE
AT NORTHERN END
OF BRIDGE

GERMAN S.S. PANZ

palacios

KADE

EISENHUS BINNEN SINGEL

EMBANKMENT

EISENHUS BUITEN SINGEL

NORTHERN RAMP

WESTERVOOTSCHE DYK

NIEUWE KADE

CAPT. ERIC MACKAY'S POSITION

GRENADIERS

N

missing companies would reach him at the bridge. In any case, he would only have to hold, at most, for another forty-eight hours— until the tanks of General Horrocks' XXX Corps arrived.

☆15☆

FROM BERLIN TO THE WESTERN FRONT, the German high command was stunned by the sudden Allied attack. Only in Arnhem, where the British 1st Airborne Division had dropped almost on top of General Bittrich's two panzer divisions, was the reaction both fierce and quick. Elsewhere, baffled and confused commanders tried to determine whether the startling events of September 17 were indeed the opening phase of an invasion of the Reich. A ground attack by the British out of Belgium had been anticipated. All available reserves, including General Von Zangen's Fifteenth Army, so worn down that men had little else but the rifles they carried, had been thrown into defense positions to hold against that threat. Trenches had been dug and strategic positions built in an all-out effort to force the British to fight for every foot of ground.

No one had foreseen that airborne forces would be used simultaneously with the British land advance. Were these airborne attacks the prelude to an invasion of Holland by sea, as Berlin feared? In the hours of darkness, while staff officers tried to analyze the situation, reports of additional airborne attacks further confused the picture. American paratroopers, their strength unknown and their units still unidentified, were in the Eindhoven-Nijmegen area; and the British 1st Airborne Division had clearly landed around Arnhem. But now new messages told of paratroopers in the vicinity of Utrecht, and a totally bewildering report claimed that airborne forces had landed in Warsaw, Poland.°

At Field Marshal Gerd von Rundstedt's headquarters in Koblenz, the general reaction was one of astonishment.† The crusty, aristocratic Von Rundstedt was not so much surprised at the nature of the attack as by the man who, he reasoned, must be directing it—Montgomery. Initially, Von Rundstedt doubted that these sudden and apparently combined land-and-air operations were the opening of Eisenhower's offensive to invade the Reich. The Field Marshal had long been certain that Patton and the American Third Army driving toward the Saar posed the real danger. To combat that threat, Von Rundstedt had committed his best troops to repulse Patton's racing tanks. Now Germany's most renowned soldier was caught temporarily off balance. Never had he expected Eisenhower's main offensive to be led by Montgomery, whom he had always considered "overly cautious, habit-ridden and systematic."

He was astounded by the boldness of Montgomery's move. The messages pouring in from Model's headquarters carried a note of hysteria attesting all the more to the surprise and gravity of the attack: "We must reckon with more airborne landings being made at night . . . the enemy obviously believes his attack to be of major importance and the British have achieved considerable initial success against Student and pushed forward to Valkens-waard . . . the position here is particularly critical . . . the lack of fast, strong reserves is increasing our difficulties . . . the general situation of Army Group B, stretched as it is to the limits, is critical . . . we require, as fast as possible, panzers, artillery, heavy mobile antitank weapons, antiaircraft units, and it is

---

° The R.A.F. did drop dummy paratroops over a wide area around Utrecht, diverting some German troops for days. No troops were dropped on Warsaw and the report may have been garbled in transmission or, more simply, may have been the result of unfounded rumor.

† "When we first informed Von Rundstedt's headquarters of the airborne attack," Colonel Hans von Tempelhof, Model's operations chief, told me, "OB West seemed hardly perturbed. In fact the reaction was almost callously normal. It quickly changed."

absolutely essential that we have fighters in the sky day and night . . ."

Model ended with these words: ". . . the main concentration of the Allies is on the northern wing of our front." It was one of the few times Von Rundstedt had ever respected the opinion of the officer he had caustically referred to as having the makings of a good sergeant major. In that fragment of his message, Model had stripped away Von Rundstedt's last doubts about who was responsible for the startling developments. The "northern wing" of Army Group B *was* Montgomery.

During the night hours it was impossible to estimate the strength of the Allied airborne forces in Holland, but Von Rundstedt was convinced that further landings could be expected. It would now be necessary not only to plug gaps all along the German front but to find reserves for Model's Army Group B at the same time. Once again, Von Rundstedt was forced to gamble. Messages went out from his headquarters transferring units from their positions facing the Americans at Aachen. The moves were risky but essential. These units would have to travel north immediately, and their commitment in the line might take forty-eight hours at minimum. Von Rundstedt issued further orders to defense areas along Germany's northwest frontier, calling for all available armor and antiaircraft units to proceed to the quiet backwater of Holland where, the Field Marshal was now convinced, imminent danger to the Third Reich lay. Even as he worked steadily on through the night to shore up his defenses, Germany's Iron Knight pondered the strangeness of the situation. He was still amazed that the officer in charge of this great Allied offensive was Montgomery.

It was late evening when the staff car carrying General Wilhelm Bittrich from his headquarters at Doetinchem arrived in the darkened streets of Arnhem. Bittrich was determined to see for himself what was happening. As he reconnoitered through the city, fires were still burning and debris littered the streets—the effect of the morning's bombing. Dead soldiers and smoldering vehicles in many areas attested, as Bittrich was later to say, to "the turbulent fighting that had taken place." Yet, he had no clear picture of what was happening. Returning to his own headquarters, Bittrich learned from reports received from two women telephone operators in the Arnhem Post headquarters—whom he was later to decorate with the Iron Cross—that the great highway bridge had been taken by British paratroopers. Bittrich was infuriated. His specific order to Harzer to hold the bridge had not been carried out. Now it was crucial that the Nijmegen bridge over the Waal river be secured before the Americans in the south could seize it. Bittrich's only chance of success was to crush the Allied assault along the corridor and squeeze the British to a standstill in the Arnhem area. The paratroopers now on the north end of the Arnhem bridge and the scattered battalions struggling to reach them must be totally destroyed.

The top-secret Market-Garden plan that had fallen into Colonel General Kurt Student's possession finally reached Field Marshal Model at his new headquarters. He had abandoned the gardener's cottage on the Doetinchem castle grounds and moved about five miles southeast near the small village of Terborg. It had taken Student the best part of ten hours to locate the Field Marshal and transmit the document by radio. Arriving in three parts and now decoded, Market-Garden lay revealed.

Model and his staff studied it intently. Before them was Montgomery's entire plan: the names of the airborne divisions employed, the successive air and resupply lifts ranging over a three-day period, the exact location of the landing and drop zones, the crucial bridge objectives—even the flight routes of the aircraft involved. Model, as Harzer was later to learn from the Field Marshal himself, called the plan "fantastic." It was so fantastic that in these critical hours Model refused to believe it.

The plans were too pat, too detailed for credibility. Model suggested to his staff that the very preciseness of the document argued against its authenticity. He stressed again his own firm conviction that the landings west of Arnhem were the spearhead of a large-scale airborne attack toward the Ruhr, via Bocholt and Münster, some forty miles east. Additional airborne landings should be expected, he warned, and once assembled would undoubtedly swerve north and then east. Model's reasoning was not without validity. As he told his staff, "If we are to believe these plans and are to assume that the Arnhem bridge is the true objective, why were not troops dropped directly on the bridge? Here, they arrive on vast open areas suitable for assembly, and moreover, eight miles to the west."

Model did not inform General Bittrich of the document. "I never realized until after the war," says Bittrich, "that the Market-Garden plans had fallen into our hands. I have no idea why Model did not tell me. In any case, the plans would simply have confirmed my own opinion that the important thing to do was prevent the link-up between the airborne troops and the British Second Army—and for that, they certainly needed the bridges."[*] One officer under Bittrich's command did learn of the document. Lieutenant Colonel Harzer seemed to be the only officer outside the Field Marshal's staff with whom Model talked about the plan. Harzer recalls that "Model was always prepared for the worst, so he did not discount it entirely. As he told me, he had no intention of being caught by the short hairs." Only time would tell the Germans whether the document was, in fact, genuine. Although the temperamental, erratic Field Marshal was not fully prepared to accept the evidence before him, most of his staff were impressed. With the Market-Garden plan in their hands, Model's headquarters alerted all antiaircraft units already on the move of the drops that the plan said would take place a few hours later.

One assumption, at least, was laid to rest. Lieutenant Gustav

---

[*] OB West was not informed of the captured Market-Garden plans either; nor is there any mention in Model's reports to Von Rundstedt of the documents. For some reason Model thought so little of the plans that he did not pass them on to higher headquarters.

Sedelhauser, the general-headquarters administrative officer, recalls that on the basis of the captured documents, Model was now of the opinion that he and his Oosterbeek headquarters had not been the objective of the airborne assault after all.

� 16 ✶

At the precise time that Lieutenant Colonel John Frost secured the northern end of the Arnhem bridge, a cautious approach to another prime objective eleven miles away was only just beginning. The five-span highway bridge over the Waal river at Nijmegen in the 82nd Airborne's central sector of the corridor was the last crossing over which the tanks of General Horrocks' XXX Corps would pass on their drive to Arnhem.

With spectacular success, Brigadier General James M. Gavin's 504th paratroopers had grabbed the crucial Grave bridge eight miles southwest of Nijmegen; and, at about 7:30 P.M., units of the 504th and 505th regiments secured a crossing over the Maas-Waal Canal at the village of Heumen, less than five miles due east of Grave. Gavin's hope of capturing all three canal crossings and a railroad bridge was in vain. The bridges were blown or severely damaged by the Germans before the 82nd could grab them. Yet, within six hours of landing, Gavin's troopers had forged a route over which the British ground forces would travel. Additionally, patrols of the 505th Regiment probing the area between the 82nd's drop zones near the Groesbeek Heights and the Reichswald encountered only light resistance; and, by nightfall, other troopers of the 508th Regiment had secured a 3½-mile stretch of woods along the Holland-German border north of the Groesbeek

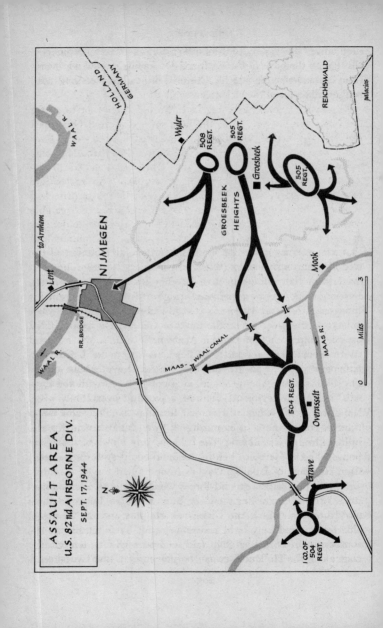

ASSAULT AREA
U.S. 82nd AIRBORNE DIV.
SEPT. 17, 1944

GERMANY

HOLLAND

REICHSWALD

palacios

WAAL R.

Wyler

508 REGT.

505 REGT.

GROESBEEK HEIGHTS

Groesbeek

505 REGT.

to Arnhem

NIJMEGEN

Lent

RR. BRIDGE

WAAL R.

Mook

MAAS-WAAL CANAL

MAAS R.

504 REGT.

Overasselt

Grave

I CO. OF 504 REGT.

N

0   1   2   3
Miles

drop zone and running to the southeastern outskirts of Nijmegen. Now, with three of the 82nd's four key objectives in hand, everything depended upon the capture of the 1,960-foot-long road bridge at Nijmegen.

Although General Browning had directed Gavin not to go for the Nijmegen crossing until the high ground around Groesbeek was secured, Gavin was confident that all the 82nd's objectives could be taken on this first day. Evaluating the situation some twenty-four hours before the jump, Gavin had called in the 508th's commander, Colonel Roy E. Lindquist, and directed him to send one battalion racing for the bridge. In the surprise and confusion of the airborne landings, Gavin reasoned, the gamble was well worth taking. "I cautioned Lindquist about the dangers of getting caught in streets," Gavin remembers, "and pointed out that the way to get the bridge was to approach from east of the city without going through built-up areas." Whether by misunderstanding or a desire to clean up his initial assignments, Lindquist's own recollection was that he was not to commit his troopers in an assault on the bridge until the regiment's other objectives had been achieved. To the 1st Battalion, commanded by Lieutenant Colonel Shields Warren, Jr., Lindquist assigned the task of holding protective positions along the Groesbeek-Nijmegen highway about a mile and a quarter southeast of the city. Warren was to defend the area and link up with the regiment's remaining two battalions to the west and east. Only when these missions were accomplished, Warren recalled, was he to prepare to go into Nijmegen. Thus, instead of driving for the bridge from the flat farming areas to the east, Warren's battalion found itself squarely in the center of those very built-up areas Gavin had sought to avoid.

It was nightfall before Warren achieved his other objectives. Now with precious time lost, lead companies began to move slowly through the quiet, almost deserted streets of Nijmegen. The main objective was to reach the traffic circle leading to the southern approaches of the bridge. There was a diversionary target as well. The Dutch underground reported that the detonating mechanism for destroying the great crossing was situated in the main post-office building. This vital information reached Warren's units only after they had begun moving toward the bridge. A platoon was hurriedly sent to the post office, where, after subduing the German guards, engineers cut wires and blew up what they believed to be the detonating controls. Whether this apparatus was, in fact, actually hooked up to explosives on the bridge, no one would ever know for certain, but now, at least, electrical circuits and switchboards were destroyed. When the platoon attempted to withdraw to rejoin the main force they found that the enemy had closed in behind them. They were cut off and for the next three days would be forced to hold out in the post office until help arrived.

Meanwhile, as the remainder of Warren's force approached a park that led toward the bridge, they came suddenly under intense machine-gun and armored-car fire. Captain Arie D. Bestebreurtje, the Dutch officer assigned to the 82nd, remembers that "guns suddenly opened up on us, and I could see the flashes of fire from the muzzles. They seemed to be all around us." Before he could raise his carbine to fire, Bestebreurtje was hit in the left hand and elbow and the right index finger.° To Corporal James R. Blue, the eerie battle raging in the blacked-out streets was like a nightmare. "Right away we were engaged in hand-to-hand combat," Blue remembers. He was moving through the streets with Private First Class Ray Johnson, both armed with M-1 rifles with fixed bayonets, when they came face to face with SS troops. As Johnson tried to get one of the Germans with his bayonet, Blue went after an officer with a trench knife. "Our orders were not to fire. If we came to close combat we were to use knives and bayonets. But," Blue recalls, "that trench knife seemed mighty short, so I used my Tommy gun. That closed that chapter, but almost immediately a self-propelled gun began to fire in our direction and we moved up to the park and tied in with other

° Several days later, Bestebreurtje was told by doctors that the finger must be amputated. "I told them absolutely not," Bestebreurtje says. "It was my finger and I was not going to have it amputated. Besides, it would have ruined my piano playing." He still has the finger.

platoons." Private James Allardyce remembers hearing a call for medics up front, but "bullets were whistling down the street and there was so much confusion in the darkness that men did not know where others were. We set up a perimeter defense around a modern brick schoolhouse. Out front we heard German voices and the moaning and cries of the wounded. We couldn't make it to the bridge. Finally it came through to us that the Jerries had stopped us."

As indeed they had. Captain Paul Gräbner's Reconnaissance Battalion, which had missed Frost at the Arnhem bridge, had arrived in Nijmegen well in advance of the late-starting Americans.

By midnight on this first day of the mightiest airborne assault in history, British and American paratroops were on, or fighting toward, their major objectives. Through long hours of march and savage encounters with an unexpectedly strong and tenacious enemy, they had gained most of the objectives that the planners had expected them to take swiftly and with ease. From the gallant men of Colonel John Frost's 2nd Battalion clinging to the north end of the Arnhem bridge, all along the corridor south to where Colonel Robert Sink's 101st troopers struggled to repair the bridge at Son, the mood was one of fierce determination; they must hold open the highway along which the British Second Army tanks and infantry would drive. On this midnight, troopers did not doubt that relief was on the way or that reinforcements and supplies, scheduled to arrive on the eighteenth, would further bolster their position. Despite heavy casualties, confusion, and communications setbacks, the men of the airborne army were completely optimistic. All in all, it had not been a bad Sunday outing.

☆17☆

THERE WAS A RED GLOW in the sky over Arnhem as the speeding car bringing Major General Heinz Harmel back from Berlin neared the city. Apprehensive and tired after the long trip, Harmel arrived at the Frundsberg Division headquarters in Ruurlo, only to find that his command post was now situated in Velp, approximately three miles northeast of Arnhem. There, he found his chief of staff, Lieutenant Colonel Paetsch, looking exhausted. "Thank God you're back!" Paetsch said. Quickly he briefed Harmel on the day's events and on the orders received from General Bittrich. "I was dumfounded," Harmel recalls. "Everything seemed confused and uncertain. I was very tired, yet the gravity of the situation was such that I called Bittrich and told him I was coming to see him."

Bittrich had not slept either. As Harmel was shown in, Bittrich began immediately to outline the situation. Angry and frustrated, he bent over his maps. "British paratroopers have landed here, west of Arnhem," he told Harmel. "We have no idea of their actual strength or intentions." Pointing to Nijmegen and Eindhoven, the corps commander said, "American airborne forces have secured lodgments in these two areas. Simultaneously, Montgomery's forces have attacked north from the Meuse-Escaut Canal. My belief is that the object is to split our forces. In my opinion, the objectives are the bridges. Once these are secured, Montgomery can drive directly up to the center of Holland and from there, into the Ruhr." Bittrich waved his hands. "Model disagrees. He still believes further airborne forces will be dropped north of the Rhine, east and west of Arnhem and march toward the Ruhr."

Harzer's Hohenstaufen Division, Bittrich went on to explain, had been ordered to mop up the British west and north of Arnhem. The armed forces commander in the Netherlands, General Christiansen, had been directed to send in his forces—a mixture of defense and training battalions—under command of Lieutenant General Hans von Tettau. Their mission was to aid the Hohenstaufen Division on the flanks in an effort to overrun the British landing and drop zones.

The Frundsberg Division, Bittrich continued, was charged with all activities to the east of Arnhem and south to Nijmegen. Stabbing the map with his finger, Bittrich told Harmel, "The Nijmegen bridge must be held at all costs. Additionally the Arnhem bridge and the area all the way south to Nijmegen is your responsibility." Bittrich paused and paced the room. "Your problems," he told Harmel, "have been made more difficult. Harzer failed to leave armored units at the north end of the Arnhem bridge. The British are now there."

As he listened, Harmel realized with growing alarm that with the Arnhem bridge in British hands, there was no way to get his armor quickly across the Rhine and down to Nijmegen. Nor was there another bridge crossing over the river east of the Arnhem bridge. His entire division would have to be taken over the Rhine at a ferry landing in the village of Pannerden, some eight miles southeast of Arnhem. Bittrich, anticipating the problem, had already ordered the ferry operations to begin. It would be a slow, tedious, roundabout way of reaching Nijmegen, and to ferry the division's trucks, armor and men would take all of Harmel's resources.

As he left Bittrich's headquarters, Harmel asked his commander, "Why not destroy the Nijmegen bridge before it's too late?" Bittrich's tone was ironic. "Model has flatly refused to consider the idea. We may need it to counterattack." Harmel stared in amazement. "With what?" he asked.

In the dark, Harmel set out once again, heading for Pannerden. His units were already on the move toward the ferry crossing and the roads were choked with troops and vehicles. In Pannerden itself, Harmel saw the reason for the chaotic conditions he had witnessed on the road. Vehicles congested the streets in one gigantic traffic jam. At the river's edge, makeshift ferries composed of rubber rafts were slowly floating trucks across the river. From his chief of staff, Harmel learned that one battalion had reached the far shore and was already en route to Nijmegen. Some trucks and smaller vehicles were also across. But as yet, heavier armored equipment had not even been loaded. In Paetsch's opinion, Harmel's Frundsberg units might not be in action in the Arnhem-Nijmegen area until September 24 if the slow, cumbersome ferrying could not be speeded up.

Harmel knew there was only one solution to the problem. He would have to retake the Arnhem bridge and open the highway route to Nijmegen. As this first day of Market-Garden, September 17, ended all the German frustrations now focused on a single obstinate man—Colonel John Frost at the Arnhem bridge.

Convinced that Holland was on the verge of liberation and completely oblivious to the dangers, the Dutch climbed on their roofs to watch the vast armada of troop carrier planes and gliders.

British troopers enplane for Holland [ABOVE], and an American Waco glider [BELOW] is loaded. · [OPPOSITE] Planes tow gliders of 101st Airborne over Eindhoven, and [NEXT PAGE] men of 82nd Airborne land over Groesbeek in mass jump.

Gliders and paratroopers of British 1st Airborne [ABOVE] *land near Arnhem, and planes drop supplies* [BELOW] *in the face of heavy anti-aircraft fire.*

A tow plane behind the Waco glider [ABOVE] *crash-lands and explodes on Arnhem drop zone. Tail of the huge Horsa glider* [BELOW] *was quickly removed to unload the cargo.*

In spite of warnings, Arnhem's German commander, General Kussin, took the wrong road and was killed by British troopers.

[ABOVE] *Artillery chief Lieutenant Colonel "Sheriff" Thompson (at left) unloads gear from Horsa glider.* · *A Guards Armored tank passes a knocked-out German armored vehicle* [BELOW]. *Terrain difficulties and narrow, one-tank-width roads hindered the advance of the armored drive.*

In the corridor [ABOVE] *a supply truck explodes after receiving direct hit. A German patrol* [BELOW] *moves up during first hours of battle.*

Flight Lieutenant David Lord [BELOW, AT RIGHT]*, in an unprecedented act of courage, witnessed by British paratroopers, circled his flaming Dakota again and again over the drop zone in a successful attempt to parachute precious supplies. The only survivor was Flying Officer Henry King* [ABOVE LEFT]*. · Typical of courageous glider pilots was Sergeant Victor Miller* [ABOVE RIGHT]*, who successfully landed his huge, unwieldy craft. His one concern was that another glider might "crash-land on top of me."*

Lieutenant Tony Jones [ABOVE LEFT], *called by General Horrocks the "bravest of the brave," rushed across Nijmegen bridge in wake of tanks and cut the German detonating explosive wires.* · *A badly wounded paratrooper* [ABOVE RIGHT] *is rushed to casualty station.* · *82nd Airborne troopers* [BELOW] *move through outskirts of Nijmegen.*

[ABOVE] British "Red Devils" move forward through the debris at Arnhem. [BELOW] Antoon Derksen's house at 14 Zwarteweg, where General Urquhart hid out when caught behind German lines.

101st Airborne troopers are greeted by Dutch [ABOVE] as they pass through Eindhoven.
· Terrain difficulties are clearly shown [BELOW] on one-tank front, where Guards
Armored column has been halted on "island" dike-top road.

On Arnhem bridge Colonel Frost's and Captain Mackay's men successfully repulsed a German armored attack, knocking out twelve lead vehicles. The German commander, Gräbner, was killed in the attack.

[BELOW, LEFT TO RIGHT] *Field Marshal Model; General Bittrich; the one-legged Major Knaust (also shown above left as he is today); and Major General Heinz Harmel confer during battle. Knaust's Tiger tanks stopped the last drive of British to relieve the Arnhem bridge defenders. · Major Egon Skalka* [ABOVE RIGHT], *Hohenstaufen Division medical officer, who cooperated in exchanging the wounded during the truce. The SS man, obviously worried about his future, requested a letter of commendation from a British medical officer.*

Dutch women who had collaborated with Germans [ABOVE] *were quickly rounded up by the Resistance and had their heads shaved* [BELOW].

[LEFT] *The Hartenstein Hotel in Ooster-beek, General Urquhart's headquarters during the battle.* [CENTER] *The Schoo-noord Hotel and* [BOTTOM] *the Tafelberg Hotel, shown before and during the battle.*

Perhaps the finest journalistic coverage of the war came out of Arnhem. Sergeants Lewis and Walker, Army cameramen [ABOVE], share a meal with Dutch girl. · London Daily Express war correspondent Alan Wood [BELOW] electrified Britain with his brilliant dispatches from the field.

The build-up of the 35,000-man Allied Airborne Army was slowed by inclement weather. Parachutes of 101st Airborne troopers [ABOVE] dot countryside on second day of attack. · At Arnhem bridge, Major Digby Tatham-Warter (shown below as he is today and in 1944) bolstered the men's morale by his eccentric charges against the enemy under an open umbrella.

In Oosterbeek perimeter, cut off and without supplies, Medic "Taffy" Brace [RIGHT] used makeshift paper bandages to save the life of machine gunner Corporal Andrew Milbourne (shown above then and now), who lost an eye and both hands. · Another British hero was Sergeant Alfred Roullier (shown below then and now), who cooked and served hot stew in the midst of battle to the hungry troops.

A major British miscalculation was the failure to use the Dutch underground. The most frustrated of all were Dutch liaison officer Lieutenant Commander Arnoldus Wolters [ABOVE LEFT] and Douw van der Krap [ABOVE RIGHT], whose efforts to form a fighting unit proved fruitless.

In Oosterbeek, baker Dirk van Beek [LEFT] saw that "things are going bad," but vowed to continue "baking to the last." · Rare book seller Gerhardus Gysbers [ABOVE], whose shop was next to the German barracks, was one of the first to realize that the British Arnhem attack was doomed to failure.

In the pre-attack bombing, Resistance worker Albertus Uijen [BELOW LEFT] saw that Nijmegen was being isolated by bombers. · Telephone technician

Nicolaas de Bode [BELOW RIGHT], using secret lines, was able to pass on vital information to the underground and Allies. · Johannus Penseel [ABOVE LEFT] took advantage of German confusion to move an arsenal of weapons "beneath Germans' noses." · Gysbert Numan [ABOVE RIGHT] wanted to surrender himself and others rather than allow twelve innocent men to be executed for the abortive sabotage of a viaduct on September 15th. Arnhem Resistance chief Kruyff refused the request.

The Germans systematically destroyed British strongholds. · [BELOW] A knocked-out German tank lies amidst the ruins, and [ABOVE] British troopers hold positions around the Hartenstein Hotel. In background is the tennis court where German prisoners were held. · [OPPOSITE] Church in lower Oosterbeek was almost totally destroyed.

"They are throwing us away," Colonel Tilly [ABOVE RIGHT] *confided to his second-i[n] command, Major Grafton* [ABOVE LEFT], *after he learned that his Dorset unit was t[o] cross the Lower Rhine and make a last stand while the remnants of Urquhart's divisio[n] were evacuated. Of 10,000 Britishers in the Arnhem attack, only 2,323 crossed th[e] river to safety. Some of the survivors are shown below.*

A cipher code hidden in a .303 cartridge was supposed to be fired before evacuation. In the excitement of escape, Signaler James Cockrill forgot his instructions and later found the code and bullet in his battle dress pocket.

In the late sixties, during a photo-mapping of Holland by KLM Airlines, experts were mystified by what appeared to be aircraft on the heaths near Arnhem [OPPOSITE]. On careful examination cartographers discovered that the ghostly images were outlines of gliders. During and after the battle in 1944, wrecked gliders were burned, indelibly branding the heath. Confirmation of the silhouettes was made by Robert Voskuil, son of Jan and Bertha, who compared the wartime aerial photographs with KLM pictures and presented his findings in the Journal of the Royal Geographic Society.

The chief personalities of the airborne attack as they are today
General James M. Gavin of 82nd Airborne [ABOVE LEFT]; *General Maxwell D. Taylor of 101st Airborne* [ABOVE RIGHT]; [BELOW, LEFT TO RIGHT, IN 1966] *General Stanislaw Sosabowski; General John Hackett; General Roy Urquhart; Colonel C. F. Gough; General John Frost; and Brigadier Graeme Warrack.* · *Refusing to return to Communist-dominated Poland at war's end, Sosabowski worked for a time in Britain as a common laborer. He died as this book was being written.*

Part Four

THE SIEGE

☼ 1 ☼

Eᴀʀʟʏ ᴍᴏʀɴɪɴɢ ᴍɪsᴛ rising from the Rhine swirled around the Arnhem bridge and the silent darkened houses surrounding it. A short distance from the northern ramp, the Eusebius Buiten Singel—a long, landscaped boulevard bordering the historic inner city—stretched back toward the outlying areas north and east and ended at the Musis Sacrum, Arnhem's popular concert hall. On this Monday, September 18, in the thin, indistinct light, the ancient capital of Gelderland appeared deserted. Nothing moved in the streets, gardens, squares or parks.

From their positions around the northern end of the bridge, Colonel Frost's men could begin to see for the first time the whole sprawl of the city with its houses and municipal buildings: the Court of Justice, Provincial Government House, State Archives buildings, the town hall, general post office and the railroad station less than a mile to the northwest. Nearer, the Church of St. Eusebius, with its 305-foot-high steeple, dominated the city. Few of Frost's men, looking warily out from shattered windows and freshly dug foxholes in a perimeter composed of eighteen houses, realized that the great church now had a sinister significance. German snipers had moved into the tower during the night. Carefully concealed, they, like the British, waited tensely for full light.

The battle for the bridge had raged all night. A midnight lull had been short-lived. When the fighting broke out again, it almost seemed that each man was engaged in individual contest. Twice during the night Frost's men had tried to rush the southern end of the bridge, only to be beaten back. Lieutenant John Grayburn, leading both charges, had been badly wounded in the face, but stayed on the bridge and oversaw the evacuation of all his men to safety.° Later, truckloads of German infantry tried to ram their way across the bridge, only to be met by the concentrated fire of the British troopers. With flamethrowers, Frost's men had set the vehicles on fire. Panzer Grenadiers were burned alive in the inferno and fell screaming to the Rhine one hundred feet below. The acrid smell of burning rubber and thick black smoke eddying up from the debris hampered rescue parties from both sides searching for their wounded among the bodies littering the bridge. Lance Corporal Harold Back, in one such party, was helping to carry wounded into the basement of one of the houses held by Frost's men. In the darkness of the cellar, he saw what he thought were a few candles burning. Injured troopers were laid out all over the floor and suddenly Back realized that what he saw were tiny fragments glowing on the bodies of some of the wounded. Hit by splinters from phosphorous shells, the men were glowing in the dark.

Inexplicably, in these first moments of daylight, the battle halted again. It was almost as though both sides were drawing a deep breath. Across the road from Frost's battalion headquarters, on a side street under the ramp itself, Captain Eric Mackay made a quiet reconnaissance of the houses that his little force of engineers and small groups of men from other units now controlled. During a vicious nighttime battle, Mackay had managed to hang on to two of the four houses in the area and set up a command post in one of them, a brick schoolhouse. The Germans, counterattacking, had crept through the landscaped grounds to toss hand grenades into the houses. Infiltrating the buildings, the Germans

---

° Grayburn was killed in the battle for Arnhem. On September 20 he stood in full view of an enemy tank and directed the withdrawal of his men to a main defense perimeter. For supreme courage, leadership and devotion to duty during the entire engagement, he was posthumously awarded Britain's highest military honor, the Victoria Cross.

fought a deadly, almost silent hand-to-hand battle with the British. Ranging through the cellars and from room to room, Mackay's men drove back swarms of the enemy with bayonets and knives. Then, taking a small group of men, Mackay went out into the bushes after the retreating Germans. Again, with bayonets and grenades, the British routed the enemy. Mackay was hit in the legs by shrapnel and a bullet punctured his helmet, grazing his scalp.

Now, checking his troopers, Mackay discovered casualties similar to his own. Adding to his problems, the supply situation was not good: There were six Bren guns, ammunition, grenades and some explosives. But Mackay had no antitank weapons, little food and no medical supplies except morphia and field dressings. Additionally, the Germans had cut off the water. Now, all that was available was what the men still had in their canteens.

Terrible as the nighttime fighting had been, Mackay maintained a fierce determination. "We were doing well and our casualties were comparatively light," he recalls. "Besides, now with the coming of daylight, we could see what we were doing and we were ready." Still, Mackay, like Frost, had few illusions. In this most deadly kind of fighting—street by street, house by house and room by room—he knew it was only a question of time before the British garrison at the bridge was overwhelmed. The Germans obviously hoped to crush Frost's small force, by sheer weight of numbers, within a matter of hours. Against such powerful and concentrated attacks, all that could save the courageous defenders at the bridge was the arrival of XXX Corps or the remaining battalions of the 1st Parachute Brigade still fighting their way into the city.

It had been a night of unceasing horror for the SS soldiers who fought near the bridge. Colonel Harzer, apparently satisfied that he had halted Urquhart's battalions, had underestimated both the number and the caliber of the men who had reached the northern end. Harzer did not even bother to order his few self-propelled guns to be brought up as support. Instead, squad after squad of SS were thrown against the British positions in the buildings around the ramp. These tough units met a foe most of them remember as the fiercest soldiers they had ever encountered.

SS Squad Leader Alfred Ringsdorf, twenty-one, an experienced soldier who had fought in Russia, was on a freight train heading toward Arnhem where, he was told, his group was to be refitted. There was utter confusion at the Arnhem station when Ringsdorf and his men arrived. Troops from a hodgepodge of units were milling about, being lined up and marched off. Ringsdorf's unit was told to report immediately to a command post in the city. There, a major attached them to a company of the 21st Panzer Grenadier Regiment. The squad had arrived without arms, but by late Sunday afternoon they were outfitted with machine guns, carbines, hand grenades and a few *Panzerfäuste.*° Questioning the limited amount of ammunition, they were told that supplies were en route. "At this time," says Ringsdorf, "I had no idea where we were going to fight, where the battle was, and I had never been in Arnhem before."

In the center of the city, there was evidence that heavy street fighting had already taken place. For the first time, Ringsdorf learned that British paratroopers had landed and were holding the northern end of the Arnhem bridge. No one seemed to know how large the force was. His squad was assembled in a church and given their orders. They were to infiltrate behind the buildings on either side of the bridge ramp and rout out the British. Ringsdorf knew how deadly this kind of fighting was. His experiences at the Russian front had taught him that. Yet, the men in his command were seasoned young veterans. They thought the battle would be brief.

All through the area leading to the bridge, the squad saw houses heavily damaged by bombing, and the men had to work their way through the rubble. As they neared the perimeter

° A German version of the American recoilless antitank bazooka capable of firing a 20-pound projectile with extreme accuracy.

positions the British had set up around the north end of the bridge, they came under intense machine-gun fire. Pinned down, the squad was unable to get within six hundred yards of the bridge approach. A lieutenant called for a volunteer to cross the square and toss a demolition charge into the house where the heaviest machine-gun fire seemed to be centered. Ringsdorf volunteered. Under covering fire, he dashed across the square. "I stopped behind a tree near a cellar window where the shooting was coming from and tossed the charge inside. Then I ran back to my men." Lying in rubble waiting for the explosion to go off, Ringsdorf looked back just as a tall house on a corner, where a number of German engineers were sheltering, was suddenly hit by shells. The entire front of the house crumbled, burying everybody. It struck Ringsdorf that had his own men been there, the entire squad would have been wiped out. At that moment, the demolition charge he had thrown into the cellar exploded on the street not far from where he lay. The British had tossed it back out the window.

At nightfall various squads began to infiltrate the buildings to dig the British out. Ringsdorf's objective was a big red building which, he was told, was a school. Heading toward it, his squad quickly encountered alert British marksmen who forced the Germans to take refuge in a nearby house. Smashing the windows, the SS men opened fire. The British immediately took cover in the house next door and a vicious fire fight began. "The British shooting was deadly," Ringsdorf recalls. "We could hardly show ourselves. They aimed for the head, and men began to fall beside me, each one with a small, neat hole through the forehead."

With losses mounting, the Germans fired a panzerfaust directly at the British-occupied house. As the shell crashed into the building, Ringsdorf's squad charged. "The fighting was cruel," he remembers. "We pushed them back room by room, yard by yard, suffering terrible losses." In the middle of the melee, the young squad leader was ordered to report to his battalion commander; the British, he was told, must be driven out at all costs. Back with his men, Ringsdorf ordered the squad to dash forward, lobbing showers of grenades to keep the English under constant attack. "Only in this way," says Ringsdorf, "were we able to gain ground and continue our advance. But I certainly had not expected when I came from Germany to find myself suddenly engaged in bitter fighting in a restricted area. This was a harder battle than any I had fought in Russia. It was constant, close-range, hand-to-hand fighting. The English were everywhere. The streets, for the most part, were narrow, sometimes not more than fifteen feet wide, and we fired at each other from only yards away. We fought to gain inches, cleaning out one room after the other. It was absolute hell!"

Advancing cautiously toward one house, Ringsdorf caught a glimpse of an English helmet with camouflage netting momentarily outlined in an open cellar doorway. As he raised his arm to throw a grenade, he heard a low voice and the sound of moaning. Ringsdorf did not lob the grenade. Silently he moved down the cellar steps, then yelled, "Hands up." The command was unnecessary. In Ringsdorf's words, "Before me was a frightening sight. The cellar was a charnel house full of wounded English soldiers." Ringsdorf spoke soothingly, knowing that the British would not understand his words, but might comprehend his meaning. "It's O.K.," he told the wounded men. "It's all right." He called for medics and, collecting his prisoners, ordered the British moved back of his own lines for attention.

As the troopers were brought out of the cellar, Ringsdorf began to search one of the walking wounded. To his astonishment, the man uttered a low moan and crumpled at Ringsdorf's feet, dead. "It was a bullet meant for me," Ringsdorf says. "The English were protecting their own. They couldn't know we were trying to save their wounded. But for one moment, I was paralyzed. Then I broke out in a cold sweat and ran."

As the British troopers hung on grimly around the school, Ringsdorf knew that even his elite unit was not strong enough to force a surrender. As dawn broke on Monday, he and the depleted squad retreated back up the Eusebius Buiten Singel. Encountering an artillery commander, Ringsdorf told him that "the only way to get the British out is to blast the buildings down, brick by brick. Believe me, these are real men. They won't give up that bridge until we carry them out feet first."

Master Sergeant Emil Petersen had good reason to reach the same conclusion. He was attached to the Reichsarbeitsdienst (Reich Work Service) and, as Germany's manpower shortage became increasingly acute, Petersen and his thirty-five-man platoon had been transferred to a heavy antiaircraft unit, then to an infantry outfit. They had retreated all the way from France.

On Sunday afternoon, waiting at the Arnhem station for transportation back to Germany where they were to be reorganized, Petersen's platoon had been mobilized and told by a lieutenant that they were to be committed against British airborne troops who had landed in the city. "The unit we joined consisted of 250 men," Petersen recalls. "No one had any weapons. Only I and four others had machine pistols."

Petersen's men were tired. They had been without food for twenty-four hours, and the sergeant remembers thinking that had the train been on time, the platoon would have been fed, would have missed the battle and would have reached home in Germany.

At an SS barracks, the group was issued weapons. "The situation was laughable," Petersen says. "First, none of us liked fighting with the Waffen SS. They had a reputation for being merciless. The arms they gave us were ancient carbines. To break open mine, I had to bang it against a table. The morale of my men was not exactly high when they saw these old weapons."

It took some time to make the guns serviceable and, as yet, the unit had not received any orders. Nobody seemed to know what was happening or where the men were to be committed.

Finally, at dusk, the group was marched off to the town commander's headquarters. Arriving, they found the building deserted. Again, they waited. "All we could think about was food," says Petersen. Eventually, an SS lieutenant arrived and announced that the men were to push through the center of the city to the Rhine bridge.

The unit marched in platoons down Markt Street toward the Rhine. In the dark they could see nothing; but, Petersen recalls, "we were conscious of movement all around us. Occasionally we heard shooting in the distance and the sound of vehicles. Once or twice I thought I saw the dull silhouette of a helmet."

Less than three hundred yards from the bridge, Petersen was aware that they were passing through lines of soldiers and he guessed the group he was with must be replacing these men. Then one of the soldiers said something that, to Petersen, was unintelligible. Instantly Petersen realized that the man had spoken English. "We were marching alongside a British unit heading, like us, for the bridge." The mistaken identity was suddenly apparent to everyone. An English voice yelled out, "They're Jerries!" Petersen remembers shouting, "Fire!"

Within seconds the street reverberated with machine-gun and rifle fire as the two forces fought face to face. A stream of bullets missed Petersen by inches, ripping through his knapsack. The force of the fire slammed him to the ground. Quickly, he took cover behind a dead comrade.

"Everywhere you looked, men were firing from scattered positions, often mistakenly at their own side," Petersen remembers. Slowly he began to crawl forward. He came to an iron fence enclosing a small park and climbed the fence. There, he found most of the other survivors of the German platoons sheltering among trees and shrubs. The British had drawn back to a group of houses on both sides of the park, and now in the little square the Germans were caught in a crossfire. "I could hear the screams of the wounded," Petersen says. "The British fired flares pinpointing our positions and cut our group to pieces. Fifteen men in my platoon were killed in less than five minutes."

Just at dawn the British stopped firing. The Germans also halted. In the early light, Petersen saw that of the 250 men who had set out for the bridge, more than half were either dead or wounded. "We never did get near the approaches to the bridge. We just lay there and suffered, without support from the vaunted SS or a single self-propelled gun. That," Petersen says, "was our introduction to the Arnhem battle. For us, it was nothing less than a massacre."

Hour by hour, men of the two missing battalions of the 1st British Airborne Division somehow reached the bridge. They had managed, by twos and threes, to fight through Colonel Harzer's defense ring to the north and west. Many were wounded, hungry and cold. They would add to the medical and supply problems of Colonel Frost's group. But in these hours, the stragglers were proud and in high spirits, despite their exhaustion and wounds. They had arrived where briefing officers back in England and their own commanders had told them to come. They streamed in from every unit that had started out so confidently for the Arnhem bridge the previous afternoon, and by dawn on the eighteenth Frost estimated that he now had between 600 and 700 men on the northern approach. But each hour that brought more troopers to the bridge brought, too, the increasing sounds of mechanized equipment as General Harmel's armored units entered the city and took up positions.

Even the German armor found Arnhem a hazardous and frightening place. Along various routes throughout the city, ordinary Dutch civilians had blocked the roads. Braving German and British bullets, men and women living in the fighting areas had begun to collect the dead—British, German, and their own countrymen. Sergeant Reginald Isherwood, of the 1st Battalion, finally found his way to the center of Arnhem at daybreak, after a hazardous night on the roads. There he saw "a sight that will live with me until the end of my days." The Dutch, emerging from basements, cellars, gardens and wrecked buildings, were collecting bodies. "They carried the wounded to makeshift dressing stations and shelters in the basements," Isherwood recalls, "but the bodies of the dead were stacked like sandbags in long rows, the heads and feet placed alternately." The proud, grieving citizens of Arnhem were laying the bodies of friend and foe alike across the streets in five-to-six-foot-high human roadblocks to prevent German tanks from reaching Frost at the bridge.

For the civilians in the inner city, dawn brought no release from the terror and confusion. Fires were out of control and spreading rapidly. Huddled in cellars and basements, few people had slept. The night had been punctuated by the crash of shells, the dull crump of mortars, the whine of snipers' bullets and the staccato burst of machine guns. Strangely, outside the older part of town, the citizens of Arnhem were untouched by what was happening, and they were totally confused. They telephoned friends in the inner city seeking information, only to learn from the frightened householders that a pitched battle was taking place on the northern end of the bridge, which the British were holding against repeated German attacks. It was obvious to the callers that German troops and vehicles were moving into the city from all directions. Yet the faith of the Dutch did not falter. They believed that liberation by the British and Americans was imminent. In these outer parts of the city, people prepared for work as usual. Bakeries opened, milkmen made their rounds, telephone operators, railroad employees, utility workers—all were on their jobs. Civil servants were planning to go to work, firemen still attempted to keep up with the ever-growing number of burning buildings and, a few miles north of Arnhem, Dr. Reinier van Hooff, director of Burgers Zoological Gardens, tended his nervous, skittish animals.* Perhaps the only Dutch who knew the extent of the battle were doctors and nurses who answered calls constantly throughout the night. Ambulances raced through the city, collecting casualties and rushing them to St. Elisabeth's Hospital on the northwestern outskirts and to smaller nursing

* In the zoo were 12,000 carrier pigeons which the Germans had collected from bird keepers throughout Arnhem. Fearing that the Dutch might use the pigeons to carry reports, the birds had been confiscated and housed in the zoo. German soldiers appeared daily to count the birds and even dead pigeons were ordered kept until the Germans could check their registration numbers.

homes within the city. No one in Arnhem realized as yet that the city was already a no man's land and that the situation would grow steadily worse. Arnhem, one of the most scenic spots in the Netherlands, would soon become a miniature Stalingrad.

The Dutch in the inner city were, however, aware almost from the beginning that liberation would not come easily. In the middle of the night at the government police station on Eusebiusplein, less than a quarter of a mile from the bridge, twenty-seven-year-old Sergeant Joannes van Kuijk heard a quiet tapping at the station door. Opening up, he saw British soldiers standing outside. Immediately Van Kuijk asked them in. "They wanted the answers to all sorts of questions bearing on the locations of buildings and landmarks," he remembers. "Then a number of them left and began digging themselves in across the road in the direction of the bridge—all of it done as silently as possible." In front of a doctor's house nearby, Van Kuijk watched as the British set up a mortar site and then positioned a 6-pounder antitank gun in a corner of the doctor's garden. By dawn, Van Kuijk saw that the British had formed a tight perimeter around the northern extremity of the bridge. To him, these soldiers acted less like liberators than like grim-faced defenders.

On the other side of Eusebius Buiten Singel, the winding, grass-stripped boulevard close by the bridge, Coenraad Hulleman, a labor mediator staying with his fiancée, Truid van der Sande, and her parents in their villa, had been up all night listening to the firing and explosions around the schoolhouse a street away, where Captain Mackay's men were fighting off the Germans. Because of the intensity of the battle, the Van der Sandes and Hulleman had taken refuge in a small, windowless cellar beneath the central portion of the house.

Now, at dawn, Hulleman and his future father-in-law stole cautiously upstairs to a second-floor room overlooking the boulevard. There, they stared down in amazement. A dead German lay in the middle of a patch of marigolds in the landscaped street, and all through the grass plots they saw Germans in one-man slit trenches. Glancing along the boulevard to his right, Hulleman saw several German armored vehicles parked beside a high brick wall, drawn up and waiting. Even as the two men watched, a new battle broke out. Machine guns on the tanks suddenly fired into the towers of the nearby Walburg Church, and Hulleman saw a fine red dust spew out. He could only assume that paratroopers were in lookout positions in the church. Almost immediately the tank fire was answered, and the Germans in slit trenches began to machine-gun the houses on the opposite side of the street. One of them was a costume shop and in its windows were knights in armor. As Hulleman looked on, the bullets shattered the show window and toppled the knights. Moved to tears, Hulleman turned away. He hoped the sight was not prophetic.

A few blocks north, in a house near the concert hall, Willem Onck was awakened shortly after dawn by the sound of troop movements in the street. Someone hammered on his door and a German voice ordered Onck and his family to stay inside and to draw the blinds. Onck did not immediately obey. Running to the front window, he saw Germans with machine guns at every corner of the street. In front of the Musis Sacrum was an 88 mm. battery, and to Onck's utter amazement, German soldiers were sitting next to it on the auditorium's chairs which they had carried into the street. Watching them chatting casually with one another, Onck thought they looked as if they were only waiting for the concert to begin.

The most frustrated and angry civilians in the area were the members of the Dutch underground. Several of them had contacted the British almost immediately at the bridge, but their help had been politely refused. Earlier, Arnhem's underground chief, Pieter Kruyff, had sent Toon van Daalen and Gijsbert Numan to Oosterbeek to establish contact with the British. They too had found that their assistance was not needed. Numan remembers warning the troopers of snipers in the area and advising them to avoid main roads. "One of them told me their orders were to proceed to the bridge only, and they would follow their indicated routes," Numan says. "I got the impression that they were in dread of provocateurs and simply did not trust us."

Now, at dawn, Johannus Penseel held a meeting in his cellar with his resistance workers. Penseel planned to take over a local radio station and broadcast a proclamation that the city was free. A telephone call from Numan changed his mind. "It goes badly," Numan reported. "The situation is critical, and I think everything is already lost." Penseel was stunned. "What do you mean?" he asked. Numan was now near St. Elisabeth's Hospital. The British were finding it impossible to get through the German lines and march to the bridge, he said. Penseel immediately telephoned Pieter Kruyff, who advised the group to hold back any planned activities—"a temporary nonintervention," as Henri Knap, who attended the meeting, recalls. But the long-term hopes of the resistance workers were crushed. "We were prepared to do any-thing," Penseel recalls, "even sacrifice our lives if necessary. Instead, we sat useless and unwanted. It was now increasingly clear that the British neither trusted us nor intended to use us."

Ironically, in these early hours of Monday, September 18, when neither SHAEF, Montgomery nor any Market-Garden com-mander had a clear picture of the situation, members of the Dutch underground passed a report through secret telephone lines to the 82nd Airborne's Dutch liaison officer, Captain Arie Bestebreurtje, that the British were being overwhelmed by panzer divisions at Arnhem. In the 82nd's message logs, the notation appears: "Dutch report Germans winning over British at Arnhem." In the absence of any direct communications from the Arnhem battle area, this message was actually the first indication that the Allied High Command received of the crisis that was overtaking the 1st British Airborne Division.

AT THE FERRY LANDING STAGE in the little village of Driel, seven
miles southwest of the Arnhem bridge, Pieter, the ferryman, prepared for his first trip of the day across the Lower Rhine. The
early-morning commuters, who worked in the towns and villages
on the northern side of the river, huddled together in small groups,
chilled by the morning mist. Pieter took no part in the talk of his
passengers about the fighting going on west of Arnhem and in the
city itself. His concern was with the operation of the ferry and the
daily schedules he must maintain, as he had done for years.

A few cars, and farm carts filled with produce for stores and
markets to the north, were loaded first. Then men and women
pushing bicycles came aboard. At exactly 7 A.M. Pieter swung out
into the river, the ferry running smoothly along its cable. The trip
took only a few minutes. Edging up to the ramp below the village
of Heveadorp on the northern bank, passengers and vehicles
disembarked. Above them, the Westerbouwing, a hundred-foot-
high hill, dominated the countryside. On the northern bank, most
commuters set off on roads leading east to Oosterbeek, whose
tenth-century church tower rose above groves of oaks and lupine-
covered moors. Beyond was Arnhem.

Other passengers waited to cross back to Driel. There, once
again, Pieter took on northbound travelers. One of them was
young Cora Baltussen. Only two weeks earlier, on September 5,
which would always be remembered by the Dutch as Mad
Tuesday, she had watched the Germans' frantic retreat. In Driel,
the conquerors had not returned. For the first time in months,

Cora had felt free. Now, once again, she was apprehensive. The joy of the news of the paratroop landings the day before had been diminished by rumors of the intense fighting in Arnhem. Still, Cora could not believe the Germans would ever defeat the powerful Allied forces that had come to liberate her country.

At the Heveadorp landing on the north side of the river, Cora pushed her bicycle off the ferry and pedaled to Oosterbeek and the local baker's shop. She had given her meager hoard of sugar rations to the pastry shop for a special occasion. On this Monday, September 18, the Baltussen preserves factory was observing its seventy-fifth year in business and Cora's mother was celebrating her sixty-second birthday. For the first time in months all of the family would be together. Cora had come to Oosterbeek early to pick up the birthday cake, which would mark both the company's anniversary and Mrs. Baltussen's birthday.

Friends had tried to dissuade Cora from making the trip. Cora refused to listen. "What can possibly happen?" she had asked one friend. "The British are in Oosterbeek and Arnhem. The war is almost over."

Her trip was uneventful. In these early hours Oosterbeek seemed peaceful. There were British troops in the streets, the shops were open, and a holiday mood prevailed. For the moment, although gunfire could be heard only a few miles away, Oosterbeek was tranquil, not yet touched by the battle. Although her order was ready, the baker was amazed that she had come. "The war is all but over," she told him. With her parcels, she cycled back to Heveadorp and waited until Pieter brought the ferry in again. On the southern bank she returned to the somnolent peace of little Driel, where, as usual, absolutely nothing was happening.

On the British landing and drop zones, the officer with perhaps the least glamorous job of all was going about it with his usual capability. All through the night the men of Brigadier Philip "Pip" Hicks's 1st Airlanding Brigade had staved off a series of vicious enemy attacks, as the motley groups under Von Tettau's command harassed the brigade. Hicks's men were dug in around the perimeters to hold the zones for the expected 10 A.M. drop of Brigadier Shan Hackett's 4th Parachute Brigade, and the resupply missions that would follow. The zones under Hicks's protection were also the supply dumps for the British airborne.

Neither Hicks nor his men had managed more than an hour or two of sleep. The Germans, attacking from the woods, had set the forest on fire in some areas in the hope of burning out the British defenders. The Red Devils promptly responded. Slipping behind the enemy, they charged with fixed bayonets and forced the Germans into their own fire. Signalman Graham Marples remembers the bitter nighttime battles vividly. He and a few others came upon a platoon of dead British troopers who had been overrun and completely wiped out. "No one said anything," Marples remembers. "We just fixed bayonets and went right on into the woods. We came out, but the Jerries didn't." Private Robert Edwards, who had seen action in North Africa, Sicily and Italy, recalls that "I had managed to come through all those actions more or less unscathed, but in one day in Holland I had been in more fire fights than all else put together."

The unending skirmishes had taken their toll. Several times

during the night Hicks had called upon Lieutenant Colonel W. F. K. "Sheriff" Thompson for artillery support to force back the persistent enemy attacks. His real fear was that German armor, which he now knew was holding up the battalions going for the bridge, would break through his meager defenses and drive him off the landing and drop zones. "I went through some of the worst few hours I have ever spent in my life," Hicks recalls. "Two things were clear: although we did not know it at the time we had landed virtually on top of two panzer divisions—which weren't supposed to be there—and the Germans had reacted with extraordinary speed." Under attack from Von Tettau's groups from the west and Harzer's armor from the east, Hicks's lightly armed paratroopers had no option but to hold until relieved, or until reinforcements and supplies were safely down.

Colonel Charles Mackenzie, General Urquhart's chief of staff, had spent the night on the Renkum Heath landing zone, about three miles away from Hicks's command post. The intense fighting had caused Division to move out of the woods and back onto the field. There the headquarters staff took shelter in gliders for the rest of the night. Mackenzie was concerned about the absence of any word from Urquhart. "For more than nine hours, we had heard nothing whatsoever from the General," he recalls. "I assumed that he was with Lathbury's 1st Brigade, but communications were out and we had heard nothing from either officer. I knew that a decision would soon have to be made about the command of the division. There always existed the possibility that Urquhart had been captured or killed."

Early Monday, still without news, Mackenzie decided to confer with two senior staff officers, Lieutenant Colonel R. G. Loder-Symonds and Lieutenant Colonel P. H. Preston. Mackenzie informed them of Urquhart's conversation with him prior to takeoff in England: the succession of command, in case anything happened to Urquhart, should be Lathbury, Hicks, then Hackett. Now, with Lathbury missing as well, Mackenzie felt that Brigadier Hicks should be contacted. The other officers agreed. Immediately they drove to Hicks's headquarters. There, in a house close by the Heelsum-Arnhem road, Mackenzie told Hicks what he knew. "We had a scanty report that Frost had taken the bridge, but that the First and Third battalions were caught up in street fighting and had not as yet been able to reinforce him," Mackenzie remembers.

The best course of action now, Mackenzie believed, was for Hicks to release one of his Airlanding battalions and send it to the bridge. It could be reinforced later by elements of Hackett's 4th Paratroop Brigade when it arrived later in the morning. At the same time, Hicks was asked to take command of the division immediately.

Hicks seemed stunned. His forces were already understrength and he did not have a full battalion to send to the bridge. Yet it appeared the British battle plan was faltering. If Frost failed to get help immediately, the bridge might be lost; and if the landing areas were overrun, Hackett's 4th Brigade could be destroyed before it was even assembled.

Additionally, there seemed to be a tacit acknowledgment that Hicks was being asked to assume command of a division already in the process of disintegration through a total breakdown of communications and the absence of the commanding officer. Reluctantly, Hicks released half of one battalion—all he could spare—for defense of the bridge.* Obviously, that decision was most urgent. The bridge had to be held. Then, as Mackenzie remembers, "We finally convinced Hicks that he must take command of the division."

Few men had ever been asked to accept battleground responsibility for an entire division under such a complexity of circumstances. Hicks quickly discovered how critically the communications breakdown was affecting all operations. The few messages from Frost at the bridge were being received via Lieutenant

---

* He ordered half of the South Staffords to start off for Arnhem. The other half of this battalion would not arrive until the second lift, when, supplementing the advance of Hackett's 11th Battalion, these units would also move out.

Colonel Sheriff Thompson, commanding the Airlanding Light Regiment artillery. From an observation post in the steeple of the Oosterbeek Laag church, two and one-half miles from the bridge, Thompson had established a radio link with Major D. S. Munford's artillery command post at Brigade headquarters in a waterworks building near the bridge. The Thompson-Munford link afforded the only dependable radio communications at Hicks's disposal.

Equally critical, Division had no communications with General Browning's Corps headquarters near Nijmegen, or with the special "Phantom Net" sets at Montgomery's headquarters. Of the few vital messages that did reach England, most were sent over a BBC set, which had been specially flown in for British war correspondents. Its signal was weak and distorted. A high-powered German station and the British set were operating on the same frequency. Ironically, Division could pick up signals from rear Corps headquarters back in England, but were unable to transmit messages back. What sparse communications did get through via the BBC set were picked up at Browning's rear Corps headquarters at Moor Park and then relayed to the Continent. The transmission took hours and when the messages arrived they were outdated and often virtually meaningless.

Frustrated and worried, Hicks had three immediate concerns: the weather over England; the inability to confirm the planned arrival time of the second lift; and his lack of a means of informing anyone of the true situation in the Arnhem area. Additionally he could not warn Hackett of the perilous hold the British had on the landing areas where the 4th Brigade would expect to drop in cleared and protected zones.

Less crucial, but nonetheless troublesome, was the forthcoming encounter with Brigadier Shan Hackett. The volatile Hackett, Mackenzie told Hicks, would be informed of Urquhart's decision regarding the chain of command the moment he landed. "I knew Hackett's temperament," Mackenzie recalls, "and I was not looking forward to the meeting. But telling him was my job and I was following General Urquhart's orders. I could no longer take the

341

chance that something had not happened to both the General and Lathbury."

At least Hicks was relieved of that delicate confrontation. The new division commander had enough on his mind. "The situation was more than just confusing," he remembers. "It was a bloody mess."

✢ 4 ✢

IN THE WESTERN SUBURBS of Arnhem, the once tidy parks and clean-swept streets were scarred and pitted by the battle as the British 1st and 3rd battalions struggled to reach the bridge. Glass, debris and the broken boughs of copper beech trees littered the cobblestone streets. Rhododendron bushes and thick borders of bronze, orange and yellow marigolds lay torn and crushed, and vegetable gardens in back of the neat Dutch houses were in ruins. The snouts of British antitank guns protruded from the shattered windows of shops and stores, while German half-tracks, deliberately backed into houses and concealed by their rubble, menaced the streets. Black smoke spewed up from burning British and German vehicles and constant showers of debris rained down as shells slammed into strong points. The crumpled bodies of the wounded and dead lay everywhere. Many soldiers remember seeing Dutch men and women, wearing white helmets and overalls emblazoned with red crosses, dashing heedlessly through the fire from both sides, to drag the injured and dying to shelter.

This strange, deadly battle now devastating the outskirts of the city barely two miles from the Arnhem bridge seemed to have no plan or strategy. Like all street fighting, it had become one massive, fierce, man-to-man encounter in a checkerboard of streets.

342

The Red Devils were cold, unshaven, dirty and hungry. The fighting had been too constant to allow men more than an occasional "brew-up" of tea. Ammunition was running short and casualties were mounting; some companies had lost as much as 50 percent of their strength. Sleep had been impossible, except in brief snatches. Many men, weary and on the move for hours, had lost all sense of time. Few knew exactly where they were or how far away the bridge still was, but they were grimly determined to get there. Years later, men like Private Henry Bennett of Colonel Fitch's 3rd Battalion, on the middle, Tiger route, would remember that throughout the constant skirmishes, sniping and mortar fire, one command was constant: "Move! Move! Move!"

Yet to General Urquhart, now absent from Division headquarters for nearly sixteen hours and without radio contact, the progress of the attack was agonizingly slow. Since 3 A.M., when he had been roused at the villa where he had spent a restless few hours, Urquhart, along with Brigadier Lathbury, had been on the road continuously with the 3rd Battalion. "Sharp encounters, brief bursts of fire, kept bringing the entire column to a stop," Urquhart says. The psychological effectiveness of German snipers disturbed the General. He had anticipated that some of his men who had not been in action before would be "a bit bullet-shy initially," but would rally quickly. Instead, along some streets, sniper fire alone was slowing up the progress of the entire battalion. Yet, rather than interfere with Fitch's command, Urquhart remained silent. "As a divisional commander mixed up in a battalion encounter . . . I was in the worst possible position to intervene, but all the time I was conscious of each precious second that was being wasted." German snipers were dealt with effectively, but Urquhart was appalled at the time it took to dig them out.

So was Regimental Sergeant Major John C. Lord. Like the General, Lord was chafing at the delay. "German resistance was fierce and continuous, but at least a large part of our delay was caused by the Dutch as well. They were out in the streets early, waving, smiling, offering us ersatz coffee. Some of them had even draped Union Jacks over their hedges. There they were, right in the midst of the fighting, and they didn't even seem to realize it was going on. They, with all their good intentions, were holding us up as much as the Germans."

Suddenly the intensive sniper fire was replaced by something far more serious: the piercing crack of the enemy's 88 mm. artillery and self-propelled guns. At this point the forward units of Fitch's battalion were close by the massive St. Elisabeth's Hospital, less than two miles northwest of the Arnhem bridge. The hospital lay almost at the confluence of the two main highways leading into Arnhem, along which the 1st and 3rd battalions were attempting to march to the bridge. Here, elements of the Hohenstaufen Division's armor had been positioned throughout the night. Both Colonel Dobie's 1st Battalion on the Ede-Arnhem road and Fitch's 3rd Battalion on the Utrecht road must pass on either side of the junction to get to the bridge. Dobie's battalion was the first to feel the force of Colonel Harzer's fanatical SS units.

From a horseshoe-shaped perimeter covering the northern and western approaches of the city, the Germans had forced Dobie's men off the upper road and into cover in the surrounding built-up areas. SS men, hidden on the rooftops, and snipers in attics had allowed forward units to pass unhindered before opening up with a murderous fire on troops coming up behind. In the confusion of the surprise attack, companies and platoons were dispersed in all directions.

Now, employing the same tactics, the Germans were concentrating on Fitch's 3rd Battalion. And, in a situation that could have disastrous consequences, four critical officers—the commanders of the 1st and 3rd battalions, the officer in charge of the 1st Parachute Brigade and the commander of the 1st British Airborne Division—all found themselves bottled up in the same small, heavily populated area. Ironically, as in the case of Model and his commanders at Oosterbeek, General Urquhart and Brigadier Lathbury were surrounded by an enemy oblivious to their presence.

Trapped by fire from ahead and behind, the British columns scattered. Some men headed for buildings along the Rhine, more took to the nearby woods and others—among them, Urquhart and Lathbury—ran for safety into narrow streets of identical brick houses.

Urquhart and his group had just reached a three-story house in a block of buildings near the main Utrecht-Arnhem road when the Germans shelled the building. The British were uninjured, but German armor, Urquhart was later to note, "moved through the streets with almost casual immunity." As one tank rumbled down the street, its commander standing in the open hatch looking for targets, Major Peter Waddy leaned out of an upper-floor window of a house next to Urquhart's and expertly dropped a plastic explosive into the open turret, blowing the tank to pieces.° Other men, following Waddy's example, demolished two more tanks. But, although the British fought fiercely, the lightly armed troopers were no match for the German armor.

Urquhart's own predicament was increasing by the minute. He was desperately anxious to get back to Division headquarters and gain control of the battle. Caught up in the fighting, he believed his only means of escape was to take to the streets and, in the confusion, try to get through the German positions. His officers, fearful for his safety, disagreed, but Urquhart was adamant. The intense fighting was, as he saw it, still only "company-size action" and, as the buildings the British occupied were not yet surrounded, he felt the group should get out quickly before German strength increased and the ring tightened.

During the hasty conference amid the noise of the battle, Urquhart and his officers were dumfounded to see a British Bren gun carrier clatter down the street, as though unaware of the German fire, and pull up outside the building. A Canadian lieutenant, Leo Heaps, who in Urquhart's words "seemed to have a charmed existence," leaped out of the driver's seat and raced for the building. Behind Heaps was Charles "Frenchie" Labouchère,

---

° A short time later, reconnoitering the British positions, Waddy was killed by a mortar blast.

of the Dutch resistance, who was acting as Heaps's guide. The carrier was loaded with supplies and ammunition which Heaps hoped to deliver to Colonel Frost on the bridge. With German armor everywhere, the small vehicle and its two occupants had miraculously survived enemy fire and en route had, by chance, discovered Urquhart's whereabouts. Now, for the first time in hours, Urquhart learned from Heaps what was happening. "The news was far from encouraging," Urquhart later recalled. "Communications were still out. Frost was on the northern end of the bridge under heavy attack, but holding, and I was reported missing or captured." After listening to Heaps, Urquhart told Lathbury that it was now imperative "before we're completely bottled up to take a chance and break out."

Turning to Heaps, Urquhart told the Canadian that if he reached Division headquarters after completing his mission at the bridge, he was to urge Mackenzie to "organize as much help as he could for Frost's battalion." At all costs, including his own safety, Urquhart was determined that Frost must get the supplies and men needed to hold until Horrocks' tanks reached Arnhem.

As Heaps and Labouchère left, Urquhart and Lathbury set about making their escape. The street outside was now being swept constantly by enemy fire and buildings were crumpling under the pounding of shells. Urquhart noted "a growing pile of dead around the houses we occupied," and concluded that any exit via the street would be impossible. The commanders, along with others, decided to leave from the rear of the building, where, under covering fire and smoke bombs, they might be able to get away. Then, taking advantage of plantings in the back gardens of the row houses, Urquhart and Lathbury hoped eventually to reach a quiet area and make their way back to headquarters.

The route was nightmarish. While paratroopers laid down a heavy smoke screen, Urquhart's group dashed out the back door, sprinted through a vegetable garden and climbed a fence separating the house from its neighbor. As they paused for a moment near the next enclosure, Lathbury's Sten gun went off accidentally, barely missing the General's right foot. As Urquhart was later to write, "I chided Lathbury about soldiers who could not keep their Stens under control. It was bad enough for a division commander to be jinking about . . . and it would have been too ironic for words to be laid low by a bullet fired by one of my own brigadiers."

Climbing fence after fence, and once a ten-foot-high brick wall, the men moved down the entire block of houses until, finally, they reached an intersecting cobbled street. Then, confused and weary, they made a drastic miscalculation. Instead of veering left, which might have given them a margin of safety, they turned right toward St. Elisabeth's Hospital, directly into the German fire.

Running ahead of Urquhart and Lathbury were two other officers, Captain William Taylor of the Brigade's headquarters staff and Captain James Cleminson of the 3rd Battalion. One of them called out suddenly but neither Urquhart nor Lathbury understood his words. Before Taylor and Cleminson could head them off, the two senior officers came upon a maze of intersecting streets where, it seemed to Urquhart, "a German machine gun was firing down each one." As the four men attempted to run past one of these narrow crossings, Lathbury was hit.

Quickly the others dragged him off the street and into a house. There, Urquhart saw that a bullet had entered the Brigadier's lower back and he appeared to be temporarily paralyzed. "All of us knew," Urquhart recalls, "that he could travel no farther." Lathbury urged the General to leave immediately without him. "You'll only get cut off if you stay, sir," he told Urquhart. As they talked, Urquhart saw a German soldier appear at the window. He raised his automatic and fired at point-blank range. The bloodied mass of the German's face disappeared. Now, with the Germans so near, there was no longer any question that Urquhart must leave quickly. Before going, he talked with the middle-aged couple who owned the house and spoke some English. They promised to get Lathbury to St. Elisabeth's Hospital as soon as there was a lull in the fighting. In order to save the owners from German reprisal, Urquhart and his party hid Lathbury in a cellar beneath a stairway until he could be removed to the hospital. Then, Urquhart remembers, "we left by the back door and into yet another maze of tiny, fenced gardens." The three men did not get far, but Urquhart's life may well have been saved by the prompt action of fifty-five-year-old Antoon Derksen, owner of a terrace house at Zwarteweg 14.

In the maelstrom of firing, Antoon, his wife Anna, their son Jan, and daughter Hermina were sheltering in the kitchen at the rear of the house. Glancing through a window, Derksen was amazed to see three British officers vault over the fence into his back garden and head for the kitchen door. Quickly, he let them in.

Unable to communicate—he didn't speak English and no one in Urquhart's party knew Dutch—Antoon, gesturing, tried to warn the Britishers that the area was surrounded. "There were Germans in the street," he later recalled, "and at the back, in the direction the officers had been going. At the end of the row of gardens there were Germans in position at the corner."

Derksen hastily ushered his visitors up a narrow staircase to a landing and from there into a bedroom. In the ceiling was a pull-down door with steps leading to the attic. Cautiously looking out the bedroom window the three men saw the reason for Derksen's wild pantomime. Only a few feet below them, in positions all along the street, were German troops. "We were so close to them," Urquhart remembers, "we could hear them talking."

Urquhart was unable to guess whether the Germans had spotted his group as they entered the rear of the house, or whether they might burst in at any moment. In spite of Derksen's warning that the area was surrounded, he pondered the twin risks of continuing through the chain of back gardens or making a dash down the front street, using hand grenades to clear the way. He was ready to take any chance to return to his command. His officers, fearful for him, were not. At the moment, the odds were simply too great. It was far better, they argued, to wait until British troops overran the sector than for the commanding general to risk capture or possible death.

The advice, Urquhart knew, was sound, and he did not want to compel his officers to take risks that might prove suicidal. Yet, "my long absence from Division headquarters was all I could think about, and anything seemed better to me than to stay out of the battle in this way."

The familiar creaking clack of caterpillar treads forced Urquhart to stay put. From the window the three officers saw a German self-propelled gun come slowly down the street. Directly outside the Derksen house, it came to a halt. The top of the armored vehicle was almost level with the bedroom window, and the crew, dismounting, now sat talking and smoking directly below. Obviously, they were not moving on and at any moment the Britishers expected them to enter the house.

Quickly Captain Taylor pulled down the attic steps and the three officers hurriedly climbed up. Crouched down and looking about him, the six-foot Urquhart saw that the attic was little more than a crawl space. He felt "idiotic, ridiculous, as ineffectual in the battle as a spectator."

The house was now silent. Antoon Derksen, as a loyal Dutchman, had sheltered the British. Now, fearing possible reprisal if Urquhart was found, he prudently evacuated his family to a neighboring house. In the nearly airless attic, and without food or water, Urquhart and his officers could only wait anxiously, hoping either for the Germans to pull back or for British troops to arrive. On this Monday, September 18, with Market-Garden only a day old, the Germans had almost brought the Arnhem battle to a halt and, compounding all the errors and miscalculations of the operation, Urquhart, the one man who might have brought cohesion to the British attack, was isolated in an attic, trapped within the German lines.

It had been a long, tedious mission for Captain Paul Gräbner and his 9th SS Panzer Reconnaissance Battalion. Allied paratroopers had not landed in the eleven-mile stretch between Arnhem and Nijmegen. Of that, Gräbner was quite certain. But enemy units were in Nijmegen. Immediately after a few of Gräbner's vehicles had crossed the great Waal river bridge, there had been a short, brisk small-arms encounter. In the darkness, the enemy had seemed to show no great inclination to continue the fight against his armored vehicles, and Gräbner had reported to headquarters that the Allies seemed to have little strength in the city as yet.

Now, his scouting mission completed, Gräbner ordered a few self-propelled guns from his forty-vehicle unit to guard the southern approaches to the Nijmegen bridge. With the rest of the patrol, he headed back north to Arnhem. He had seen neither paratroopers nor any enemy activity when crossing the Arnhem bridge the night before. However, from radio messages, he had learned that some British troops were on one side of the bridge. Harzer's headquarters had merely called them "advance units." Gräbner halted once more, this time at the town of Elst, approximately midway between Arnhem and Nijmegen. There again, to be within striking distance of either highway bridge, he left off part of his column. With the remaining twenty-two vehicles, he sped back toward the Arnhem bridge to clear it of whatever small enemy units were there. Against paratroopers armed with only rifles or machine guns, Gräbner expected little difficulty. His powerful armored units would simply smash through the lightly held British defenses and knock them out.

At precisely 9:30 A.M., Corporal Don Lumb, from his rooftop position near the bridge, yelled out excitedly, "Tanks! It's XXX Corps!" At Battalion headquarters nearby, Colonel John Frost heard his own spotter call out. Like Corporal Lumb, Frost felt a moment's heady exhilaration. "I remember thinking that we would have the honor of welcoming XXX Corps into Arnhem all by ourselves," he recalls. Other men were equally cheered. On the opposite side of the northern approach, the men under the ramp near Captain Eric Mackay's command post could already hear the sound of heavy vehicles reverberating on the bridge above.

Sergeant Charles Storey pounded up the stairs to Corporal Lumb's lookout. Peering toward the smoke still rising from the southern approach, Storey saw the column Lumb had spotted. His reaction was immediate. Racing back downstairs, the pre-Dunkirk veteran shouted, "They're Germans! Armored cars on the bridge!"

At top speed, the vanguard of Captain Paul Gräbner's assault force came on across the bridge. With extraordinary skill, German drivers, swerving left and right, not only avoided the smoldering wreckage cluttering the bridge, but drove straight through a mine field—a string of platelike Teller mines that the British had laid during the night. Only one of Gräbner's five lead vehicles touched off a mine—and only superficially damaged, kept on coming. On his side of the ramp, Captain Mackay stared with amazement as the first of the squat camouflaged cars, machine guns firing constantly, barreled off the ramp, smashed through the British perimeter defenses, and kept on going straight toward the center of Arnhem. Almost immediately, Mackay saw another go past. "We had no antitank guns on our side," Mackay says, "and I just watched helplessly as three more armored cars sped right past us and took off up the avenue."

Gräbner's daring plan to smash across the bridge by force and speed was underway. Out of the sight of the British, on the southern approach to the bridge, he had lined up his column. Now, half-tracks, more armored cars, personnel carriers and even a few truckloads of infantry, firing from behind heavy sacks of grain, began to advance. Crouching behind the half-tracks were other German soldiers, firing steadily.

The sudden surprise breakthrough of Gräbner's lead vehicles had stunned the British. They recovered quickly. Antitank guns from Frost's side of the bridge began to get the range. From the entire northern area a lethal fire enveloped the German column. From parapets, rooftops, windows and slit trenches, troopers opened fire with every weapon available, from machine guns to hand grenades. Sapper Ronald Emery, on Mackay's side of the ramp, shot the driver and codriver of the first half-track to cross.

As the second came into view, Emery shot its drivers, too. The half-track came to a dead halt just off the ramp, whereupon the remainder of its crew of six, abandoning the vehicle, were shot one by one.

Relentlessly, Gräbner's column pressed on. Two more half-tracks nosed across the bridge. Suddenly, chaos overtook the German assault. The driver of the third half-track was wounded. Panicked, he threw his vehicle into reverse, colliding with the half-track behind. The two vehicles, now inextricably tangled, slewed across the road, one bursting into flames. Doggedly the Germans coming up behind tried to force a passage. Accelerating their vehicles, frantic to gain the northern side, they rammed into one another and into the growing piles of debris tossed up by shells and mortar bursts. Out of control, some half-tracks hit the edge of the ramp with such force that they toppled over the edge and down into the streets below. Supporting German infantrymen following the half-tracks were mercilessly cut down. Unable to advance beyond the center of the bridge, the survivors raced back to the southern side. A storm of fire ricocheted against the girders of the bridge. Now, too, shells from Lieutenant Colonel Sheriff Thompson's artillery, situated in Oosterbeek, and called in by Major Dennis Munford from the attic of Brigade headquarters near Frost's own building, screamed into Gräbner's stricken vehicles. Through all the din came the yelling of the now-exuberant British paratroopers as they shouted the war cry, "Whoa Mohammed," which the Red Devils had first used in the dry hills of North Africa in 1942.*

The fierceness of the raging battle stunned the Dutch in the area. Lambert Schaap, who lived with his family on the Rijnkade —the street running east and west of the bridge—hurried his wife and nine children off to a shelter. Schaap himself remained in his

* In that campaign, paratroopers noted that the Arabs, shouting messages to one another, seemed to begin each communication with these two words. In Arnhem, the war cry was to take on special meaning. It enabled paratroopers on both sides of the northern ramp to determine who was friend or foe in the various buildings and positions, since the Germans seemed unable to pronounce the words. According to Hilary St. George Saunders in *By Air to Battle*, the war cry "seemed to rouse the men to their highest endeavours."

house until a hail of bullets came through the windows, pitting walls and smashing furniture. Under this intense barrage Schaap fled. To Police Sergeant Joannes van Kuijk, the battle seemed endless. "The firing was furious," he recalls, "and one building after another seemed to be hit or burning. Telephone calls from colleagues and friends were constant, asking for information about what was happening. We were having a hard time of it in our building, and neighboring premises were catching fire. The houses on Eusebius Buiten Singel were also alight."

On that wide boulevard near the northern approach, Coenraad Hulleman, in his fiancée's house only a few doors away from Captain Mackay's command post, now stayed with the rest of the Van der Sande family in their basement shelter. "There was a funny sound overriding all the other noise and someone said it was raining," Hulleman remembers. "I went up to the first floor, looked out, and saw that it was fire. Soldiers were running in every direction, and the entire block seemed to be in flames. The battle moved right up the boulevard, and suddenly it was our turn. Bullets smacked into the house, smashing windows, and upstairs we heard musical notes as the piano was hit. Then, amazingly, a sound like someone typing in Mr. Van der Sande's office. The bullets were simply chewing up the typewriter." Hulleman's fiancée, Truid, who had followed him up, saw that shots were hitting the tower of the massive Church of St. Eusebius. As she watched in amazement the gold hands of the huge clock on the church spun crazily as though, Truid remembers, "time was racing by."

To the bridge fighters, time had lost all meaning. The shock, speed and ferocity of the battle caused many men to think that the fight had gone on for many hours. Actually, Gräbner's attack had lasted less than two. Of the armored vehicles that Colonel Harzer had jealously guarded from General Harmel, twelve lay wrecked or burning on the northern side. The remainder disengaged from the carnage and moved back to Elst, minus their commander. In the bitter no-quarter fighting, Captain Paul Gräbner had been killed.

Now the British, in pride and triumph, began to assess the damage. Medics and stretcher-bearers, braving the unrelenting sniper fire, moved through the smoke and litter, carrying the wounded of both sides to shelter. The Red Devils on the bridge had repulsed and survived the horror of an armored attack and, almost as though they were being congratulated on their success, 2nd Battalion signalmen suddenly picked up a strong clear message from XXX Corps. The grimy, weary troopers imagined that their ordeal was all but over. Now, beyond any doubt, Horrocks' tanks must be a scant few hours away.

From airfields behind the German border, swarms of fighters took to the air. To amass and fuel the planes, the nearly depleted Luftwaffe had mounted an all-out effort. Now, after a frantic, sleepless night, during which fighters had been rushed in from all over Germany, some 190 planes gathered over Holland between 9 and 10 A.M. Their mission was to destroy the second lift of Market. Unlike the skeptical Field Marshal Model, the Luftwaffe generals believed the captured Market-Garden plans to be authentic. They saw a glittering opportunity to achieve a major success. From the plans, German air commanders knew the routes, landing zones and drop times of the Monday lift. Squadrons of German fighters patrolling the Dutch coast across the known Allied flight paths and drop zones waited to pounce on the airborne columns, due to begin their drops at 10 A.M. Zero hour passed with no sign of the Allied air fleet. The short-range fighters were ordered to land, refuel and take off again. But the sky remained empty. None of the anticipated targets materialized. Baffled and dismayed, the Luftwaffe high command could only wonder what had happened.

What had happened was simple. Unlike Holland, where the weather was clear, Britain was covered by fog. On the bases, British and American airborne troops, ready to go, waited impatiently by their planes and gliders. On this crucial morning, when every hour mattered, General Lewis H. Brereton, the First Allied Airborne Army commander, was, like the men of the second lift, at the mercy of the weather. After consultation with the meteorologists, Brereton was forced to reschedule zero hour. The men in and around Arnhem and the Americans down the corridor—all holding against the increasing German buildup—must now wait four long hours more. The second lift could not reach the drop zones before 2 P.M.

✻ 5 ✻

AT VALKENSWAARD, fifty-seven miles south of Arnhem, ground fog had held up the planned 6:30 A.M. jump-off time for the tanks of XXX Corps. Scout cars, however, had set out on schedule. Patrolling ahead and to the east and west since daybreak, they were feeling out the German strength. To the east, heather-covered sand and small streams made the area barely negotiable even for reconnaissance vehicles. West of the village, wooden bridges over streams and rivers were considered too light to support tanks. As scout cars in the center moved along the narrow, one-tank-wide main road out of Valkenswaard, they suddenly encountered a German tank and two self-propelled guns, which drove off toward Eindhoven as the patrol approached. From all reports it seemed clear that the quickest route into Eindhoven was still the highway, despite the sighting of German armor and the expectation of running into more as the British approached the city. Now, three hours later, General Horrocks' tanks were only just beginning to roll again. As Colonel Frost's men engaged Captain Gräbner's units at the Arnhem bridge, the spearheading Irish Guards were

355

finally on the move, heading up the main road toward Eindhoven.

Stiff German resistance had thwarted Horrocks' plan to smash out from the Meuse-Escaut Canal on Sunday and link up with General Taylor's 101st Airborne Division in Eindhoven in less than three hours. By nightfall on the seventeenth, Lieutenant Colonel Joe Vandeleur's tankers had come only seven miles to Valkenswaard, six miles short of the day's objective. There had seemed little reason to push on during the night. Brigadier Norman Gwatkin, chief of staff of the Guards Armored Division, had told Vandeleur that the Son bridge beyond Eindhoven was destroyed. Bridging equipment would have to be brought up before Vandeleur's tanks could cross. As Vandeleur remembers, Gwatkin said, "Push on to Eindhoven tomorrow, old boy, but take your time. We've lost a bridge."

Unaware of the setback, men were impatient at the delay. Lieutenant John Gorman, who had attended General Horrocks' briefing in Leopoldsburg prior to the break-out, had thought at the time that there were too many bridges to cross. Now Gorman, recipient of the Military Cross a few weeks earlier, was edgy and irritable. His original fears seemed justified. Anxious to be off, Gorman could not understand why the Guards Armored had spent the night in Valkenswaard. Habit, he noted, "seemed to dictate that one slept at night and worked by day," but now, Gorman felt, such behavior should not apply. "We must get on," he remembers saying. "We can't wait." Lieutenant Rupert Mahaffey was equally disturbed at the Guards' slow advance. "I began having the first faint traces of conscience," he says. "Our advance seemed slower than intended, and I knew that if we did not pick up the pace soon we weren't going to get to Arnhem on time."

Although the scouting patrols of the Household Cavalry had warned of waiting German armor and infantry, the tanks of the Irish Guards met little opposition until they reached the village of Aalst, halfway to Eindhoven. Then, from the pinewood forests flanking the highway, a hail of infantry fire engulfed the column, and a lone self-propelled gun engaged the leading tanks. It was quickly put out of action and Vandeleur's force rumbled on through the village. Two miles north, at a small bridge over the river Dommel, the Irish were held up again, this time by heavy artillery fire. Four 88 mm. guns covered the bridge. Infantry with heavy machine guns were hidden in nearby houses and behind concrete walls. Immediately the lead vehicles halted and British troops, jumping from the tanks, fought back.

To move on as quickly as possible, Vandeleur decided to call in the rocket-firing Typhoons that had aided the column so expertly during the previous day's advance. Flight Lieutenant Donald Love, now in complete charge of ground-to-air communication, put through the request. To his astonishment, he was turned down. In Belgium, the squadrons were weathered in by fog. Vandeleur, Love recalls, "was livid." Squinting into the bright weather over Holland, he asked Love sarcastically "if the R.A.F. is frightened by sunshine."

By now the entire column, stretching back almost to the Belgian border, was stalled by the well-sited enemy guns. Lead tanks tried to edge forward, and one gun, firing directly down the road, stopped them at point-blank range. As his tanks opened up against the Germans, Vandeleur called for heavy artillery and quickly ordered patrols to move out west along the river in search of a bridge or ford where his vehicles might cross, outflank the German battery and attack from the rear.

A barrage of steel whistled over the lead tanks as British batteries began to engage the enemy. Well positioned and fiercely determined, the Germans continued to fire. For two hours the battle went on. Fuming at the delay, Vandeleur was helpless. All he could do was wait.

But, barely four miles to the north, one of the reconnaissance units had met with unexpected success. After a circuitous cross-country trip through water-veined terrain and marshes, and across fragile wooden bridges, one troop of scout cars, skirting the German positions, came suddenly upon American paratroopers north of Eindhoven. Shortly before noon, Lieutenant John Palmer, commanding the Household Cavalry scout unit, was warmly greeted by Brigadier General Gerald Higgins, deputy commander of the 101st Screaming Eagles. By radio, Palmer jubilantly informed his headquarters that the "Stable Boys have contacted our Feathered Friends." The first of three vital link-ups along the corridor had been made, eighteen hours behind Market-Garden's schedule.

With contact finally established, discussion immediately turned to the Son bridge. Waiting British engineering units needed complete details in order to bring forward the materials and equipment needed to repair the damaged crossing. Sappers, moving up alongside Vandeleur's lead columns, prepared to rush to the bridge the moment the advance picked up again. Information could have been passed by radio, but the Americans had already discovered a simpler method. The surprised British were radioed to ask their engineers to telephone "Son 244." The call went immediately through the German-controlled automatic telephone exchange, and within minutes the Americans at the Son bridge had given British engineers the vital information they needed to bring up the proper bridging equipment.

In the village of Aalst, Vandeleur's tankers were startled by a sudden abrupt end to the German fire which had kept them immobilized so long on the main road. One of their own squadrons had opened the way. Working slowly down the western bank of the Dommel river, a British reconnaissance force came upon a crossing a mile north of Aalst and behind the German positions. The squadron charged the German guns from the rear, overran their positions and ended the battle.

Unaware of the move, the stalled tankers at Aalst thought the sudden silence was a lull in the fighting. Major Edward Tyler, in charge of the lead Number 2 Squadron, was debating whether he should take advantage of the cessation and order his tanks to smash on, when he spotted a man cycling down the main road toward the column. Stopping on the far bank, the man jumped off the bicycle and, waving frantically, ran across the bridge. The astounded Tyler heard him say: "Your General! Your General! The Boche have gone!"